ALAN RANGER

DUNKIRK 1940
THROUGH A GERMAN LENS

STRATUS

Published in Poland in 2017
by STRATUS sp.j.
Po. Box 123,
27-600 Sandomierz 1, Poland
e-mail: office@wydawnictwostratus.pl

as

MMPBooks,
e-mail: office@ mmpbooks.biz
© 2017 MMPBooks.
http://www. mmpbooks.biz

ISBN

978-83-65281-72-2

Editor in chief
Roger Wallsgrove

Editorial Team
Bartłomiej Belcarz
Robert Pęczkowski
Artur Juszczak

Cover
Dariusz Grzywacz

Book layout
Dariusz Grzywacz

DTP
Stratus sp.j.

Printed by
Drukarnia Diecezjalna,
ul. Żeromskiego 4,
27-600 Sandomierz
www.wds.pl
marketing@wds.pl

PRINTED IN POLAND

In this series of books I have no intention of trying to add to what is a very well documented history in well research texts elsewhere. Here I hope to give an impression of the battlefield through the battles aftermath as seen by the camera lens of normal German soldiers not the professional PK cameramen who's well posed shots are well known and have been seen by most interested parties by now, but the images taken by individual soldiers that show a more personal view, the views that interested the co mmon soldier not the professional properganderist. For the most part these photographs have been part of private collections and have only recently come on to the market, most images we have used here were taken from prints made on old German Agfa paper stock and most were originally no more than 25 mm by 45 mm in size.

'Operation Dynamo'
The Dunkirk evacuation 26th May to 4th of June 1940

The necessity for the evacuation of the BEF (British Expeditionary Force) has been a matter of controversy for many years and has divided opinion of historians down party lines since the evacuation its self. My general view is that mistakes were made on all of the allied sides British, French and Belgian senior offices stuck in the thinking of the first world war failed to grasp the concept of mobile warfare and were simply out witted and outmaneuvered by the German's concept of Blitzkrieg (Lightening War). The allies fell for the German diversionary attack which thrust into Holland and advanced their forces into northern Belgium to stop the advancing Germans. Meanwhile the main German thrust came through the Ardennes region of Sothern Belgium and Northern France going around the northern end of the French Maginot line which had not been placed along the Belgian border for fear of upsetting the Belgian's. The French had left only second line units in the Ardennes region and these failed completely to stop the German advance. It was these French forces that formed the southern flank of the allied armies and with this flanks disintegration becoming a full blown rout the British and French forces to the north had to retreat back into northern France to protect themselves from being surrounded and cut off from any means of resupply. As the German Southern Army Group moved further west into France they moved faster than the allies retreated and turned north to cut the allies off. At this point the one major British counter attack was put into place and on the 21st of May the attack was made in the area around the town of Arras against German Units co mmanded by Erwin Ro mmel. The counter attack very nearly succeeded as it court the Germans by surprise and only Ro mmel utilizing his 88 mm anti-aircraft guns in an anti-tank role at the last minute stopped the British attack.

As the German attack proceeded the French morale became extremely low in many units and indeed within their own government. This lead the British High co mmand to believe that France was a lost course, Many French units surrendered on mass; however a few did stand and fight extremely bravely. Indeed the French 2nd Light Mechanized Division and the 68th Infantry Division fighting with the British 51st Highland Division formed the rear guard that held the Germans at bay right until the final evacuations took place. The British tried to retreat to a port but Boulogne had already fallen and Calais was already under attack and was not expected to be held. So the port of Dunkirk became the only option to evacuate any of the army back to the England to enable them to defend Britain against what was thought to be Hitler's obvious next move the invasion of the British Isles.

On the 20th of May Vice admiral Bertram Ramsey was asked to form a plan to evacuate 45,000 men in 48 hours from the first departure as this was seen to be the best that could be hoped for at the time. However Ramsey's ability to think outside the box and involve all the armed services and indeed proceed to co-opt civilians into the plan as well made for a different outcome. The situation as it stood on the 20th of May induced General Alan Brooke co mmander of the British Army to say 'Nothing but a Miricle can save the BEF now'. On the 26th of May Lord Gort CO of the BEF ordered the start of the evacuation and the operation got underway. Ramsey had enlisted the assistance all available ships from the British, French and Belgian Navies to take part however by the 27th of May only 8000 had been evacuated. Due to the Ports facilities being destroyed by German artillery and bombing as well as sunken ships blocking access to the dock side it soon became clear that the only deep water point of egress for the troops would be the ports outer most breakwater known as 'The Mole' and ships life boats would have to be used to ferry men from the shore to the larger boats in deeper water. Unfortunately there just was not enough small, shallow draft boats available to get any meaningful amount of men from the shore out to the larger ships. An urgent call went out across southern England for shallow draft boats to get to the southern ports to assist in the evacuation. The call was answered by boats from as far away as the Isle of Man in the Irish sea to Skegness on the east coast of the North Sea. It was answered by civilian life boats & crews and pleasure boats owners. To add to that many fishing boats and crews were temporary called up for service in the navy, as well, even the wind sail powered Themes coal barges were called upon to serve. Together this fleet over 700 small craft became famously known as the little ships of Dunkirk. Among this unique fleet were some that became especially noteworthy: a Ferry Paddle Steamer called *Medway Queen* made 7 round trips to France and back, of the 20 RLNI Life boats that took part only the Hythe Life boat the *Viscountess Wakefield* was lost permanently. The *Jean Holland* from Eastbourne was abandoned in mid channel due to damage and total engine failure following attacks from German aircraft and being ra mmed by an

E-Boat, however it was salvaged and towed to a British port days later. Over the next few days until the last evacuation on the night of the 4th of June a total of 338,226 soldiers had been evacuated among them 140,000 French and Belgian troup's. As well as these troups 200,000 troups had been evacuated form 'The Mole' the rest from 3 beaches to the east of the Town its self named Malo, Bray and La Panne where trucks were driven into the surf at low tide parked up in long rows and then strapped together in order to form temporary jetties. This enabled the troups to climb along them in order to get themselves out into deeper water closer to the bigger vessels. Sadly after this huge effort all but 3,000 wounded French troup's of the many thousands evacuated were subsequently ordered back to France to continue the battle for France and were repatriated to France on French orders via the port of Cherbourg only to be subsequently surrendered to the Germans in France's eventual capitulation only days later.

The evacuation came at a huge cost to Dunkirk its self over 1000 French Civilians were killed by the bombing and shelling, an estimated 3,500 British soldiers were killed on the beaches. By the end of the operation 68,111 troups had been killed or wounded and 4,000 captured. Many of the small ships had been lost. In all 243 ships of all sizes had been lost during the operation amongst them 9 Destroyers, 6 British: HMS *Keith*, HMS *Havant*, HMS *Basilisk*, HMS *Grafton*, HMS *Grenade* and HMS *Wakeful* and 3 French the *Bourrasque*, *Sirocco* and *Le Foudroyant*, the loss of HMS *Wakeful* was particularly tragic as it was loaded with evacuated solders and 600 lost the lives when it sank. In all the BEF left in France large amounts of equipment. The BEF lost 2,400 artillery guns of all sizes and calibres, 65,000 support vehicles (trucks, cars and tracked carriers) 68,000 tons of a mmunition and all of its 445 Tanks. If you add to this loss the thousands of French tanks Trucks and Guns left abandoned along the roadside leading to Dunkirk you can imagine the sight that met the German soldiers as they advanced many still in horse drawn infantry units, to see such equipment abandoned by the thousands. Mile upon mile of vehicles left abandoned on both sides of the road must have left a huge impression of invincibility and achievement on the individual soldiers, indeed the OKH (The German High command) issued the statement, that in the history of warfare this was 'The greatest annihilation battle of all time'.
In the defence of Dunkirk the RAF flew 3,500 sorties across the channel and lost 145 aircraft, the Germans lost 156 against them. It is often said that the evacuation or escape from Dunkirk dependent upon your view was only made possible due to Hitler taking Goering at his word that he could finish off the British using air power alone and be allowed and take the glory of victory for the Luftwaffe. However this often held belief is just not true. In fact German Field Marshall Von Rundstedt who was in overall co mmand of the German attacking forces ordered a halt to offensive operations of the land forces due to 30% and up to 50% of German tanks in some units being out of service due to battle damage and or mechanical failure. In short they needed a time out to repair/service their equipment before resuming the advance. Despite this order both Rommel and Heinz Guderian still pushed their units on to Dunkirk town's outer limits and pounded the occupants within unremittingly.

The photographs in this publication have been split up into the following sections 'The Beaches' and 'The Docks', 'The Town', 'The Roads Leading to Dunkirk', 'The Wreckage of Crashed Aircraft' and 'The Captured Rearguard' (The POW's) We hope that you find the chosen images both interesting and thought provoking, as we dedicate this book to all who were caught up in this historical action, both civilian and military alike and end with the words of Winston Churchill on the subject 'Dunkirk was indeed a miracle but wars are not won by evacuation'.

Die
Schlacht in Flandern und im Artois
Durchbruch zum Ärmelkanal
Tagesverlauf der deutschen Operationen am
29. Mai 1940
30. Mai 1940

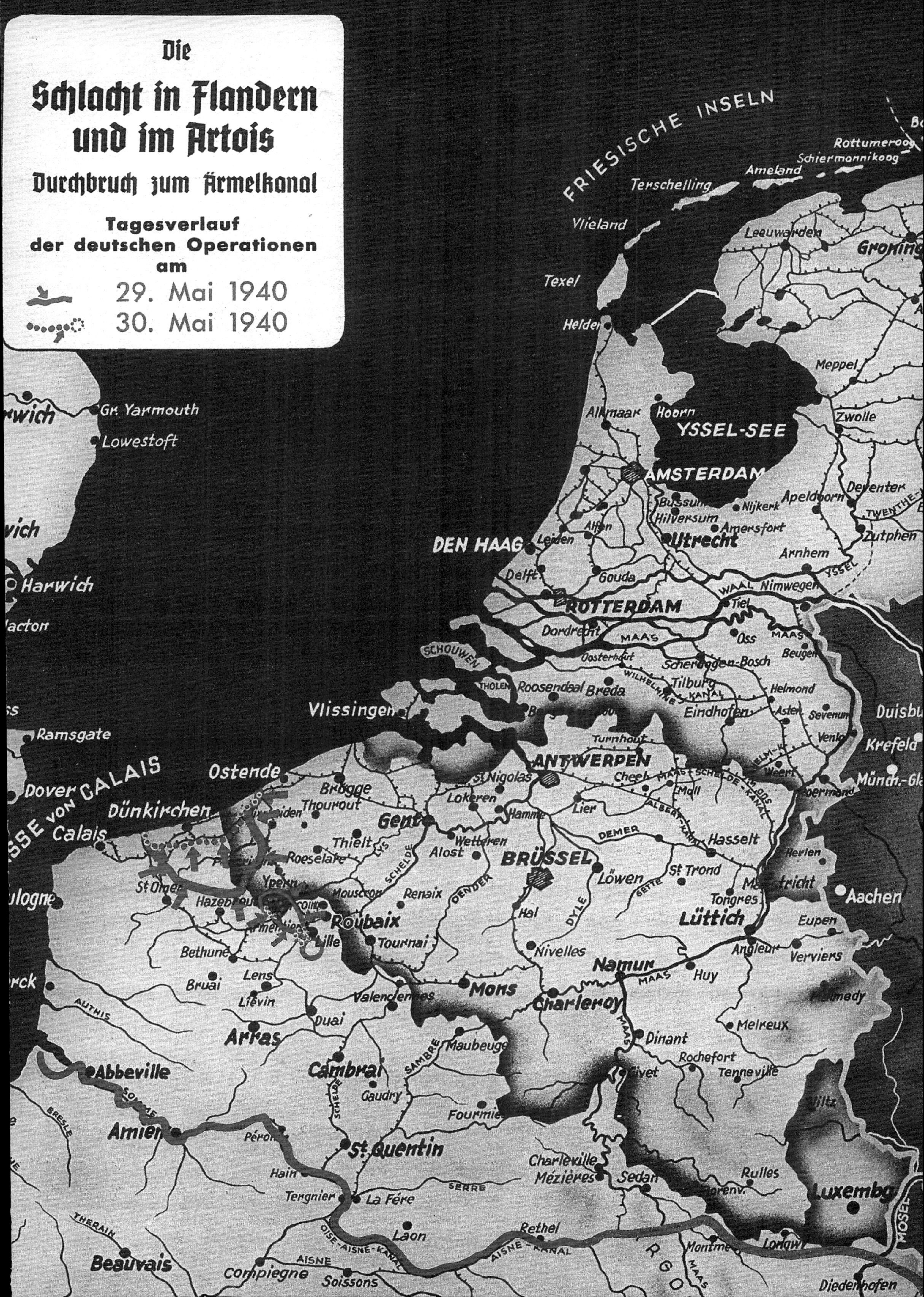

FRIESISCHE INSELN
Rottumeroog
Schiermonnikoog
Ameland
Terschelling
Vlieland
Leeuwarden
Groningen
Texel
Meppel
Helder
Zwolle
Alkmaar
Hoorn
YSSEL-SEE
AMSTERDAM
Deventer
Bussum
Nijkerk
Apeldoorn
Hilversum
Amersfort
TWENTHE
DEN HAAG
Leiden
Alfen
Utrecht
Zutphen
Delft
Gouda
Arnhem
YSSEL
ROTTERDAM
WAAL
Nimwegen
Tiel
Dordrecht
MAAS
Oss
MAAS
Beugen
SCHOUWEN
Oosterhout
Schertogen-Bosch
THOLEN
Roosendeal
Breda
WILHELMINE
Tilburg
Helmond
Vlissingen
Bergen op Zoom
KANAL
Eindhoven
Asten
Sevenum
Duisburg
Ramsgate
Turnhout
Venlo
Krefeld
GOLF VON CALAIS
Ostende
ANTWERPEN
Cheeb
MAAS-SCHELDE-KANAL
Weert
Münch.-Gla
Dover
Brügge
St Nigolas
Moll
Roermond
Dünkirchen
Thourout
Lokeren
Lier
ALBERT-KANAL
Calais
Gent
Hamme
DEMER
Hasselt
Thielt
LYS
Wetteren
BRÜSSEL
Herlen
Roeselare
SCHELDE
Alost
Löwen
St Trond
Maastricht
St Omer
Ypern
OENDER
Tongres
Aachen
Boulogne
Hazebrouck
Mouscron
Renaix
DYLE
Lüttich
Eupen
Armentieres
Roubaix
DENDER
Hal
Verviers
Bethune
Lille
Tournai
Nivelles
Angleur
Dunkerque
Lens
Namur
MAAS
Huy
Malmedy
Bruai
Lievin
Valenciennes
Mons
Charleroy
Arras
Duai
Maubeuge
Dinant
Melreux
Abbeville
Cambrai
SAMBRE
Rochefort
Tenneville
SOMME
Gaudry
Givet
Wiltz
BRESLE
Fourmies
Amiens
SCHELDE
Charleville
Sedan
Rulles
Péronne
Mézières
Florenv.
Luxemburg
Hain
St. Quentin
SERRE
THERAIN
Tergnier
La Fère
Rethel
Montme
Longwy
OISE-AISNE-KANAL
AISNE-KANAL
Beauvais
AISNE
Laon
MOSEL
Compiegne
Diedenhofen
Soissons

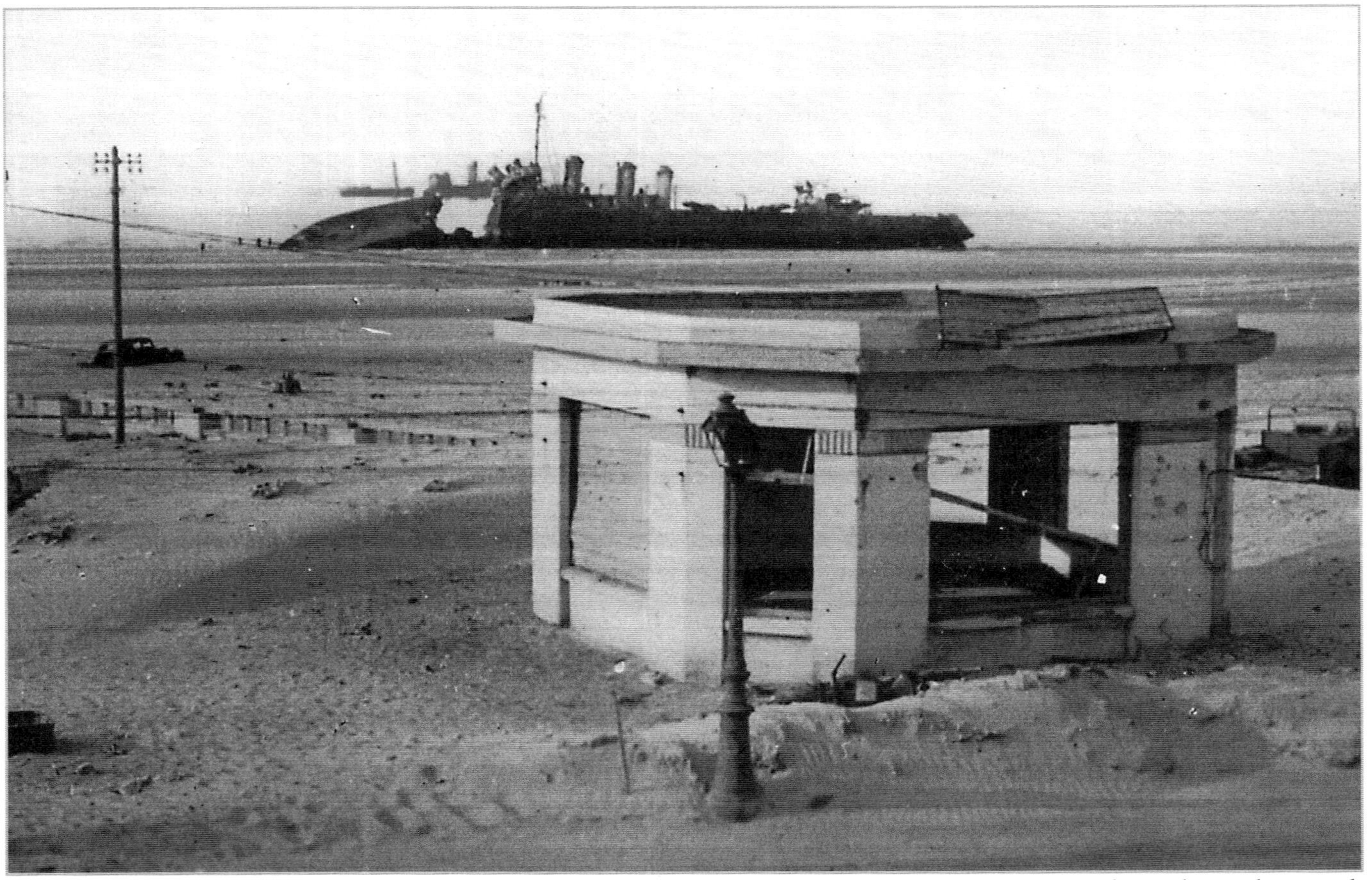

An iconic image of the ice-cream parlour, part of the grounds of the Malo Les Bains casino with, in the mid-ground, the wreck of the French destroyer *L'Adroit* and in the very background the wreck of the *Scotia*.

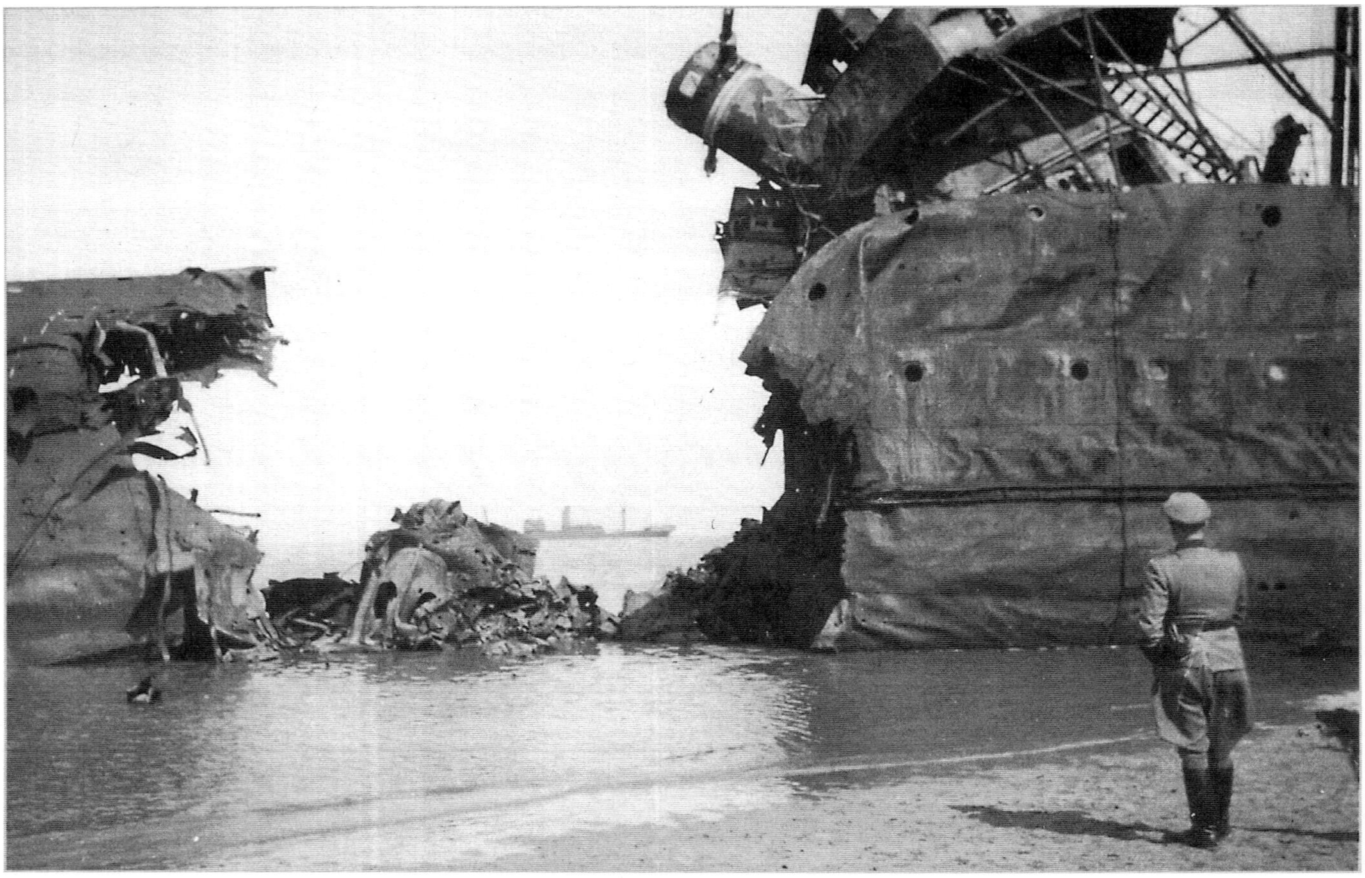

A close-up view of the bomb damage to the French destroyer *L'Adroit* and again the *Scotia* in the background.

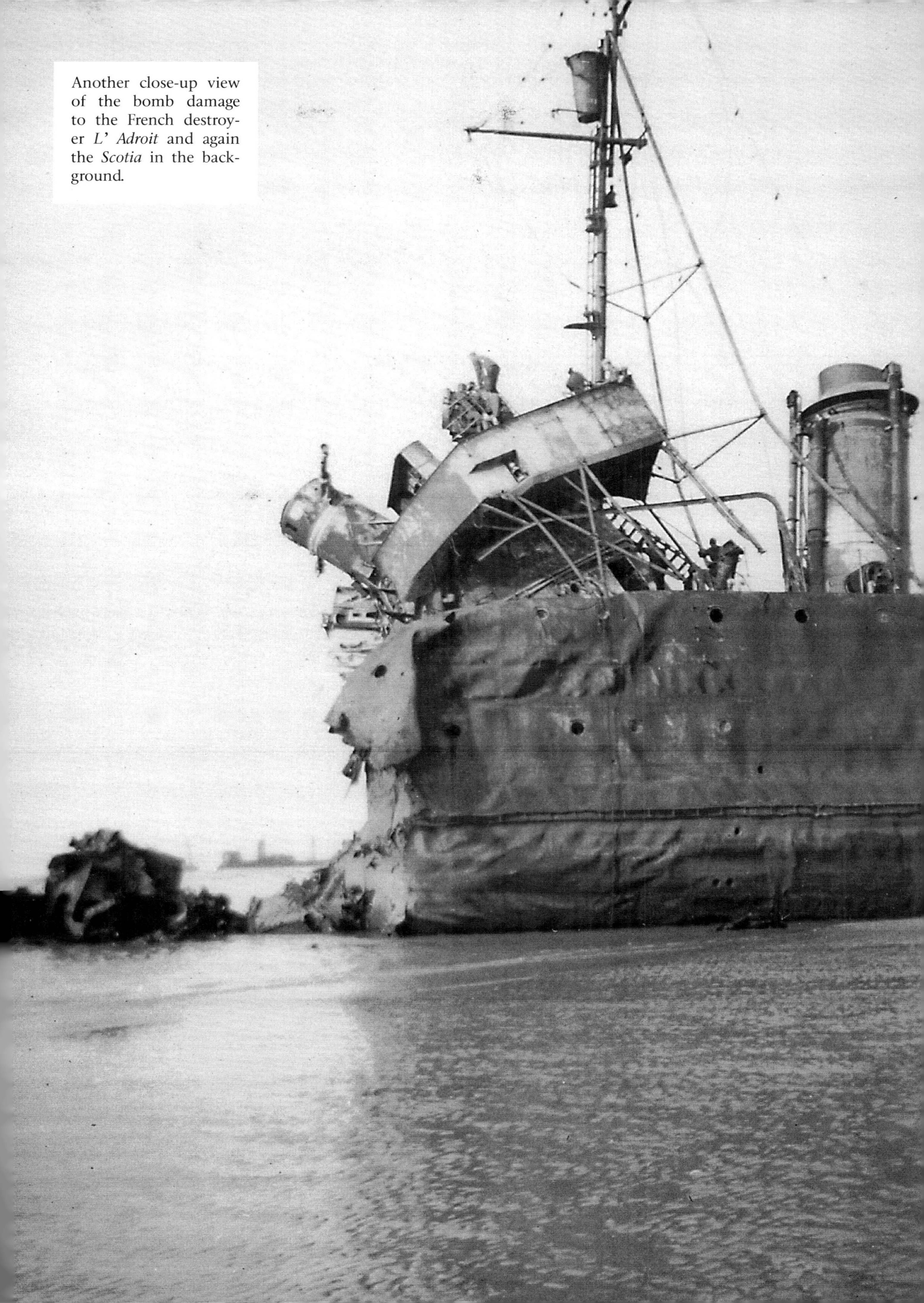

Another close-up view of the bomb damage to the French destroy-er *L' Adroit* and again the *Scotia* in the background.

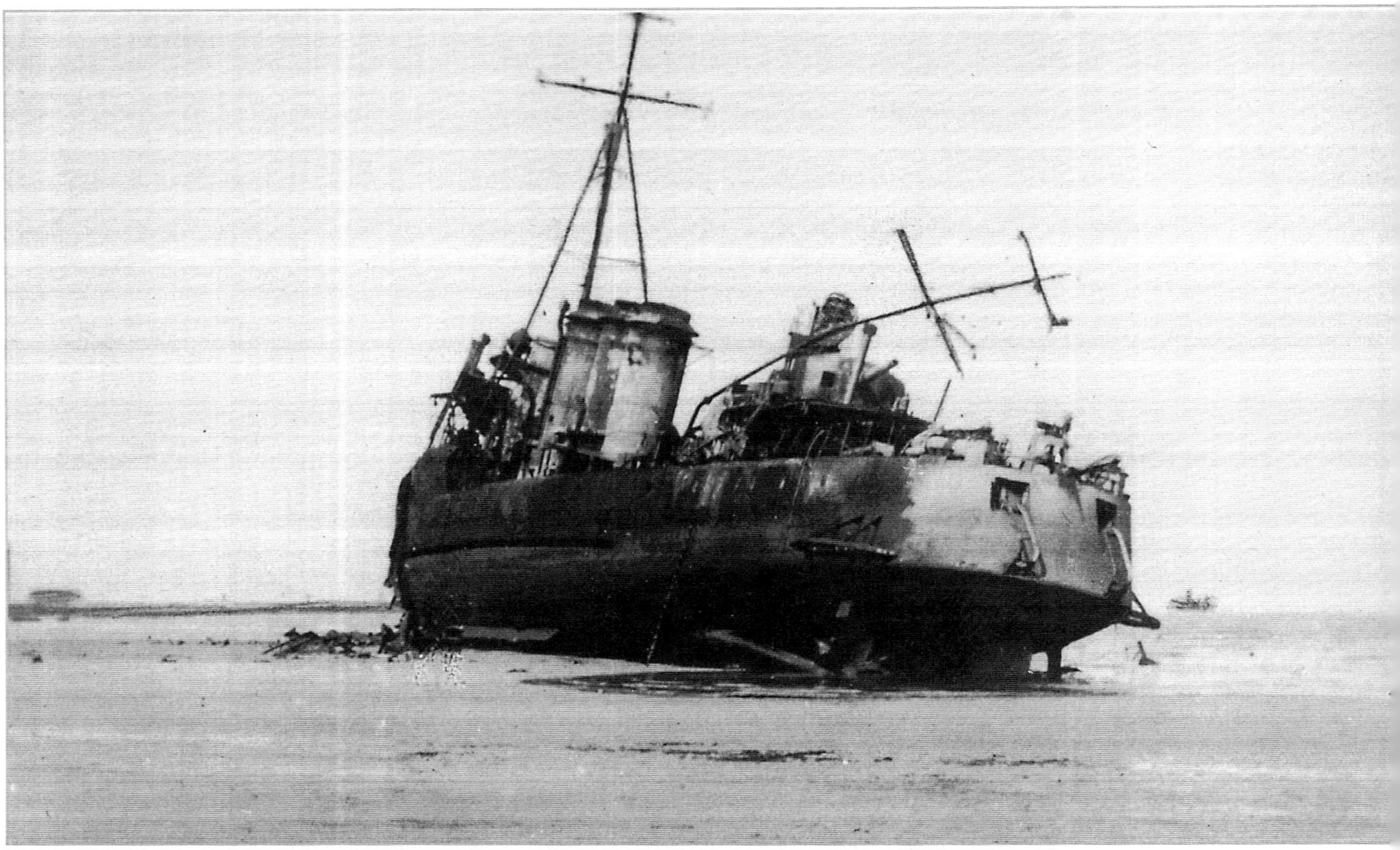

A view of the stern of the *L'Adroit* (the skilful one). She was laid down on the 26th of May 1925.

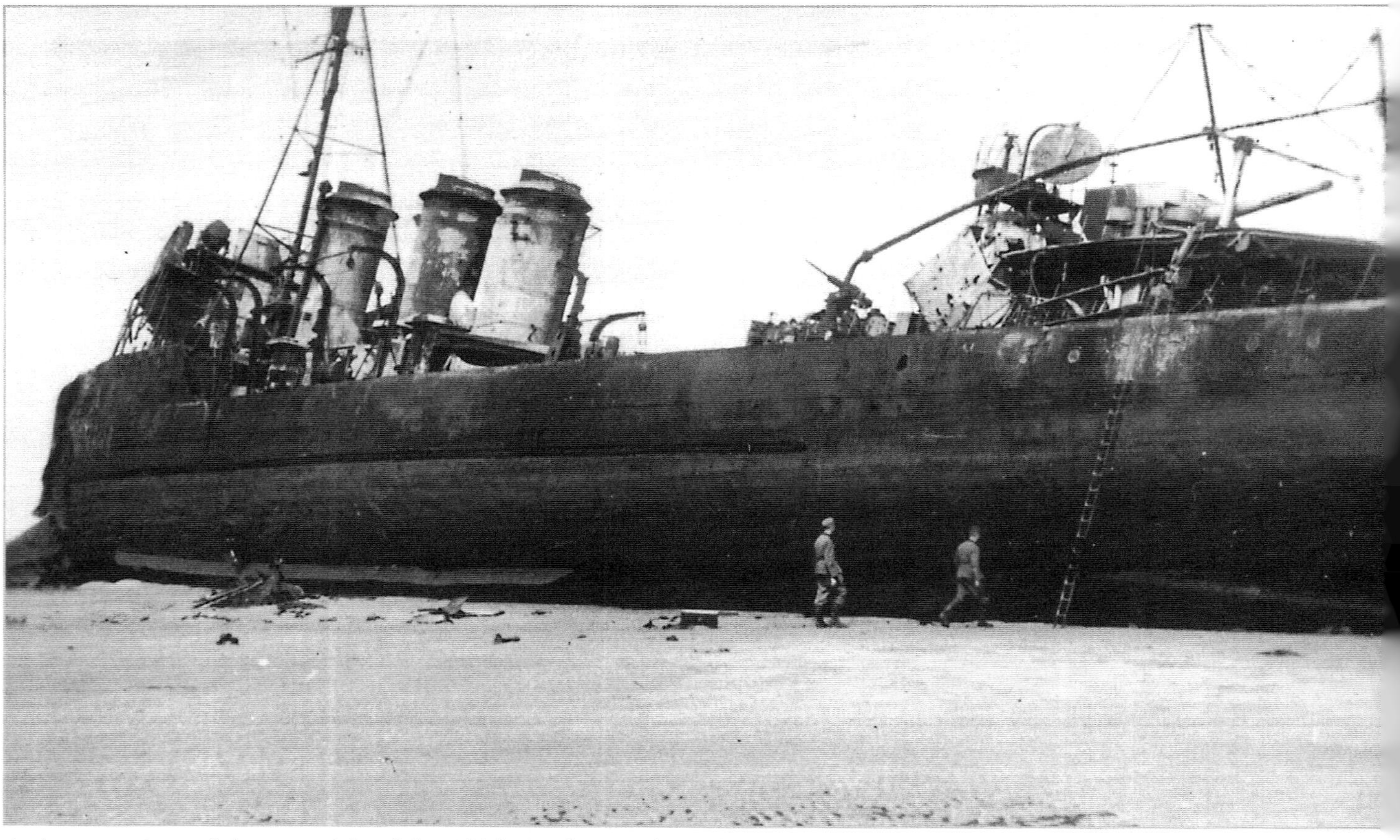

A close-up view of the port side of the *L'Adroit*. She was launched on the 1st of April 1927.

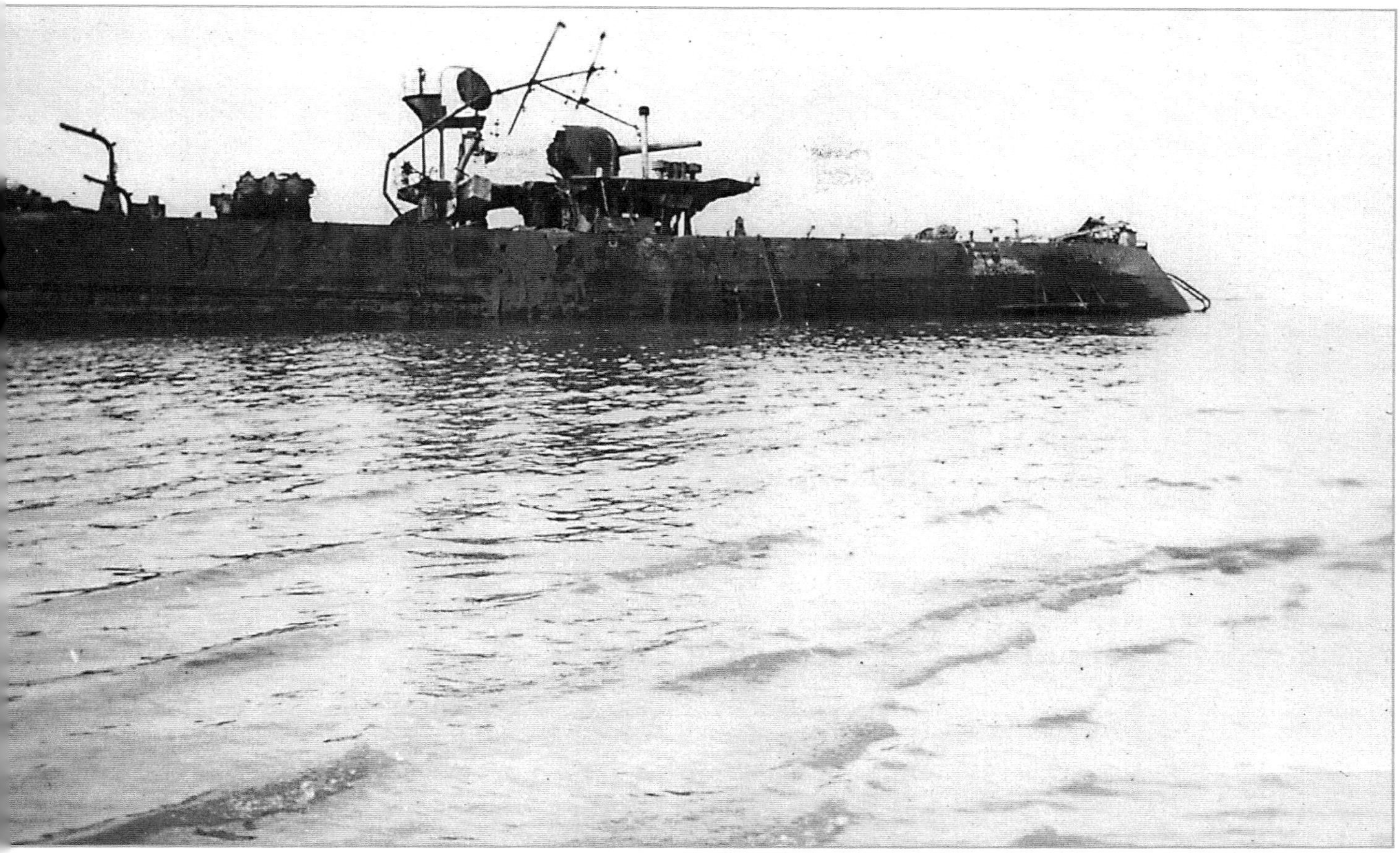

The stern of the *L'Adroit* with a good view of her one remaining gun turret. She was commissioned into service on the 1st of July 1929.

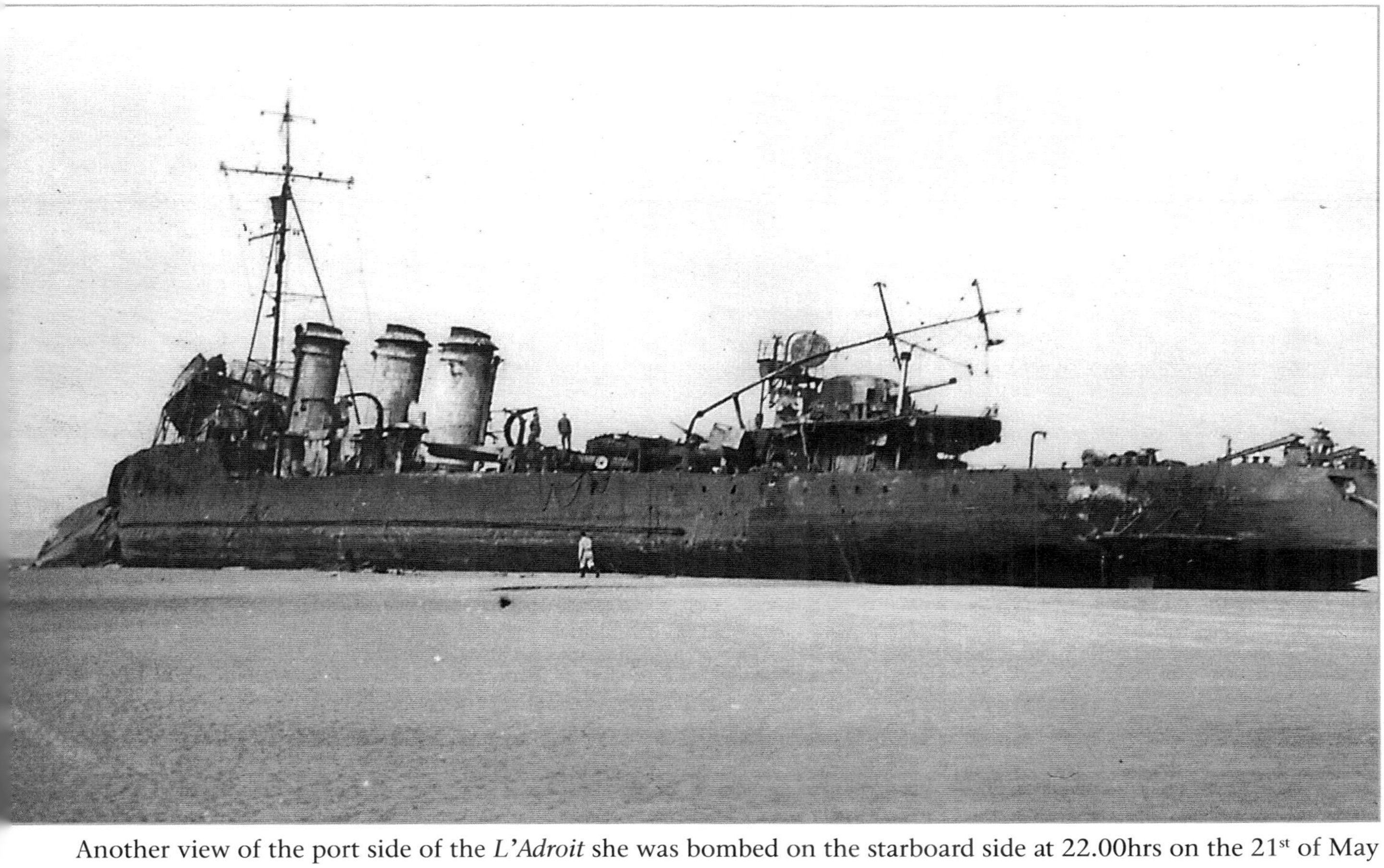

Another view of the port side of the *L'Adroit* she was bombed on the starboard side at 22.00hrs on the 21st of May 1940 by a Heinkel He 111.

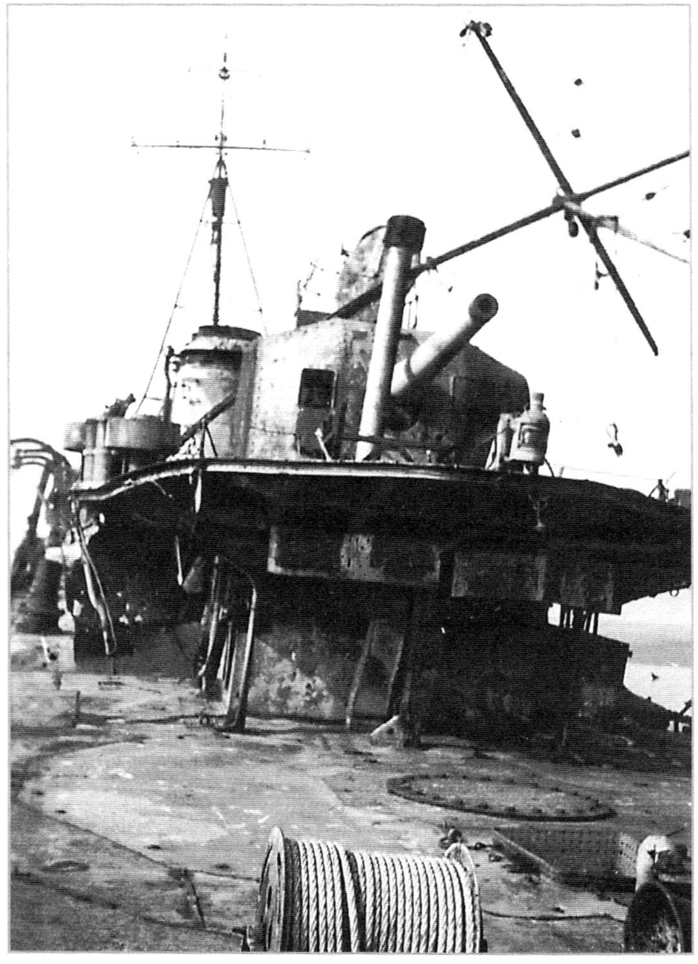

A close-up of the rear upper turret of the *L'Adroit* she was armed with 4 such turrets each mounting a single 130 mm cannon. She also had two 37 mm Anti-aircraft guns.

The *L'Adroit* and the *Scotia* at low tide. After the *L'Adroit* was run aground by her captain, Lt.Cdr HMA Dupin De Saint Cyr, his crew was disembarked and took up residence in the casino. The captain and the anti-aircraft gun crews remained, as he intended to use the wreck as an anti-aircraft battery in defence of the beaches. The ship was bombed again on the 25th of May and the whole bow section was blown off when the remaining ammunition exploded, destroying the thin strip of the keel holding the parts together.

The *Scotia*, a British steamer of 3454grt, was sunk at 13.00hrs by German bombing of Dunkirk on the 1st of June 1940. Thirty two crew members and up to three hundred troops were lost on the steamer, her survivors were picked up by the destroyer *Esk* and the drifters *Fisherboy*, *Fidget* and *Jaketa*.

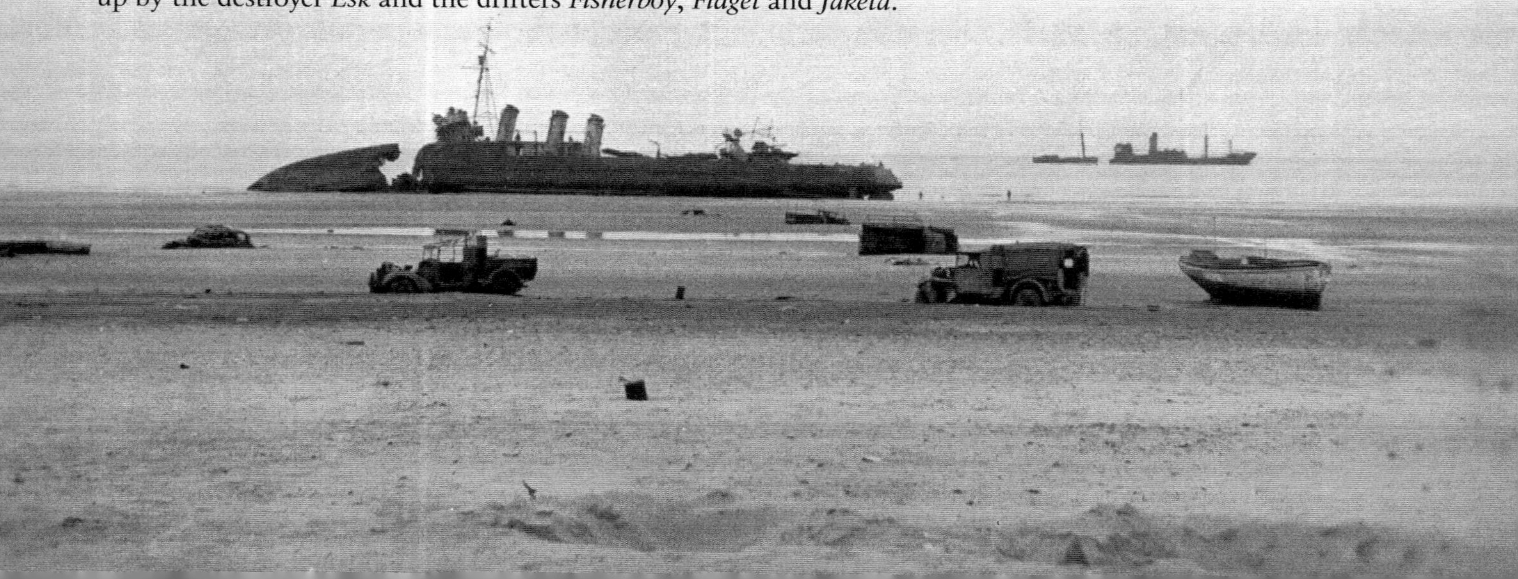

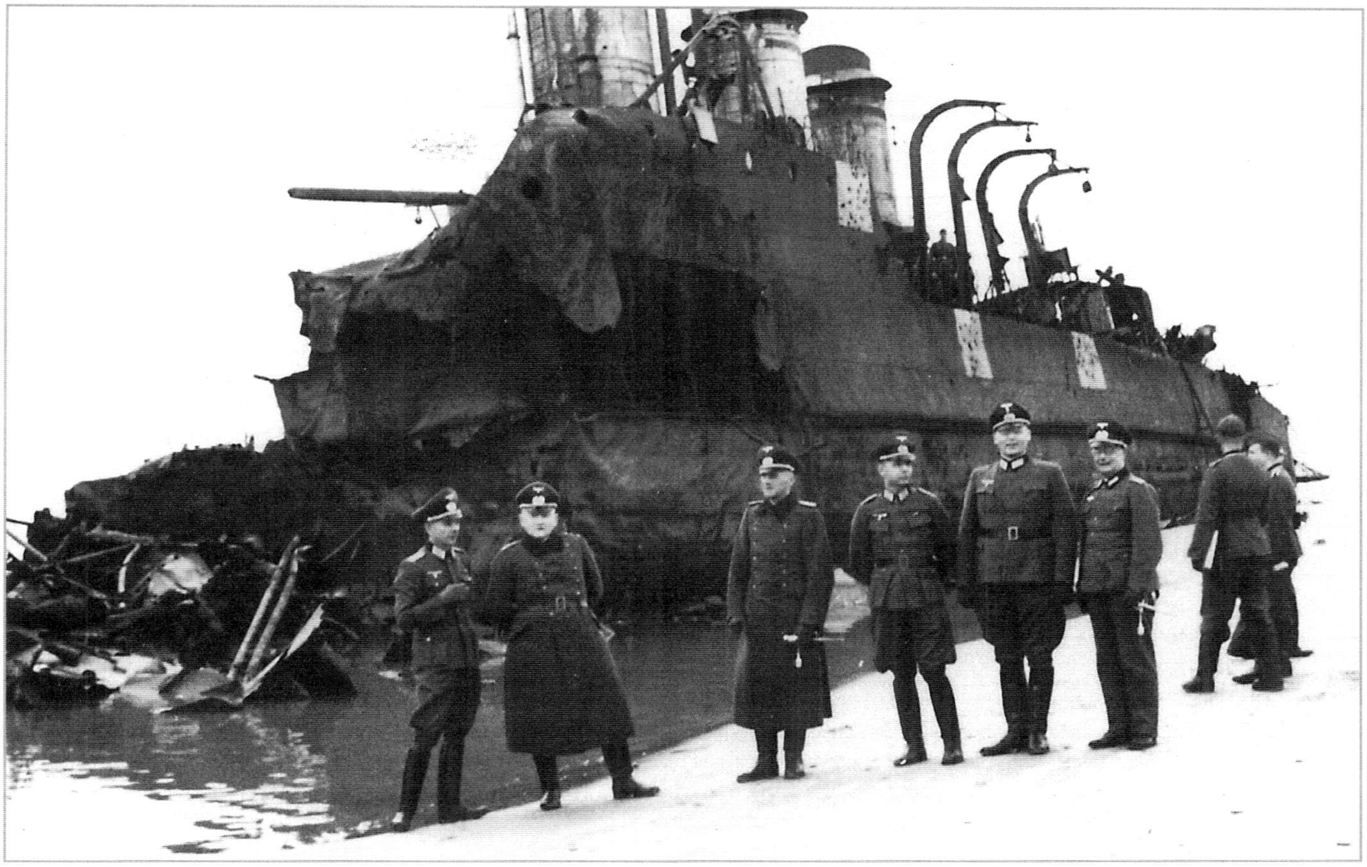

The wreck of the *L'Adroit* after being used as a target for 20 mm German flak guns, note the white painted squares that have been hit many times, indeed the whole bridge section has been blown away.

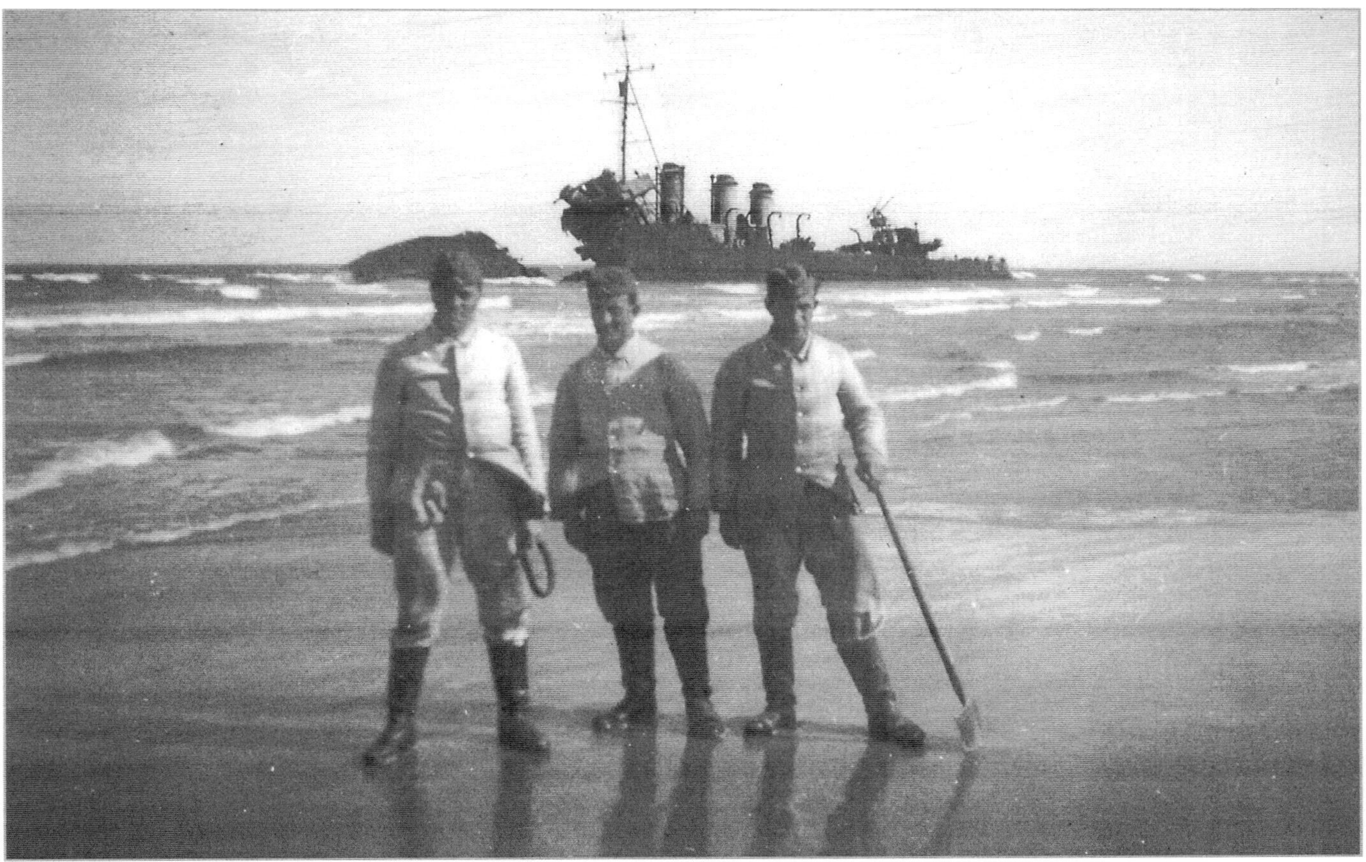

A group of three soldiers from a German sanitary unit pose for a photograph with the wreck of the *L'Adroit* behind them.

The lightship *Wandelaar*. One of the many casualties of the channel war in 1940, beached just east of Dunkirk, west of Ostend in Belgium.

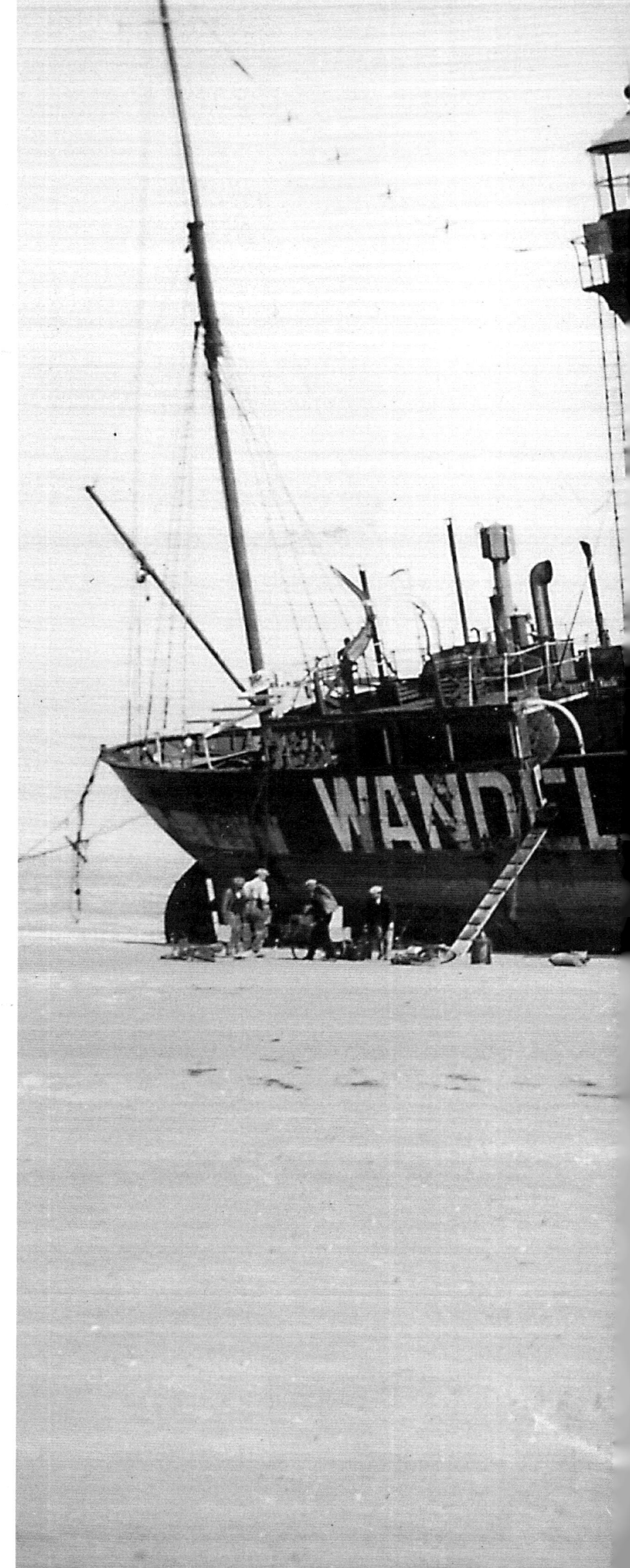

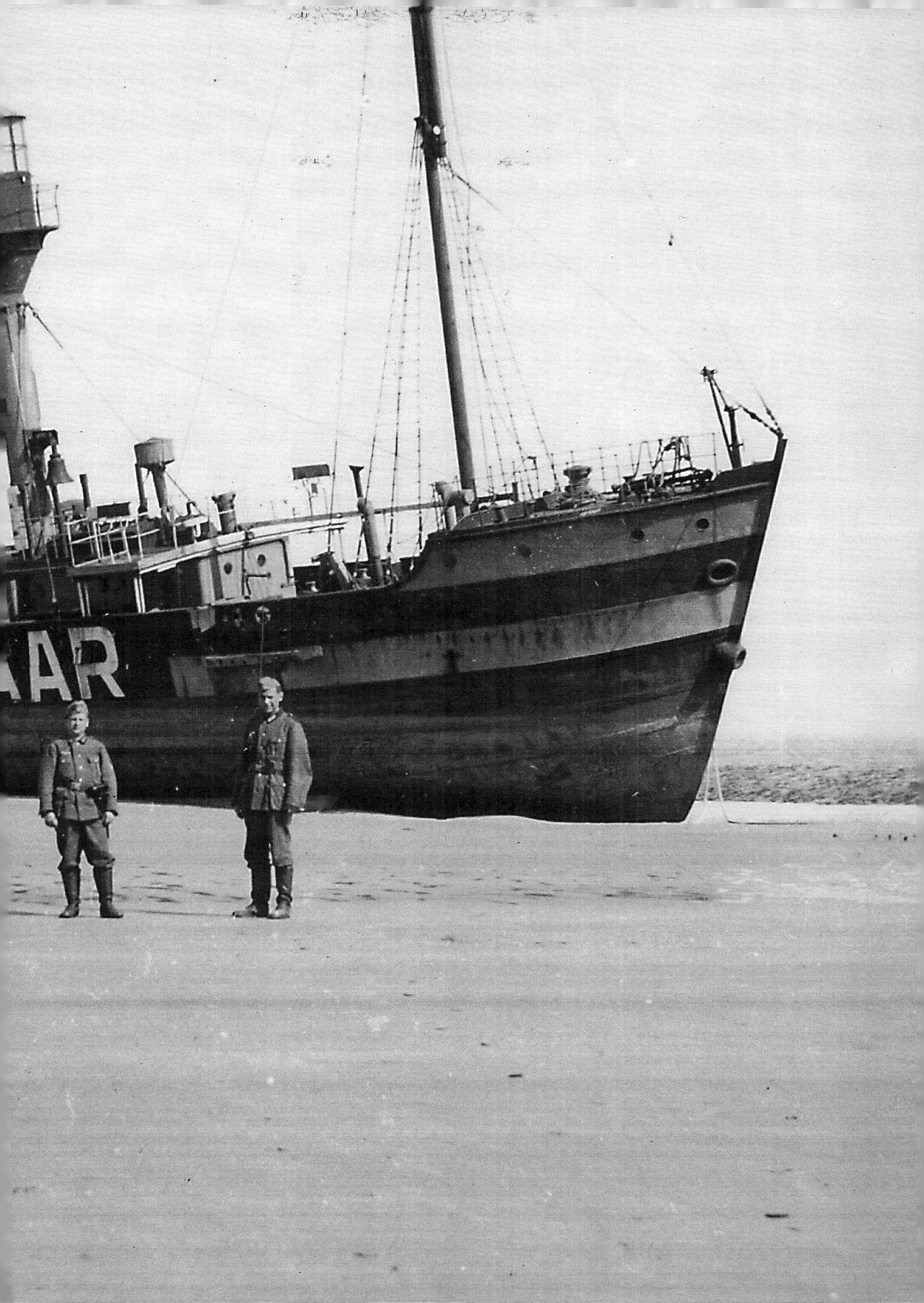
AAR

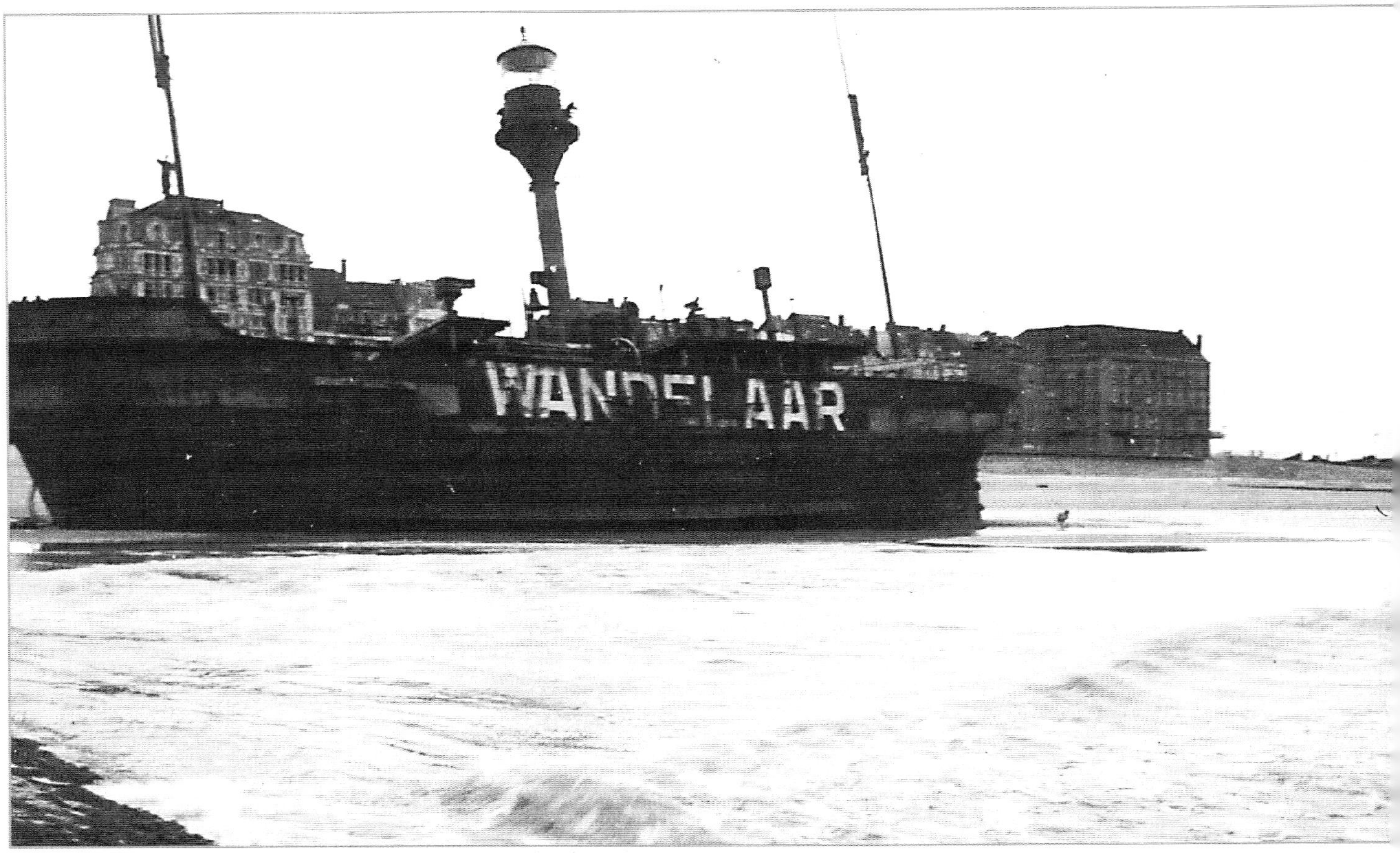

The lightship *Wandelaar* like many of the Dunkirk wrecks was pushed further and further up the coast east, towards Ostend, by successive tides.

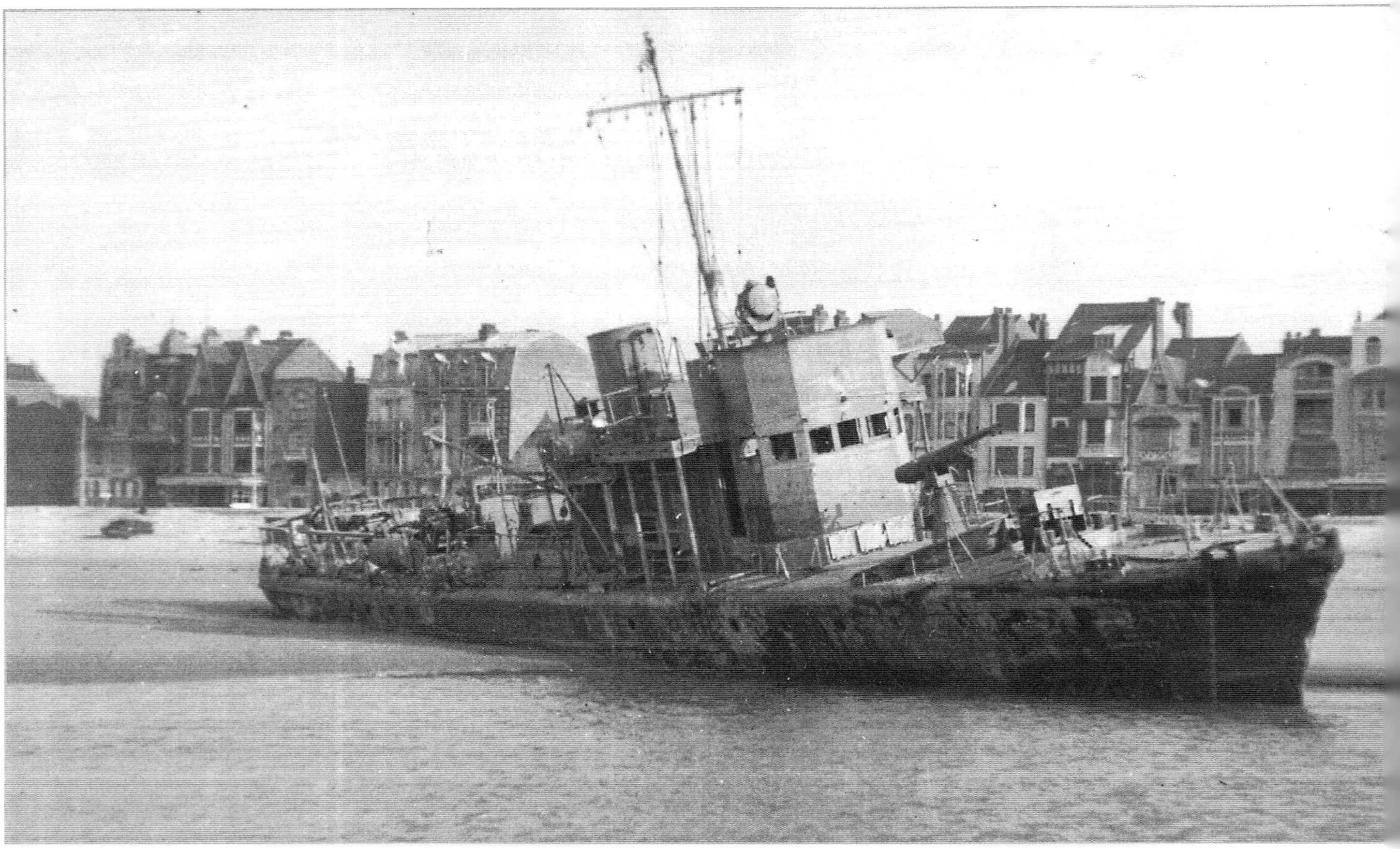

A nice view of the beached French anti-submarine coastal patrol boat (CH-9) *Chasseur 9*. Commissioned in 1940.

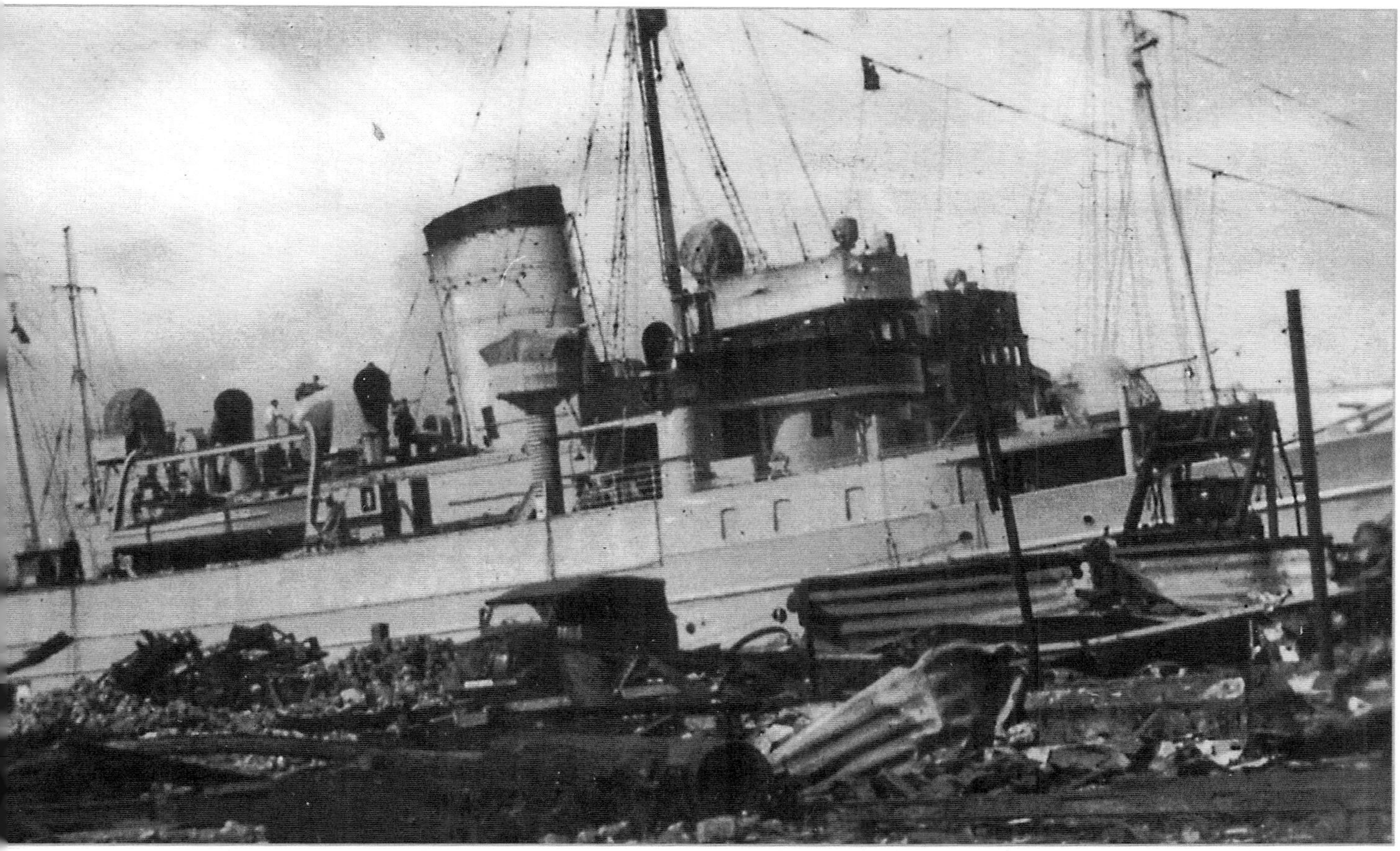

HMS *Skipjack*, a Mine-Sweeper seen here in Dunkirk harbour. She was sunk on the 1st of June just outside the harbour's mole.

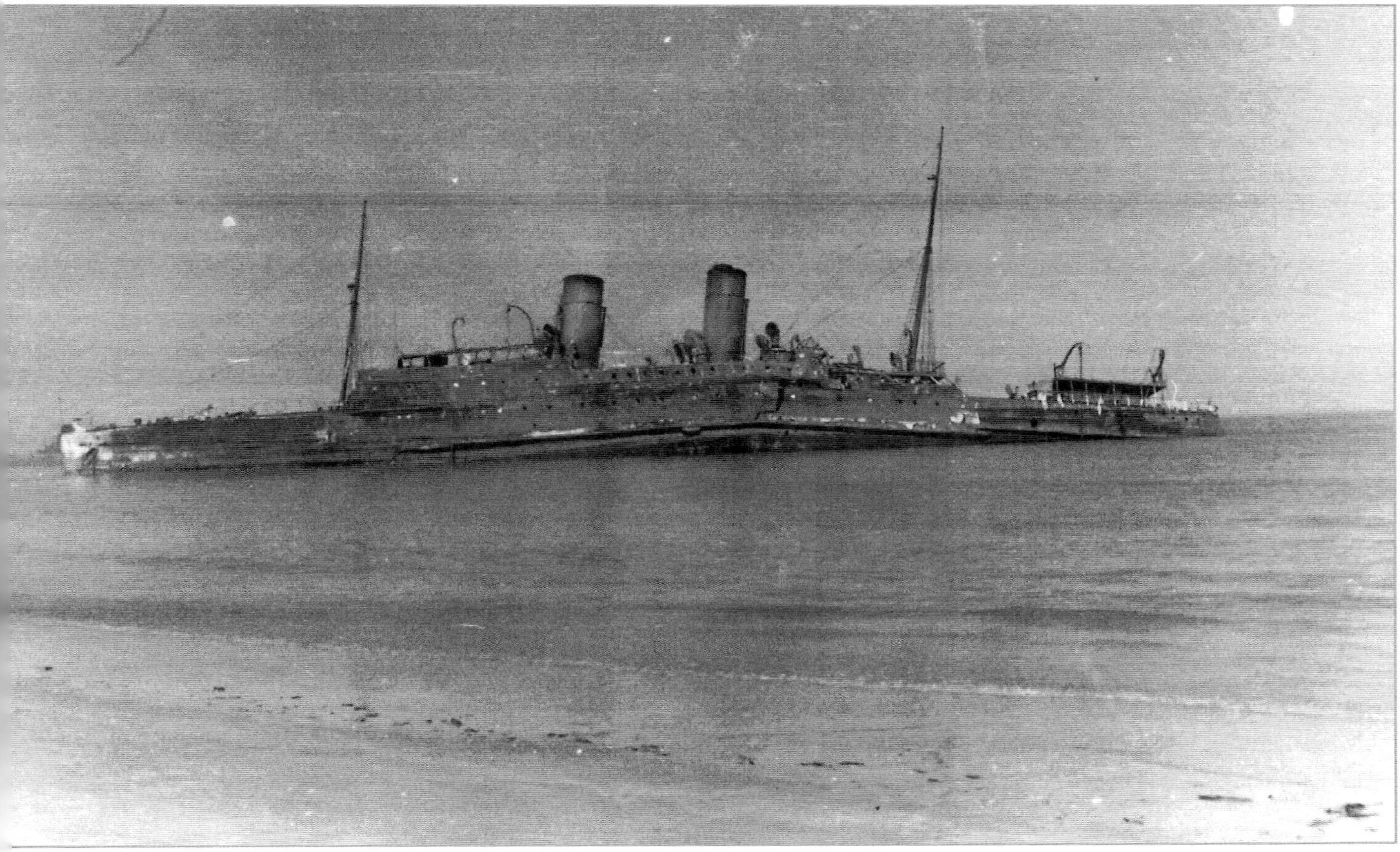

Another of the many ships lost during operation 'Dynamo'.

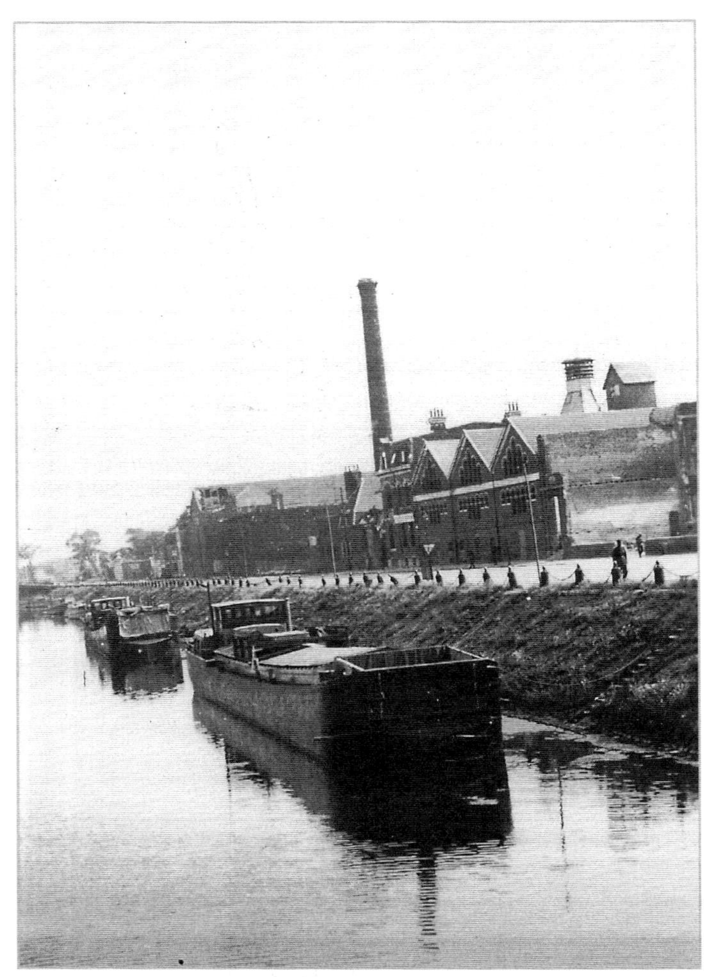

Coal barges tied up at the side of one of Dunkirk's many interconnecting channels.

The coastal freighter *Horst Gronngen*

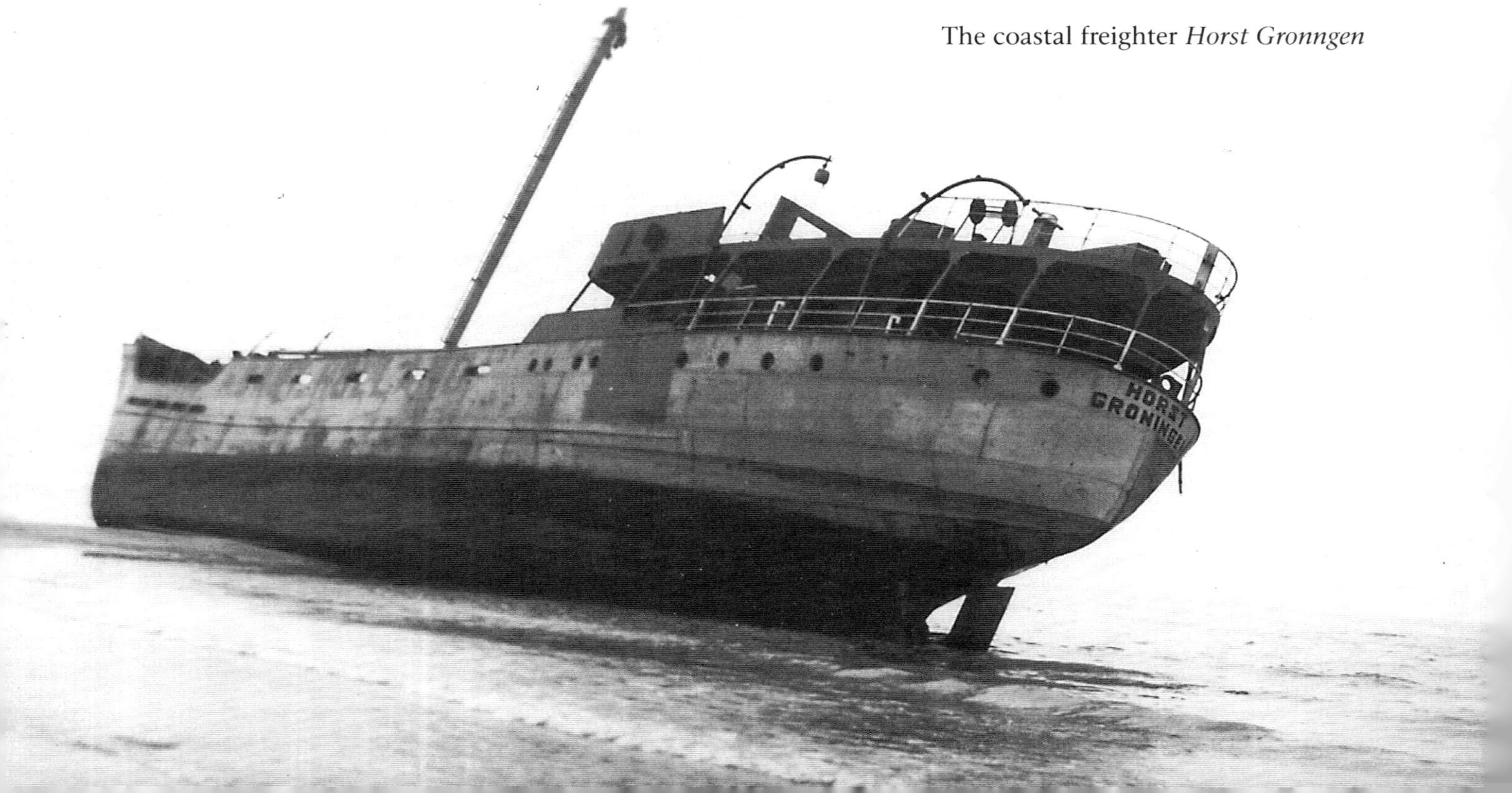

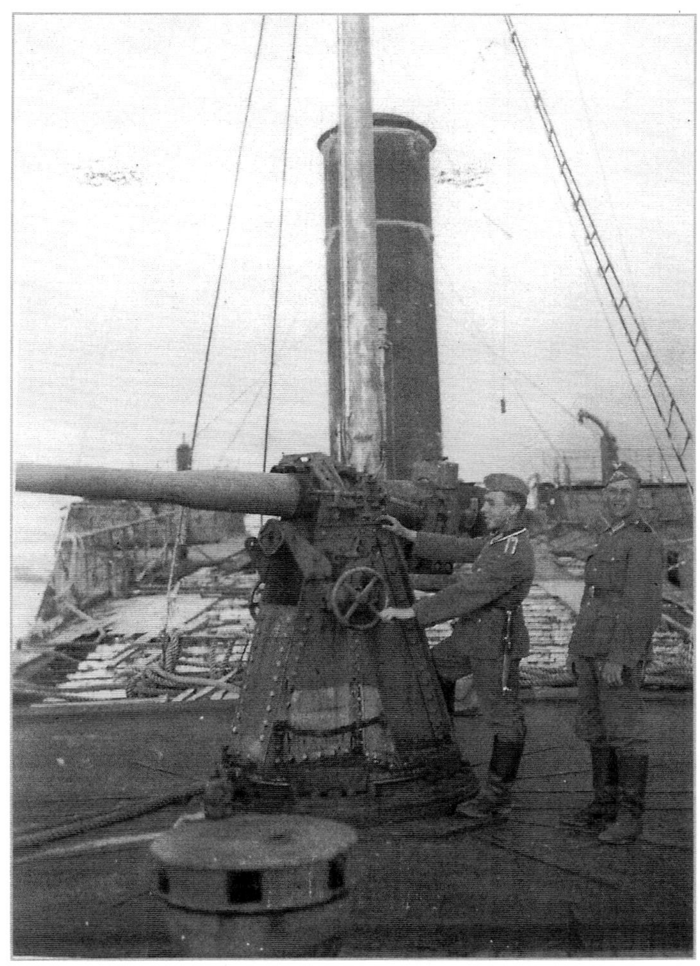

The weapon of an armed merchantman also lost during operation 'Dynamo'.

The French anti-submarine coastal patrol boat (CH-9) *Chasseur 9*. She was armed with 2 x 75 mm Schneider cannons and 8 machine guns. Bombed and badly damaged on the 22nd of May 1940, her master Captain Lv Le Templier ran the boat aground just east of the harbour rather than have it sink in the harbours mouth. All 23 of the crew survived.

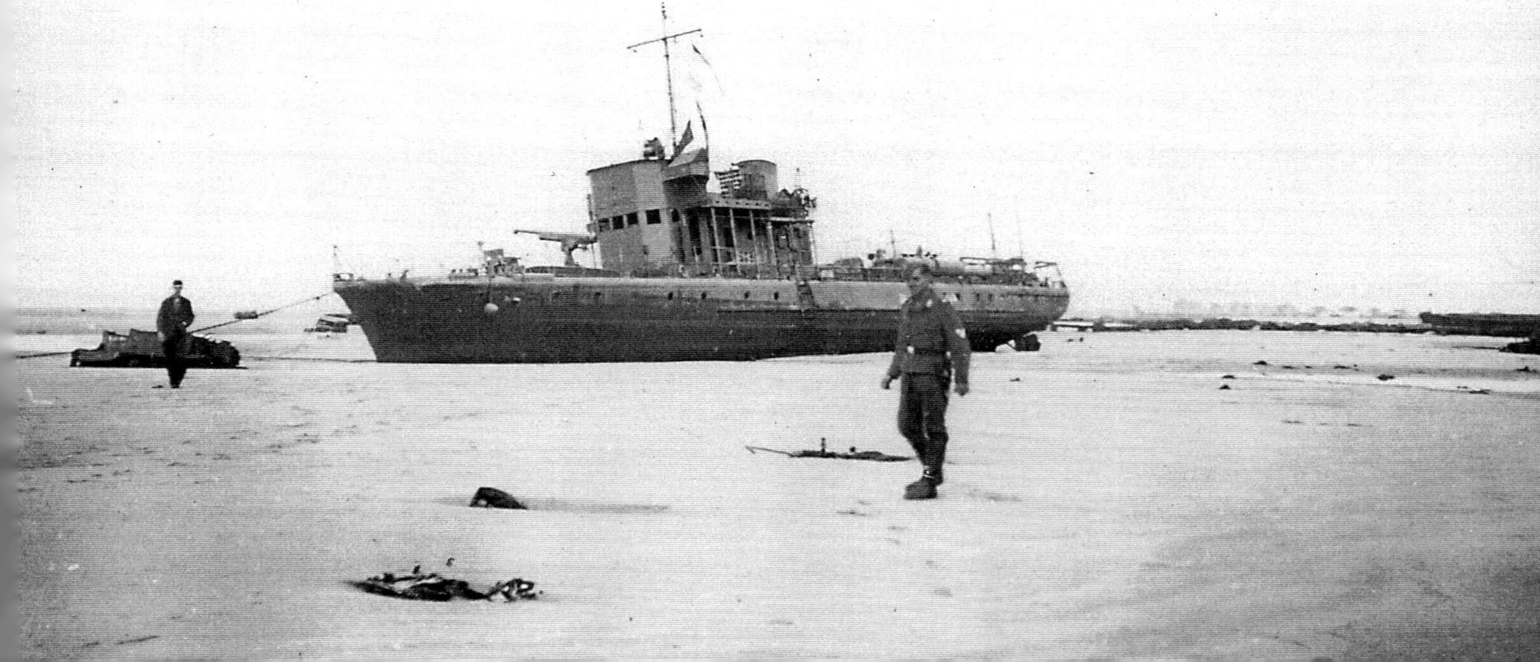

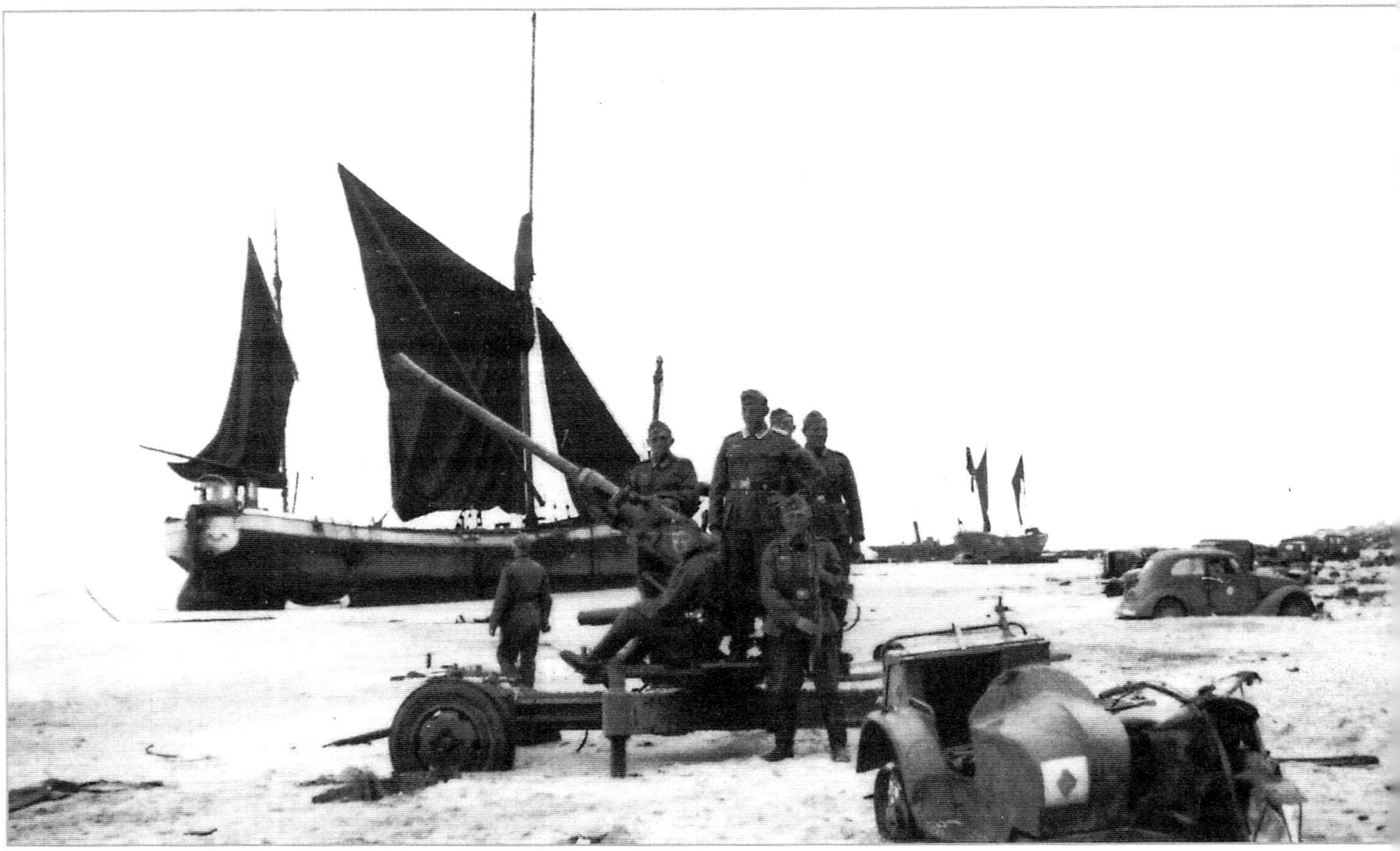

The Thames barges *Ethel Everard*, *Lark* & *The Brighton Queen* paddle steamer in the background. In the foreground a 40 mm Bofers gun and a badly damaged Gnome-Rhône motorcycle and sidecar.

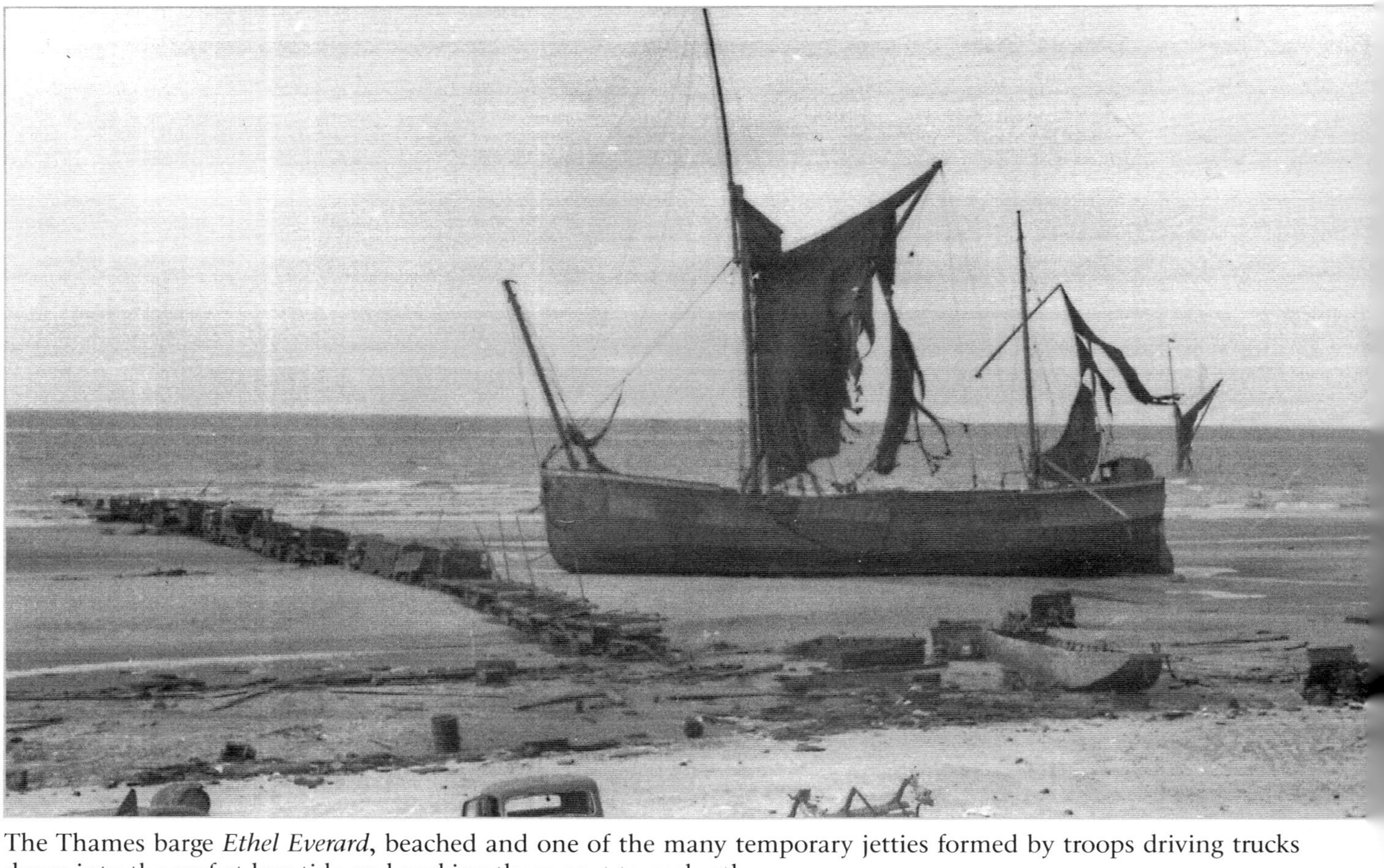

The Thames barge *Ethel Everard*, beached and one of the many temporary jetties formed by troops driving trucks down into the surf at low tide and parking them next to each other.

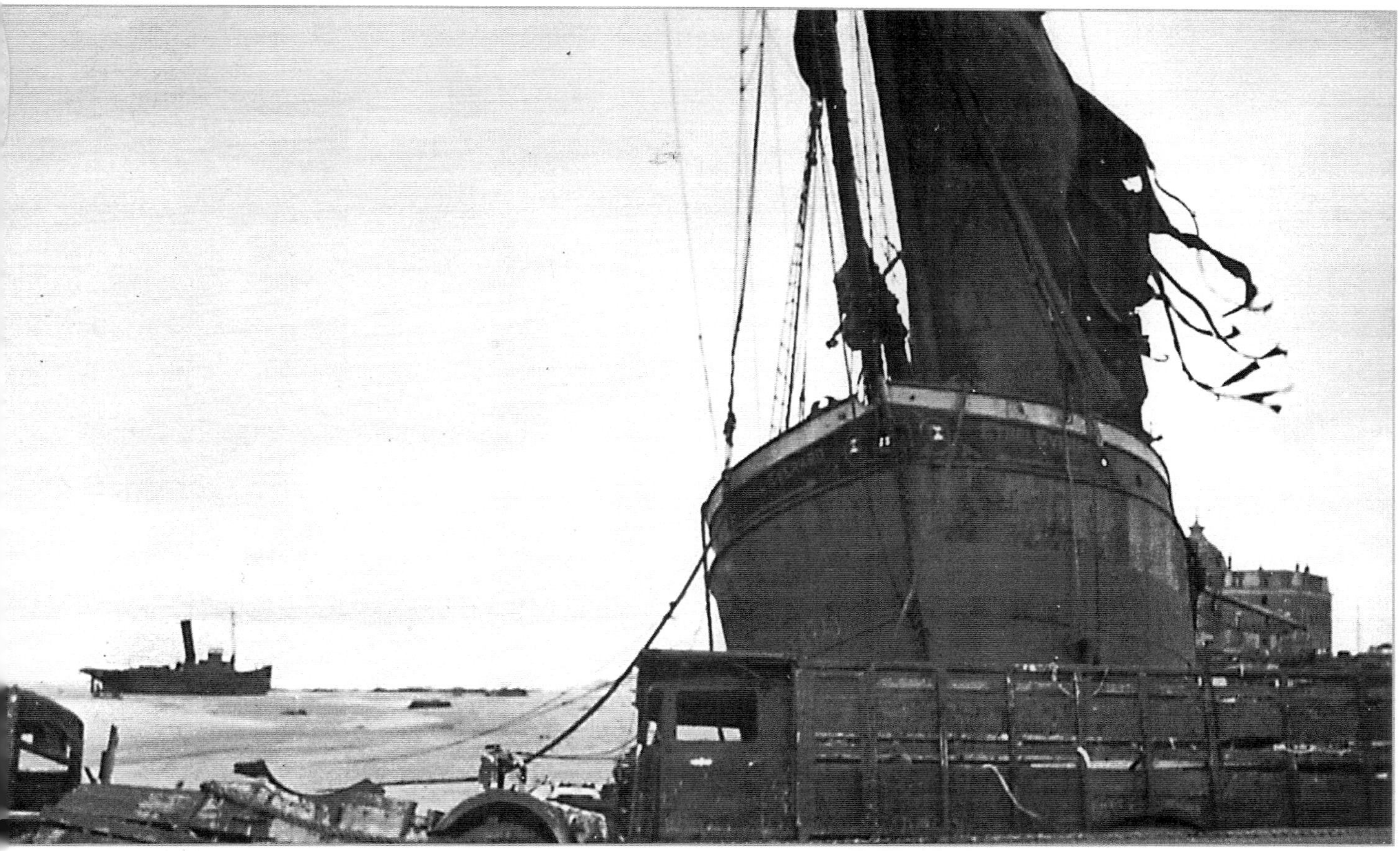

The Thames barge *Ethel Everard* from the front & the tug *Fossa* in the background.

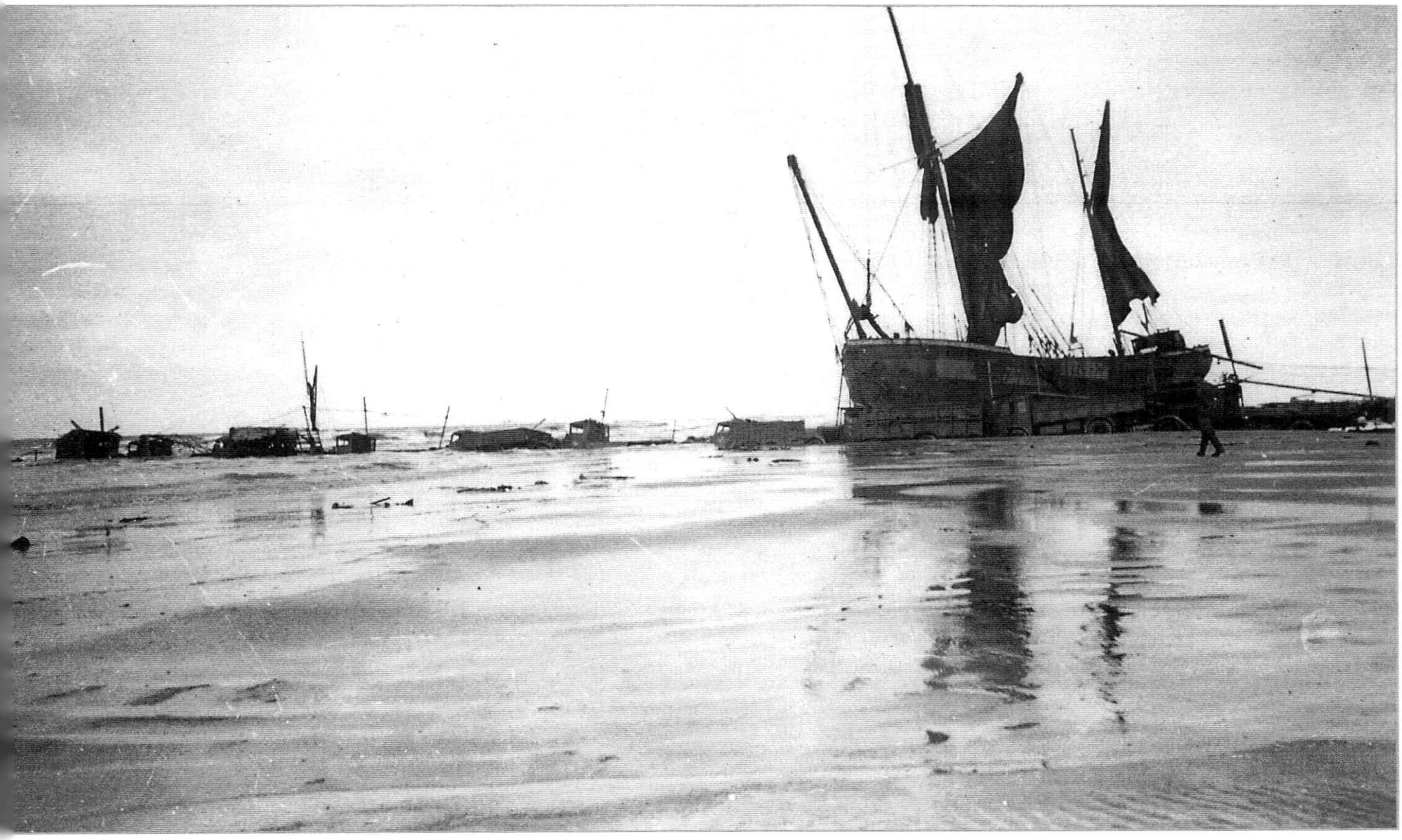

The Thames barge *Ethel Everard*. Only days after the evacuation the trucks that formed the temporary jetty are already beginning to sink into the sand.

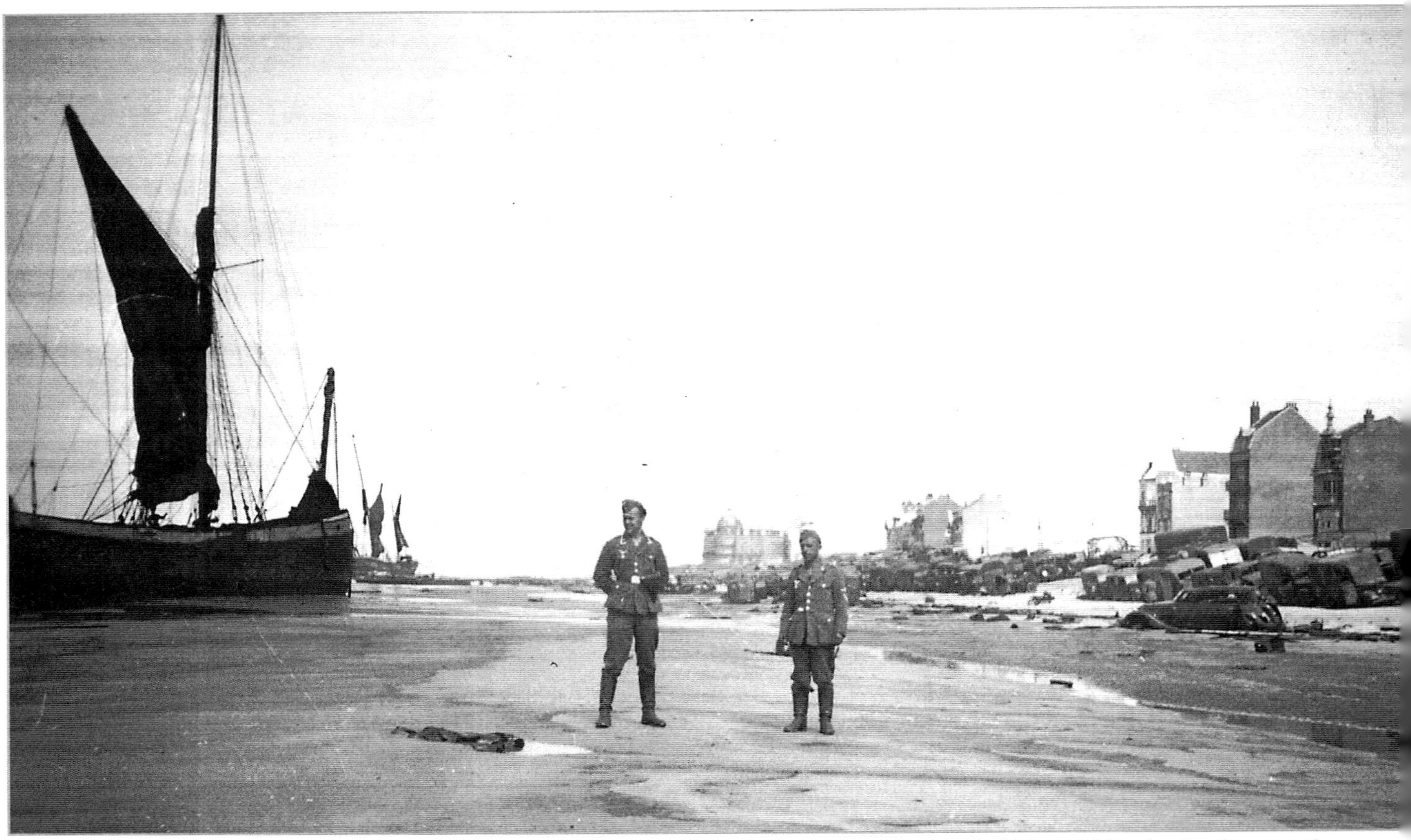

Two German infantry NCOs pose on the beach with the Thames barges *Lark* & *Ethel Everard* in the background. This photograph is rare as it is shot looking from the beach up to the promenade and gives us a glimpse of the number of vehicles abandoned on the promenade.

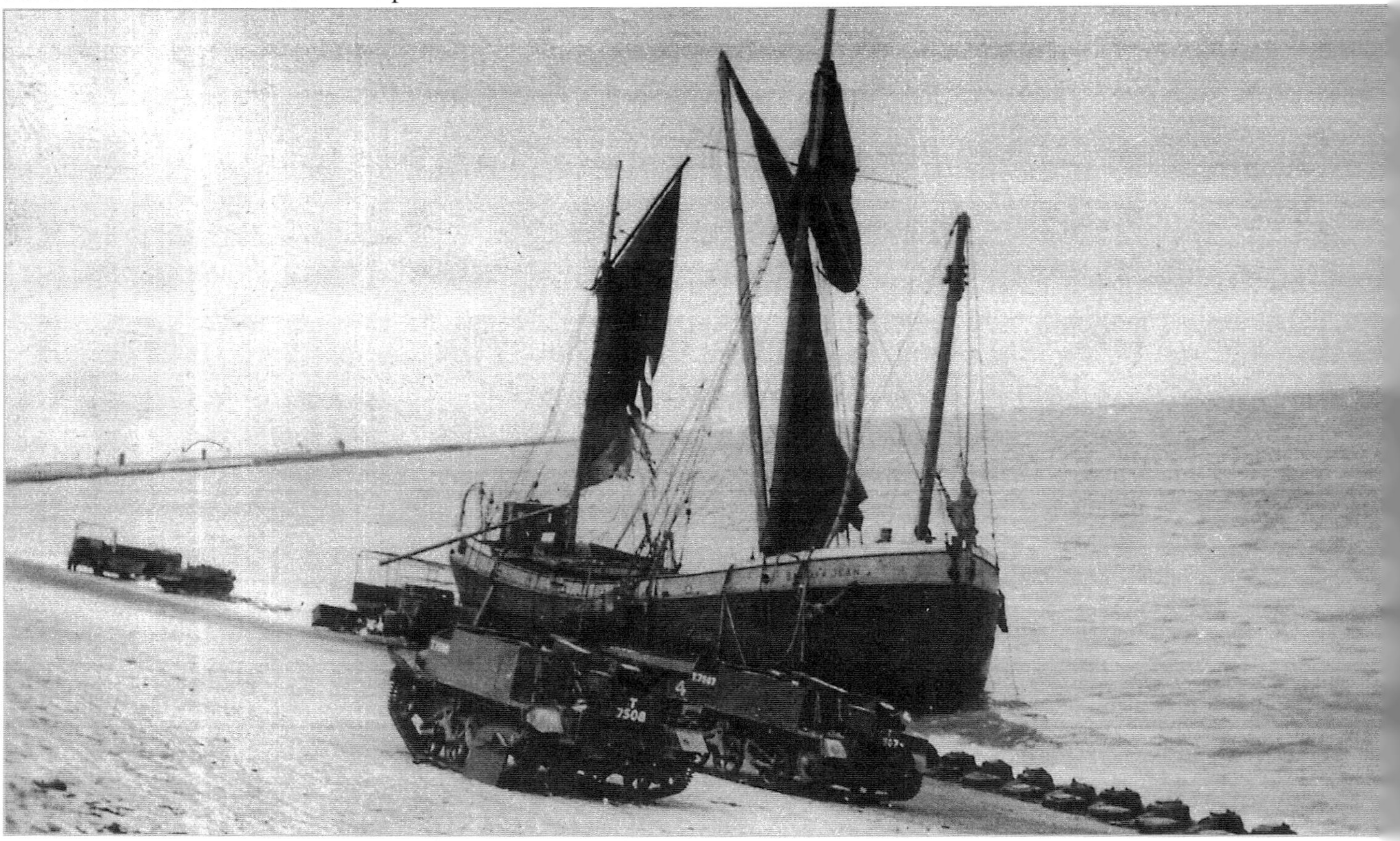

The Thames barge *Barbara Jean* lies further east along the coast on La Panne beach, notice the abandoned British universal carriers also left there in apparently good order.

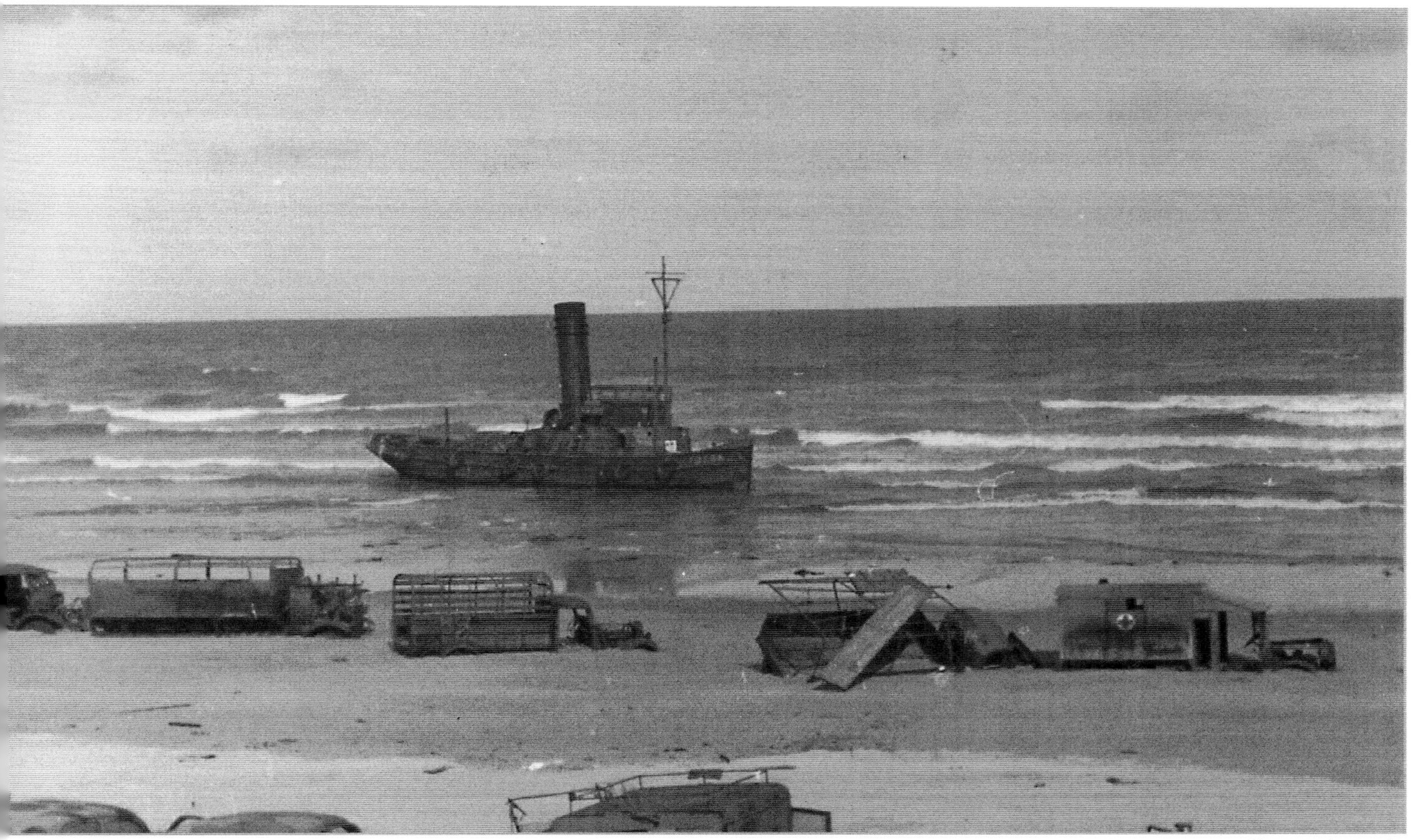

The tug *Fossa* later recovered and put back into service by the German KMD (*Kriegsmarine Dienststelle*) and made ready for use in operation 'Sea-Lion', the planned German invasion of England.

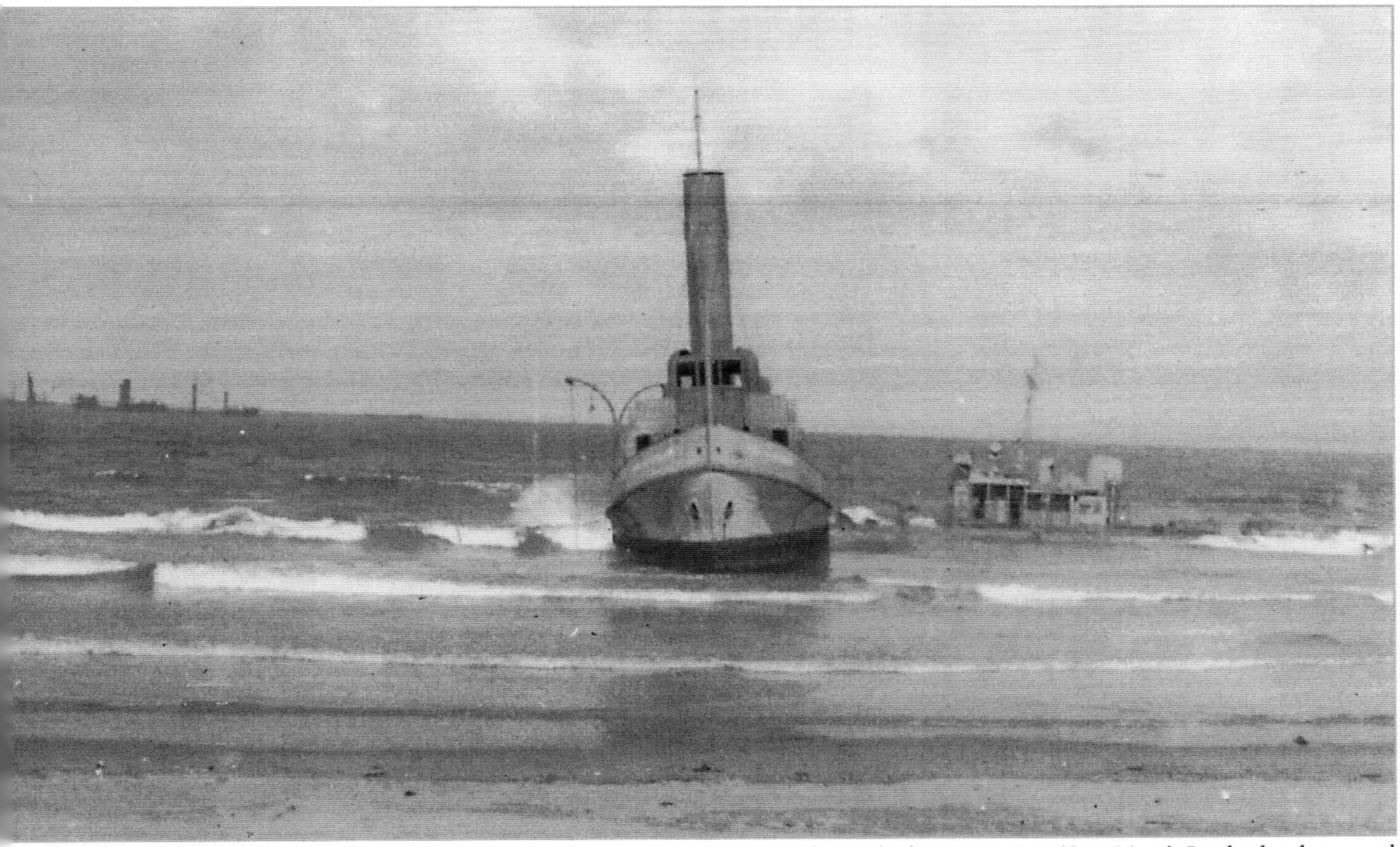

Another tug, the Dutch *Port De Beyrouth*, also recovered and made ready for operation 'Sea-Lion'. In the background the French coastal patrol boat (CH-9) *Chasseur 9*.

A beached fishing trawler one of the many
conscripted little boats lost during operation
'Dynamo'.

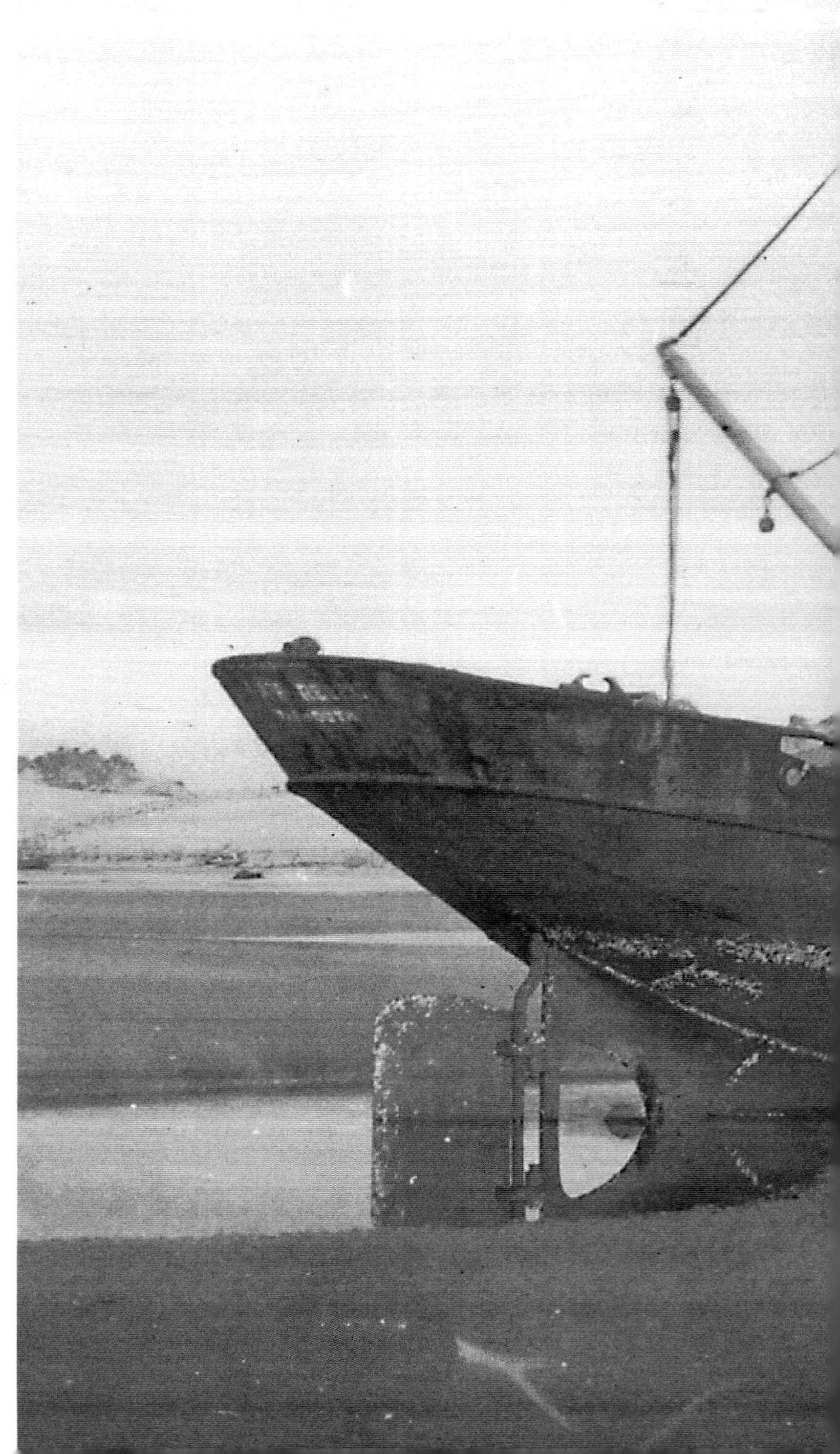

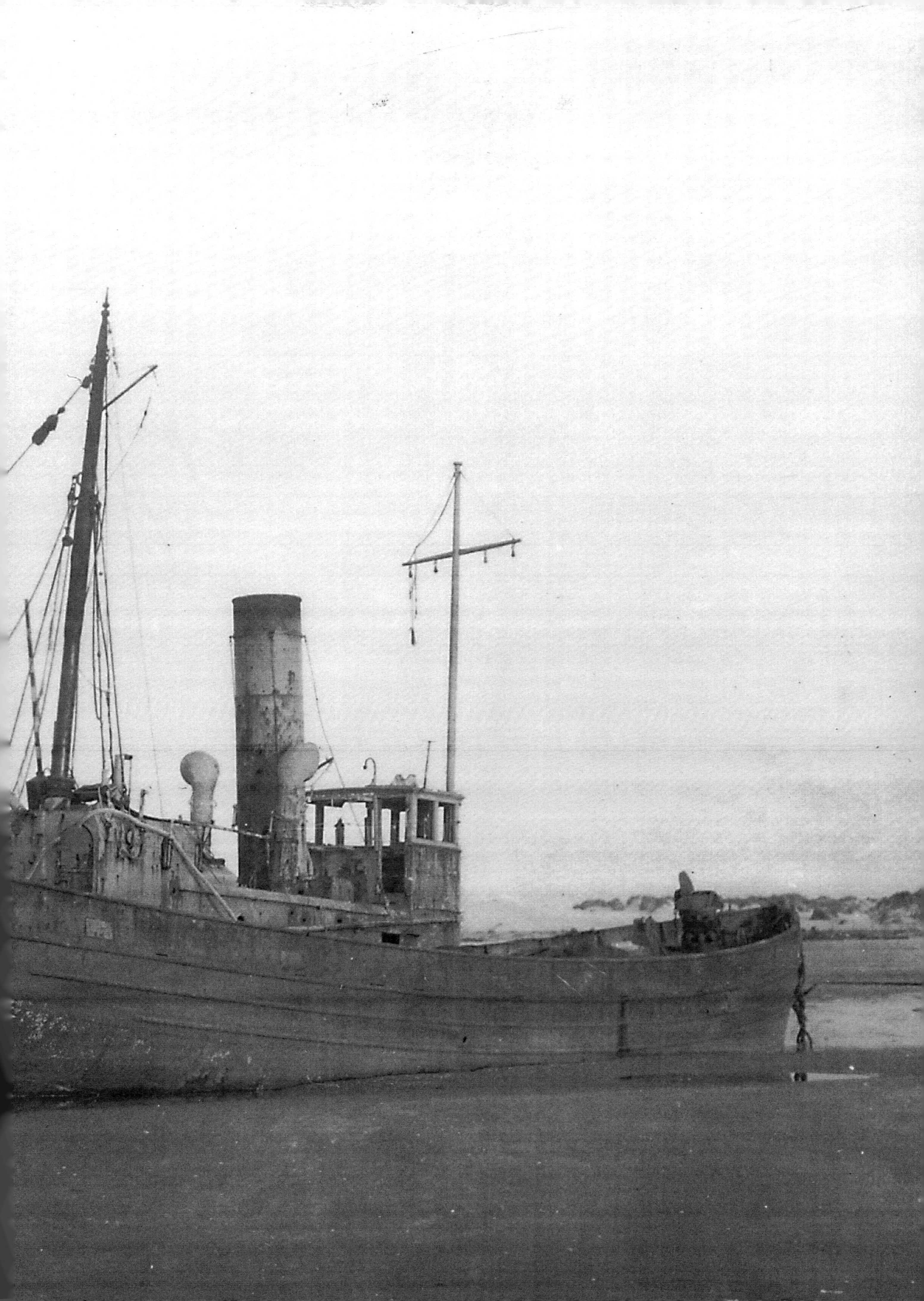

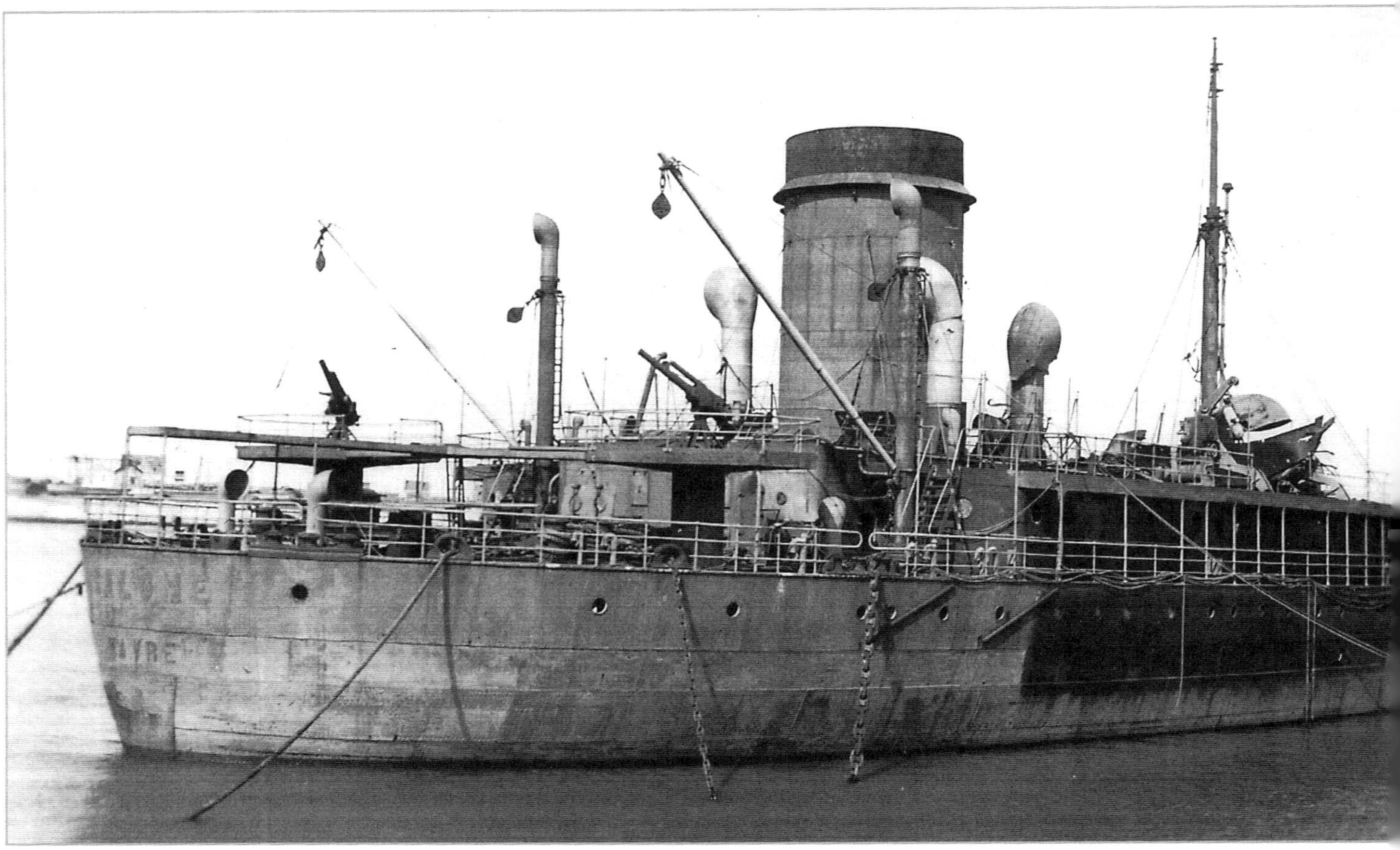

Beached armed merchantman from the operation 'Dynamo' fleet.

The often photographed French coastal patrol boat (CH-9) *Chasseur 9*, clearly shown is damage caused by the Germans taking pot shots at the wrecks for target practice and also one of the 75 mm Schneider cannons being inspected by a curious German.

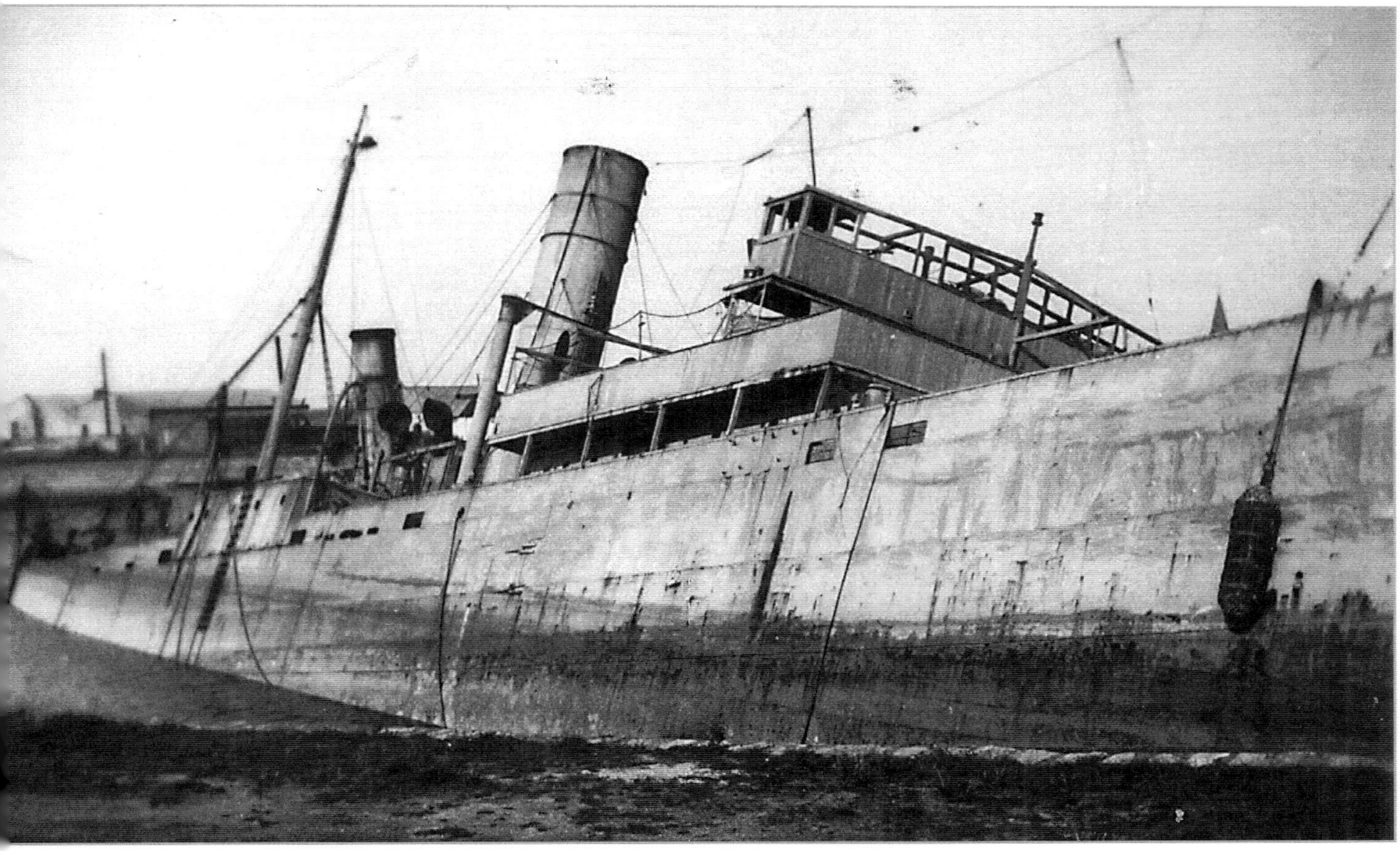

One of the tramp steamers sunk inside Dunkirk harbour.

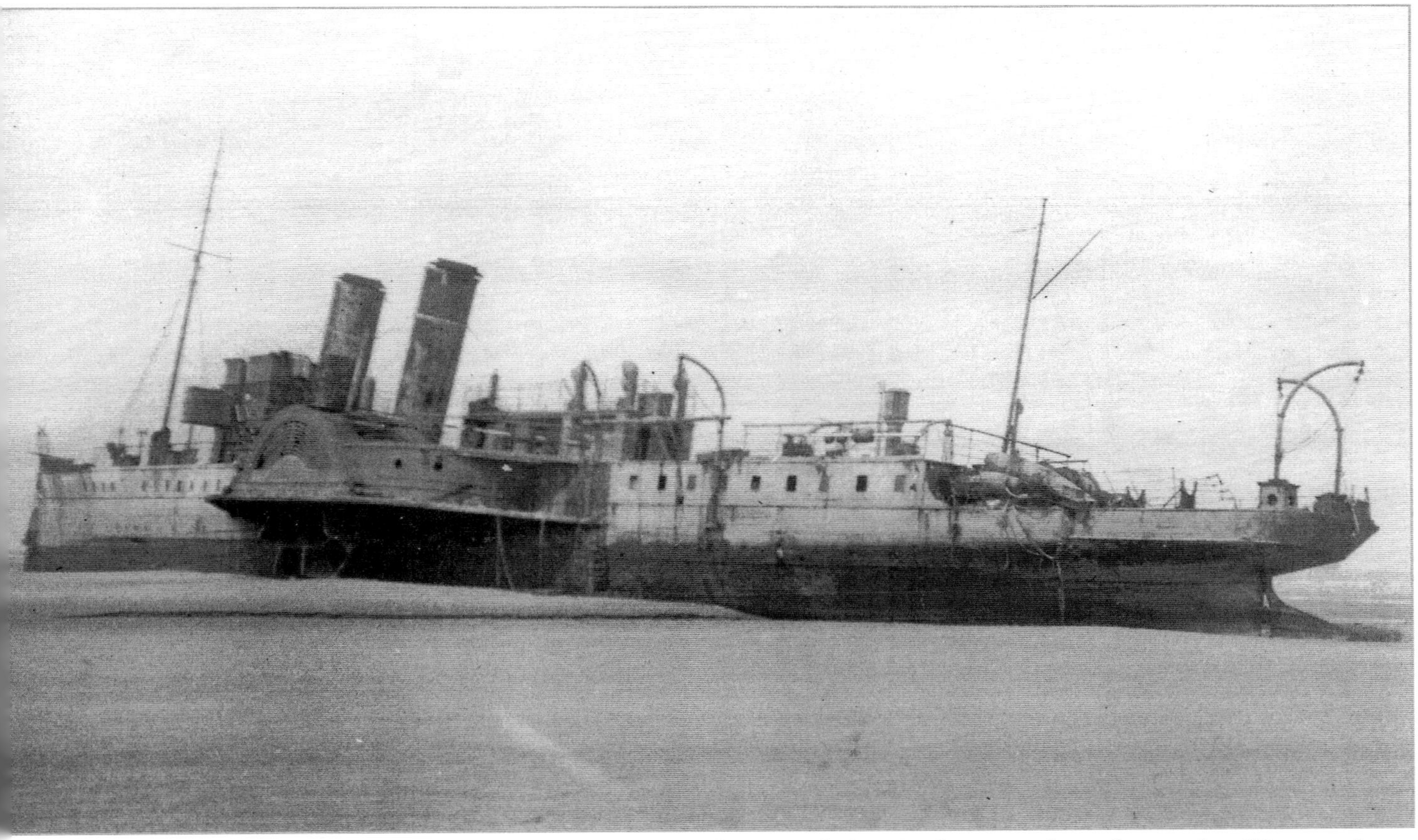

The Brighton Queen a commandeered ferry that was subsequently lost in the execution of operation 'Dynamo'.

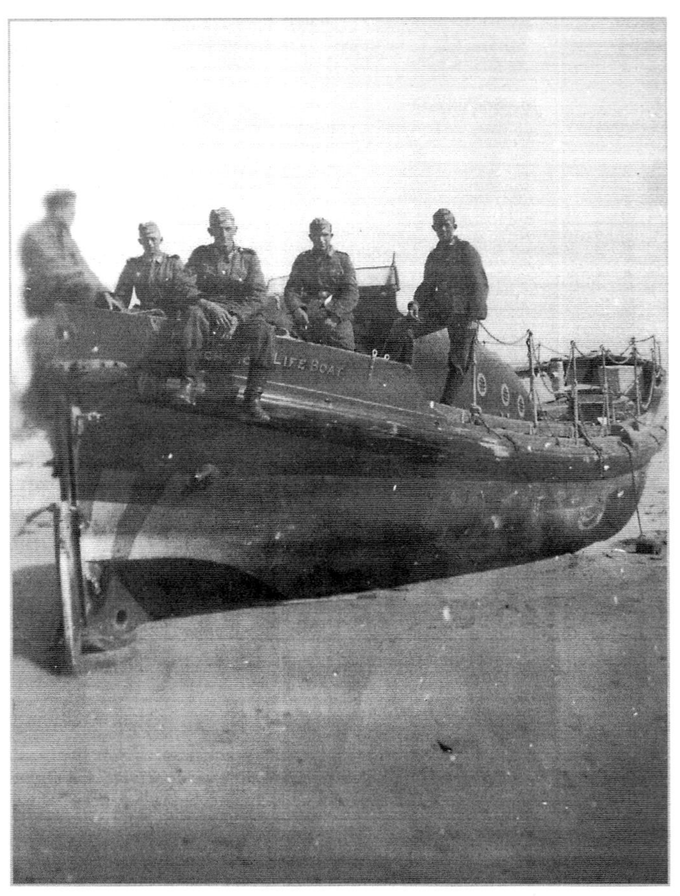 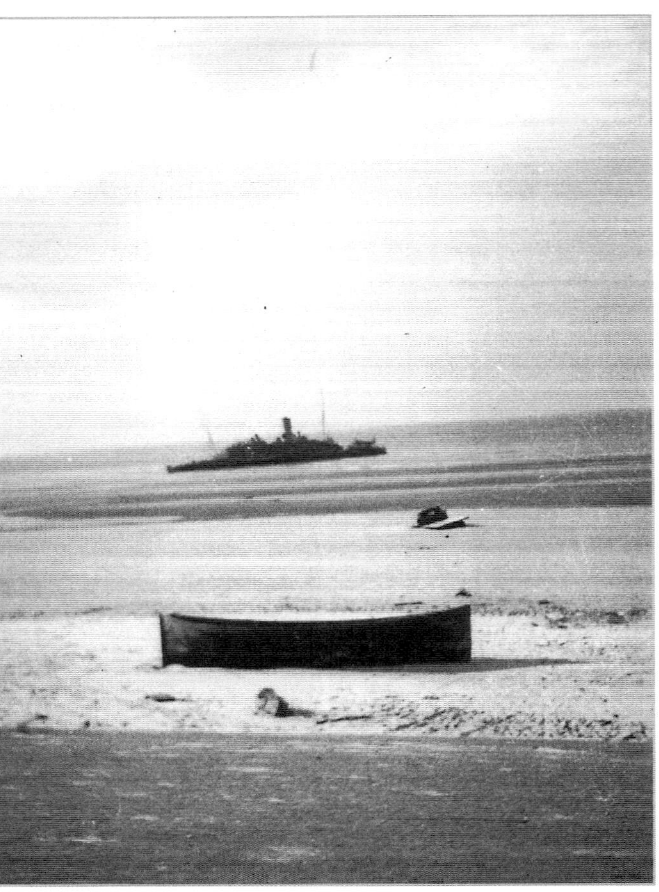

Of the nine R.N.L.I. lifeboats that took part in the evacuation only one was permanently lost, one other suffered engine failure on the return journey but was recovered and towed home before drifting back to France.

The Brighton Queen paddle steamer beached at the very limit of low tide.

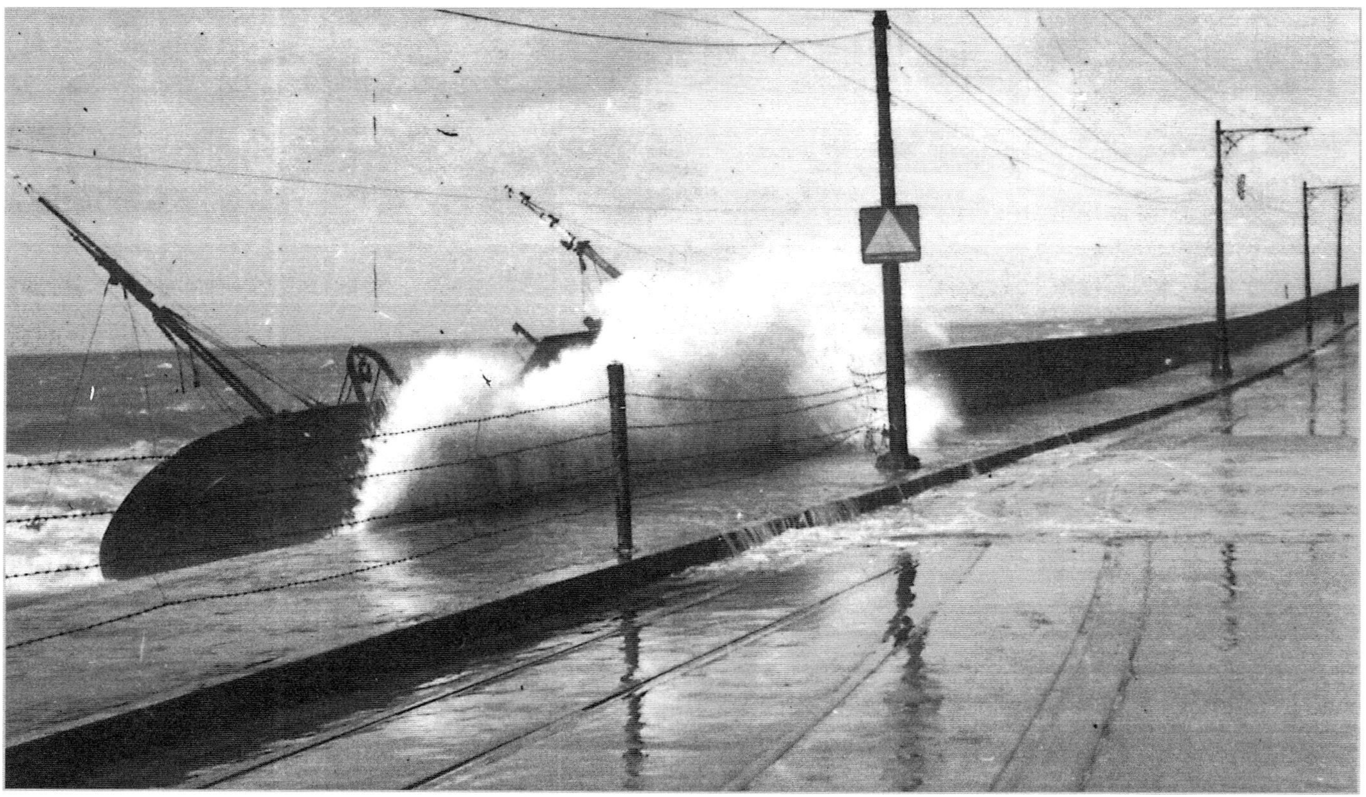

One of the many fishing trawlers lost, this one being bashed by a storm further up the coast towards Ostend. As time passed the prevailing tides moved many of the wrecks down the coast to the east of Dunkirk.

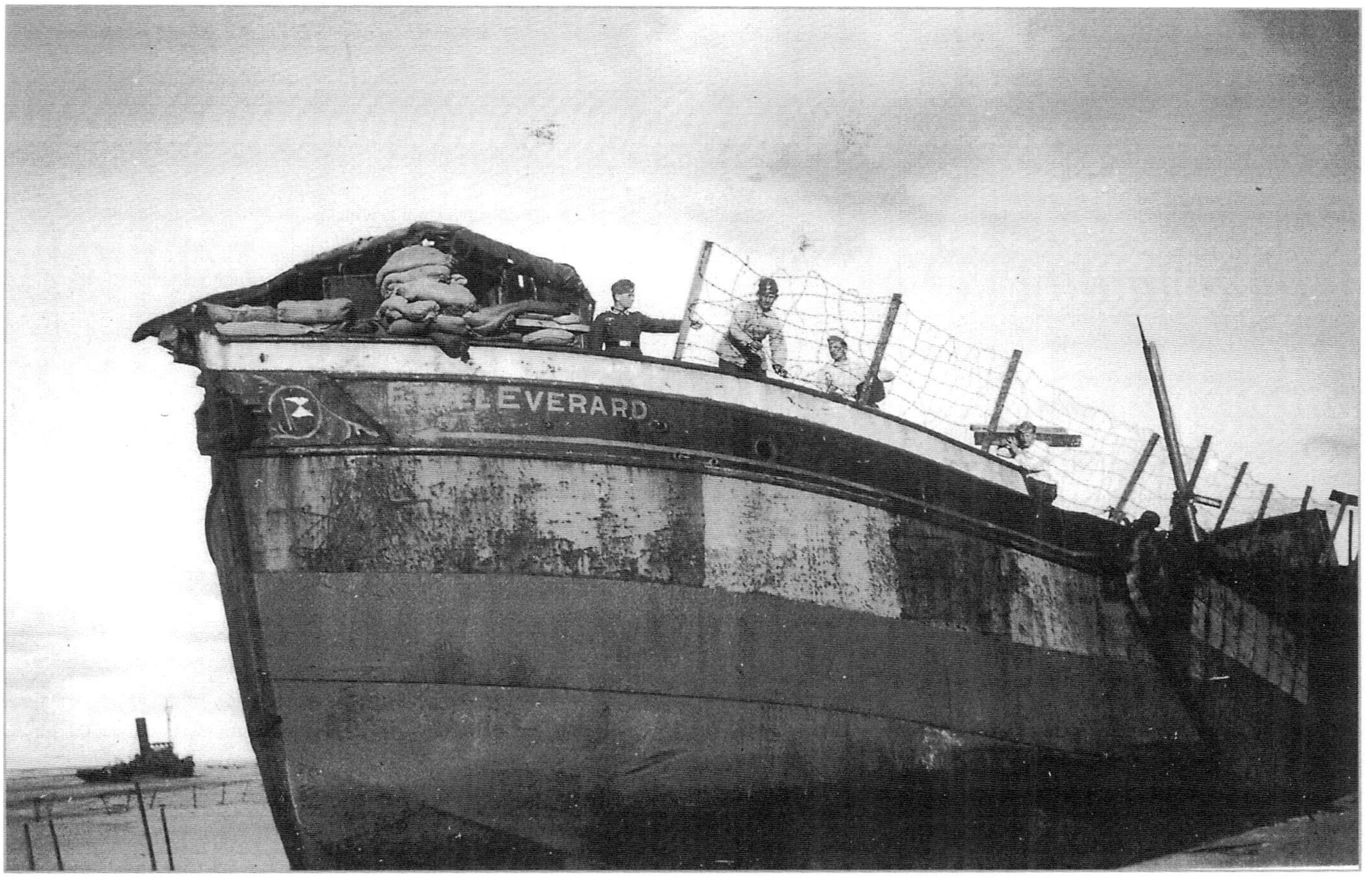

The bow of the Thames barge *Ethel Everard* with the tug *Fossa* in the background.

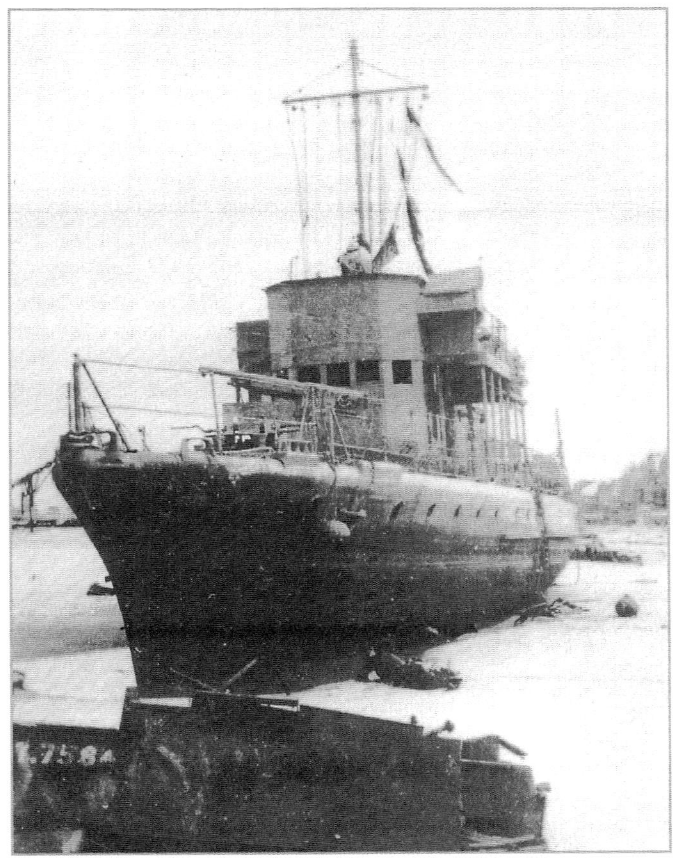

More of the often photographed French Coastal Patrol Boat (CH-9) *Chasseur 9*.

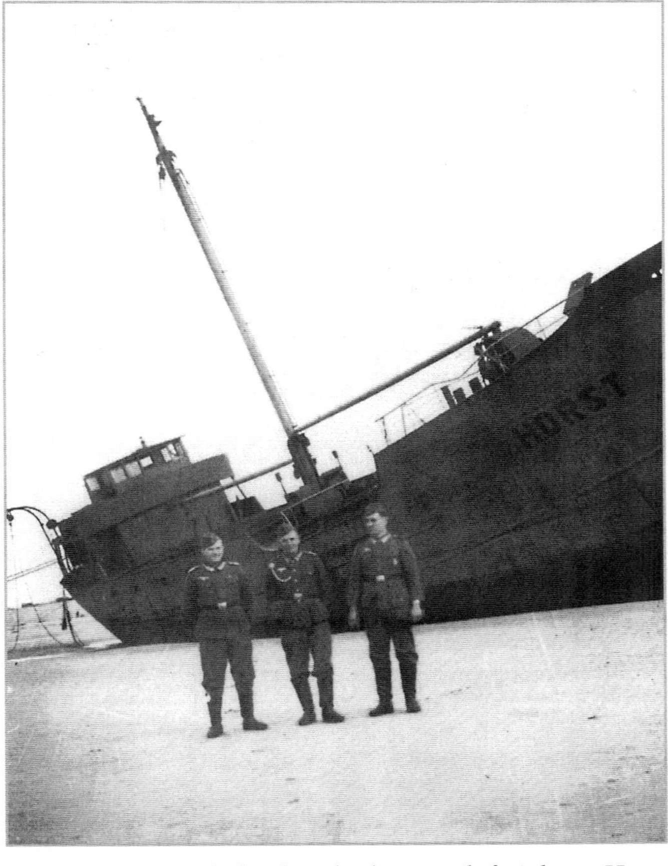

Another view of the beached coastal freighter *Horst Gronngen*.

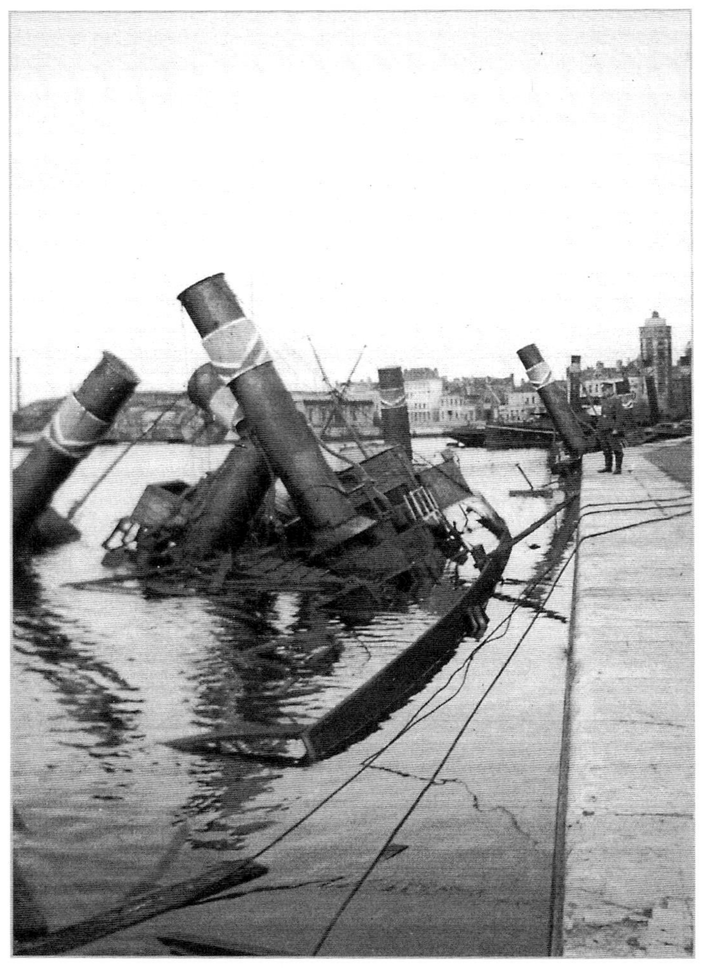

A whole flotilla of tugs were sunk whilst tied up in the inner harbour by constant bombing, artillery strikes and German aircraft strafing them with heavy machine gunfire.

Dunkirk's inner harbour entrance with the harbour master's office in the foreground.

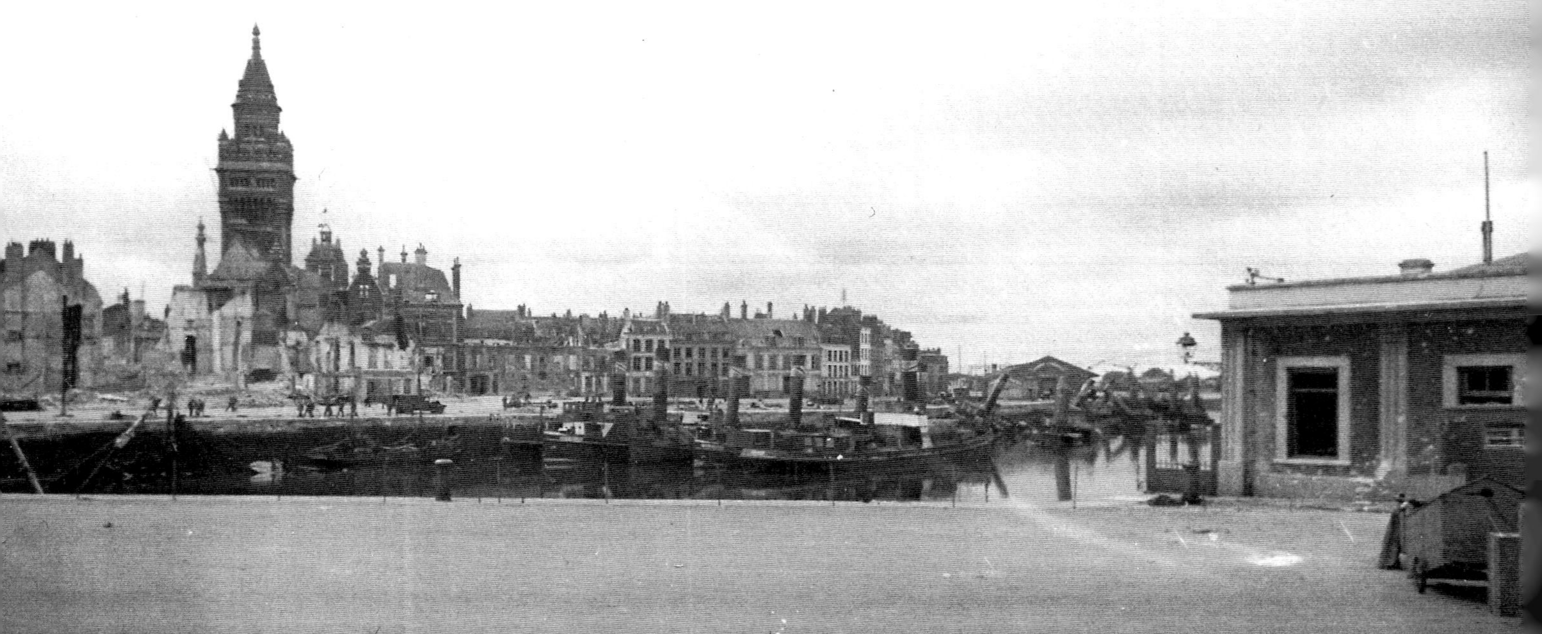

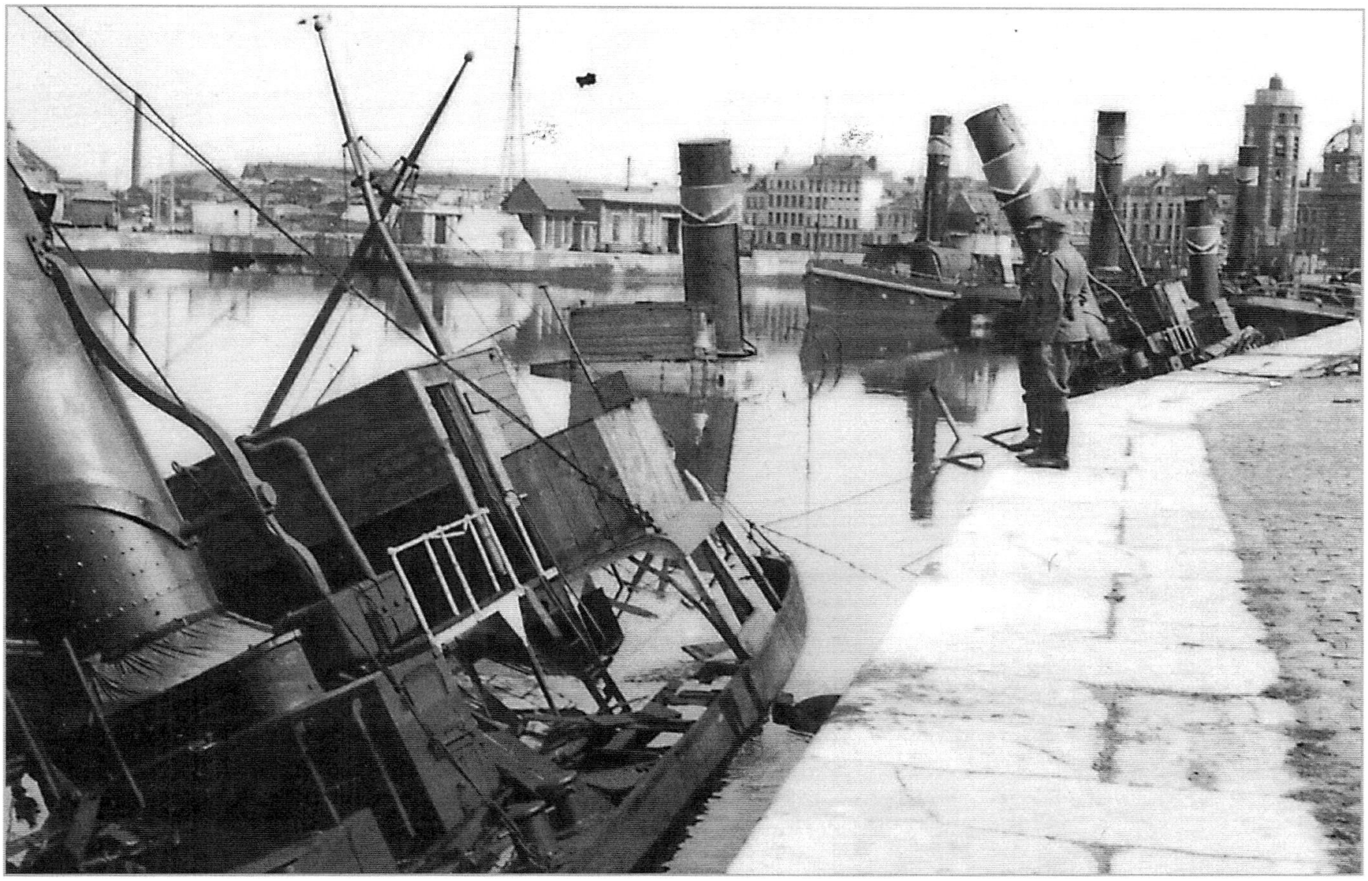

The next four pages give various views of the tug flotilla sunk in the inner harbour of Dunkirk during early June of 1940.

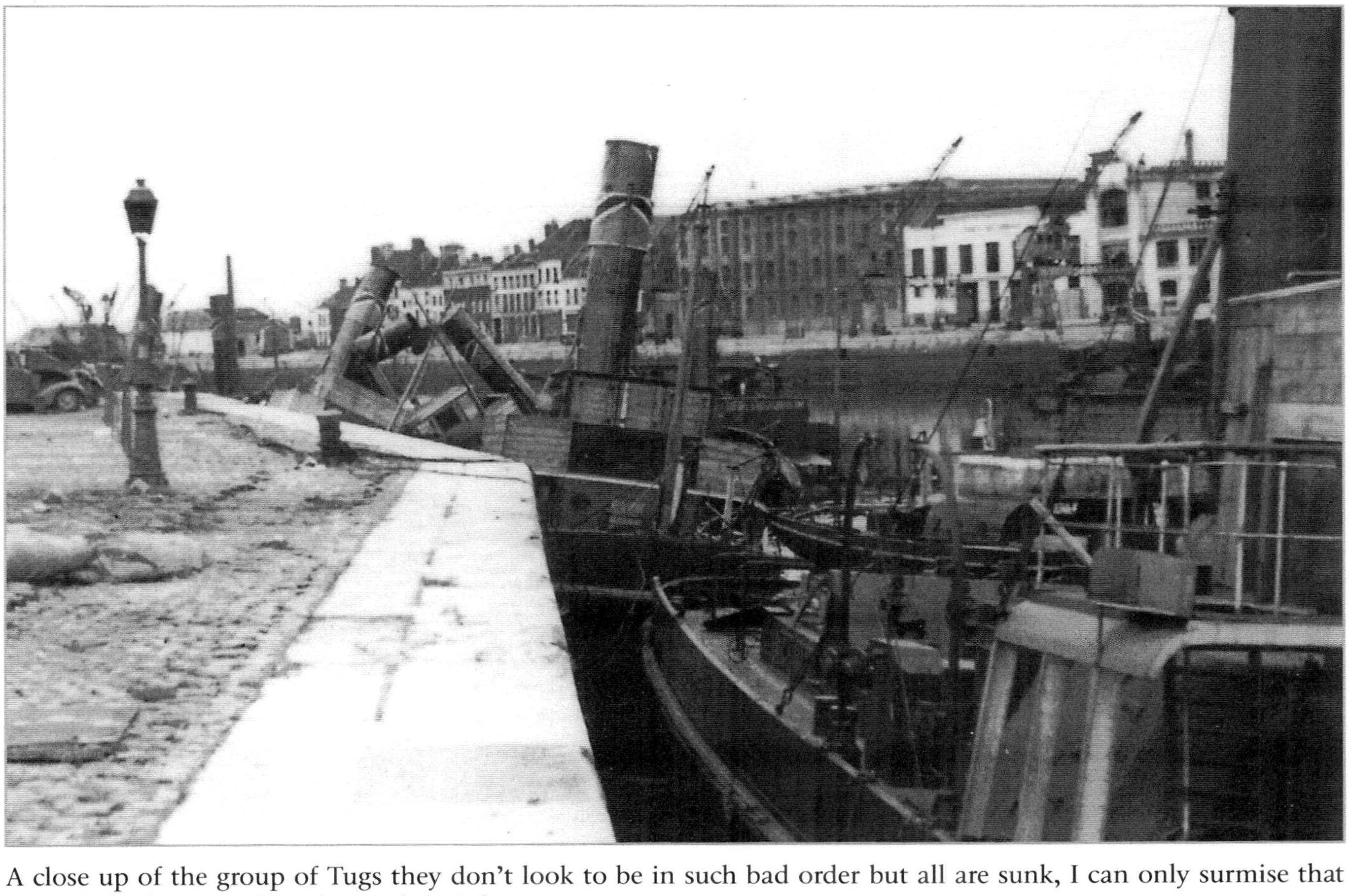

A close up of the group of Tugs they don't look to be in such bad order but all are sunk, I can only surmise that many holes have combined to seal their fate.

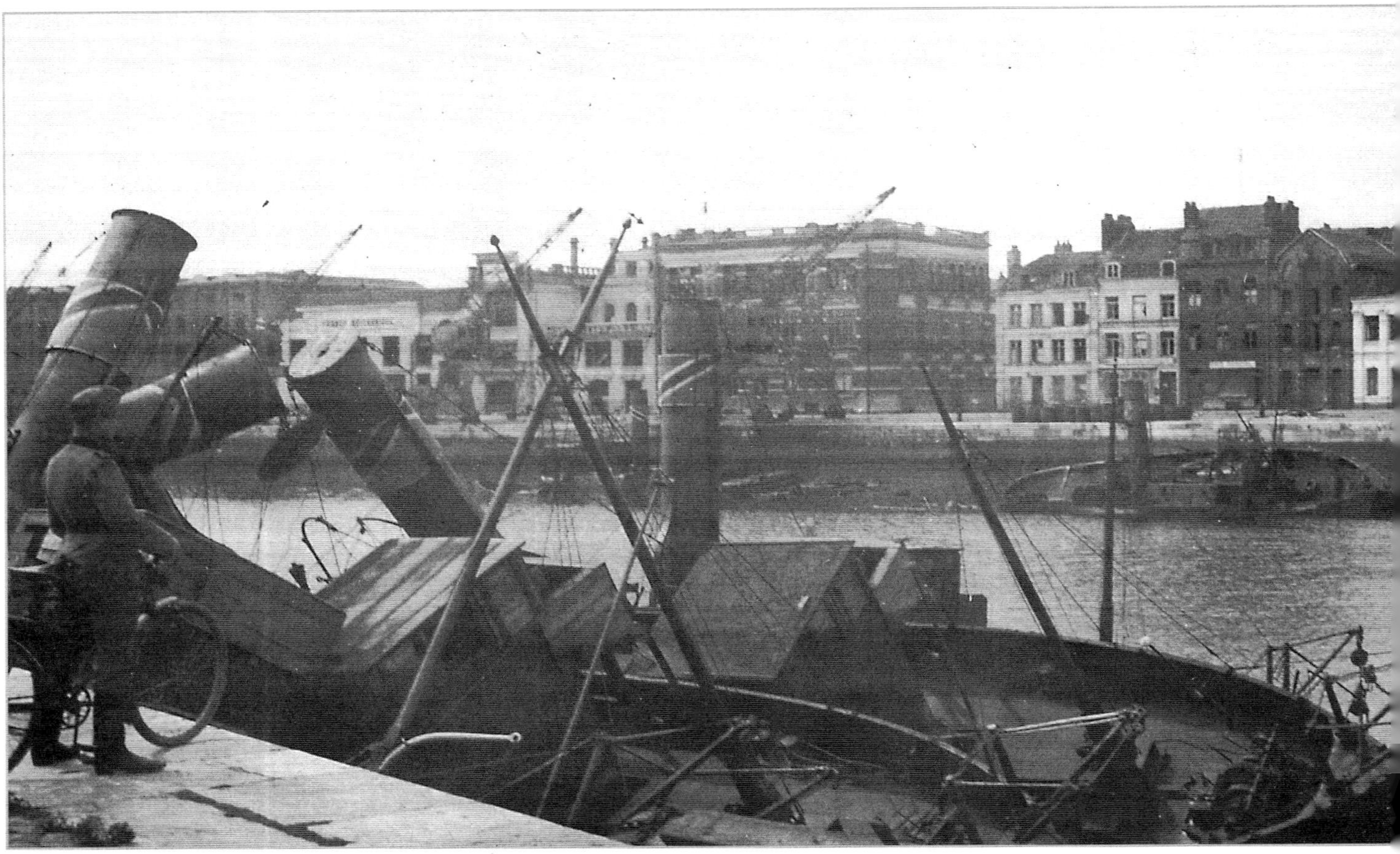

Tug Flotilla at low tide.

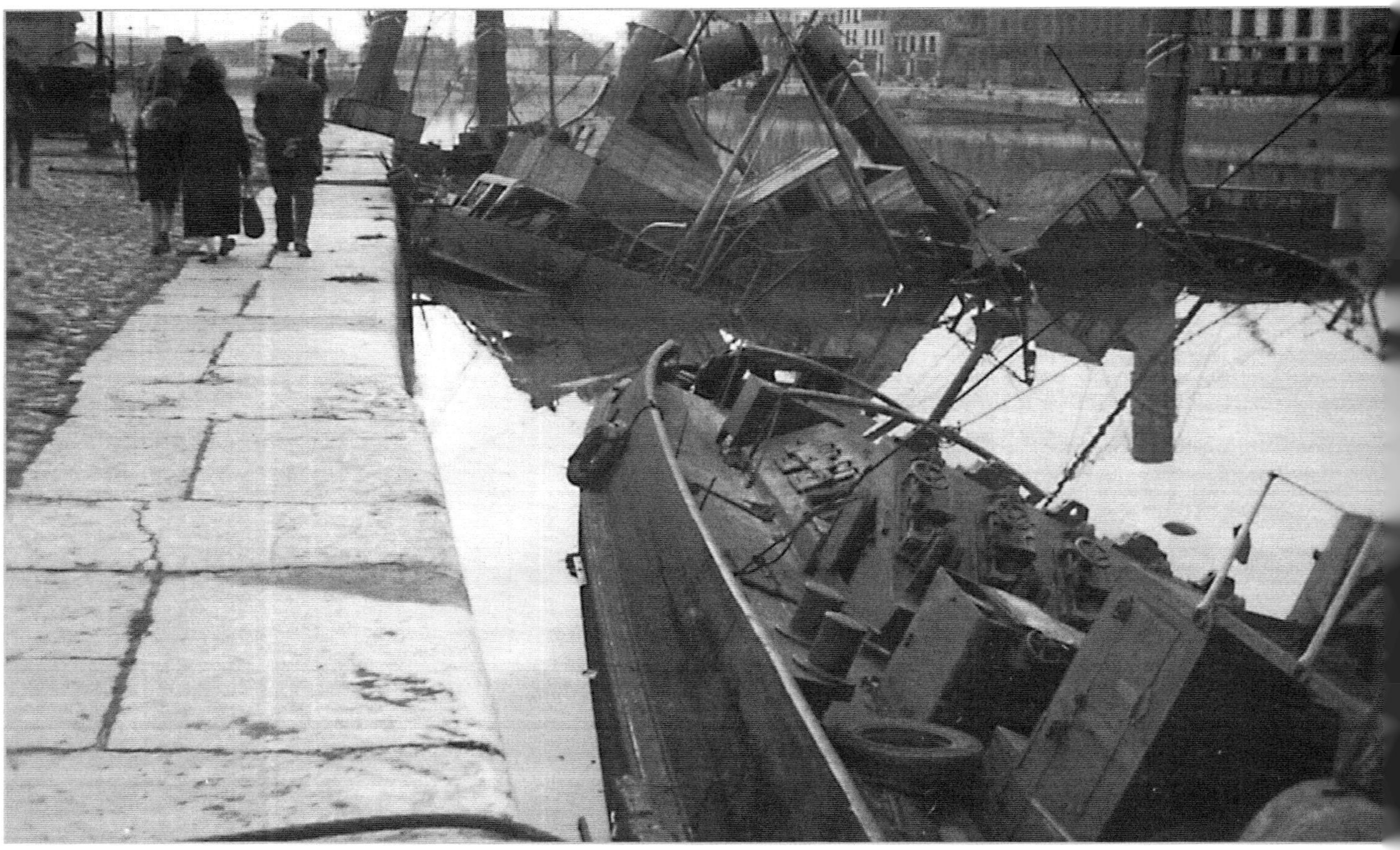

Tug Flotilla at high tide.

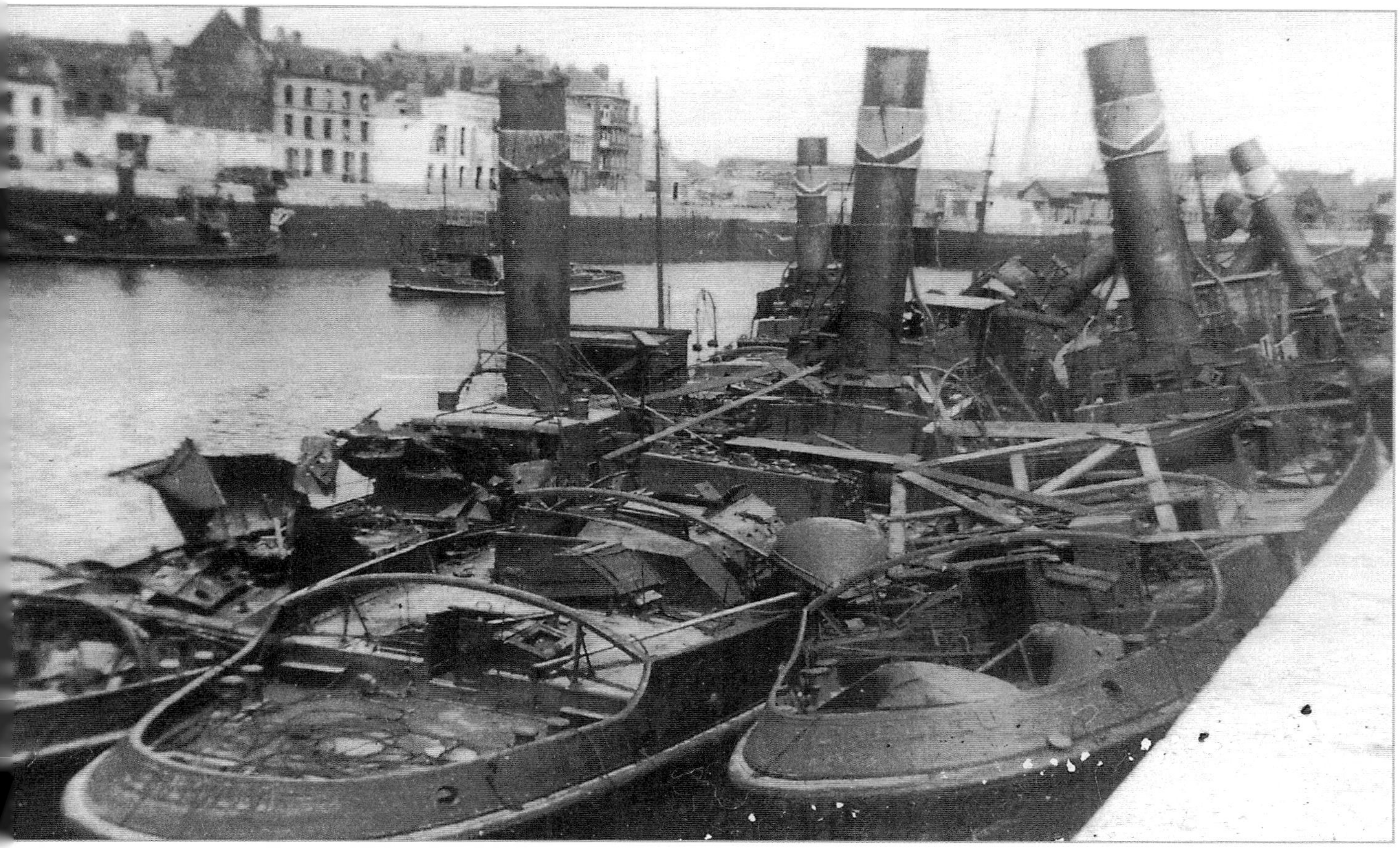

The tugs resting on the seabed of Dunkirk's inner harbour.

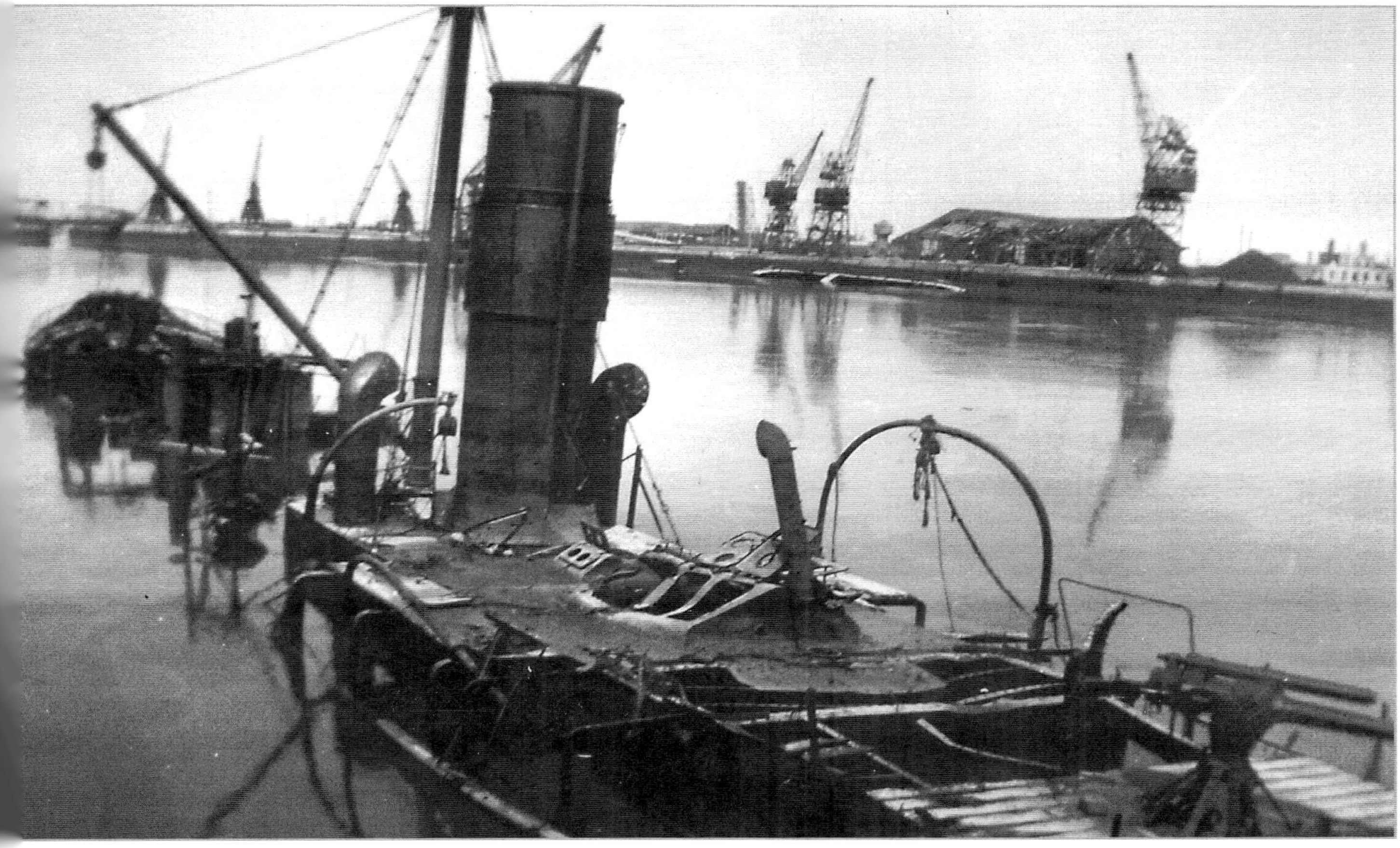

One of the coastal traders sunk in the harbour by German aircraft.

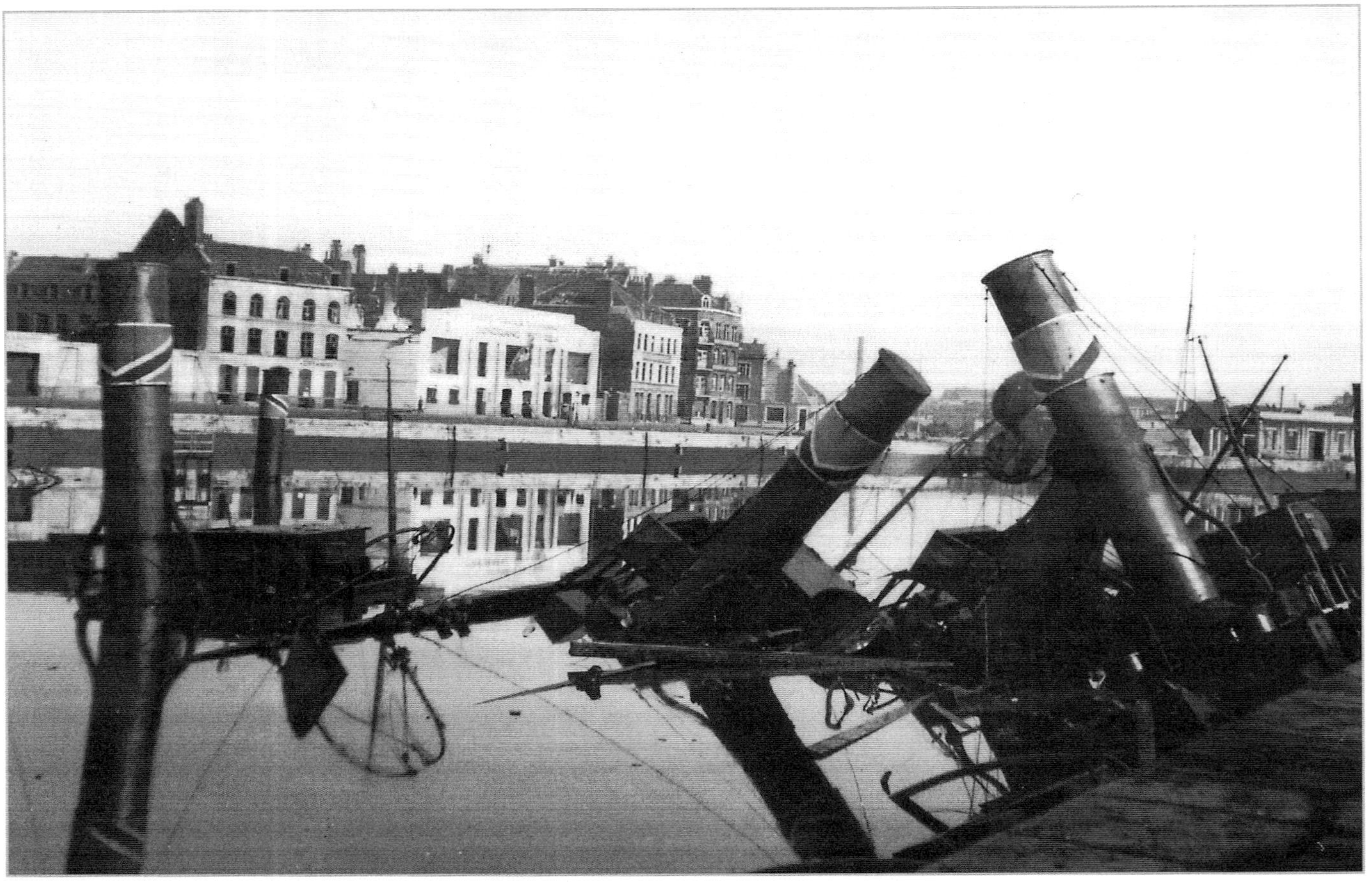

The sunken tugs looking back towards the town.

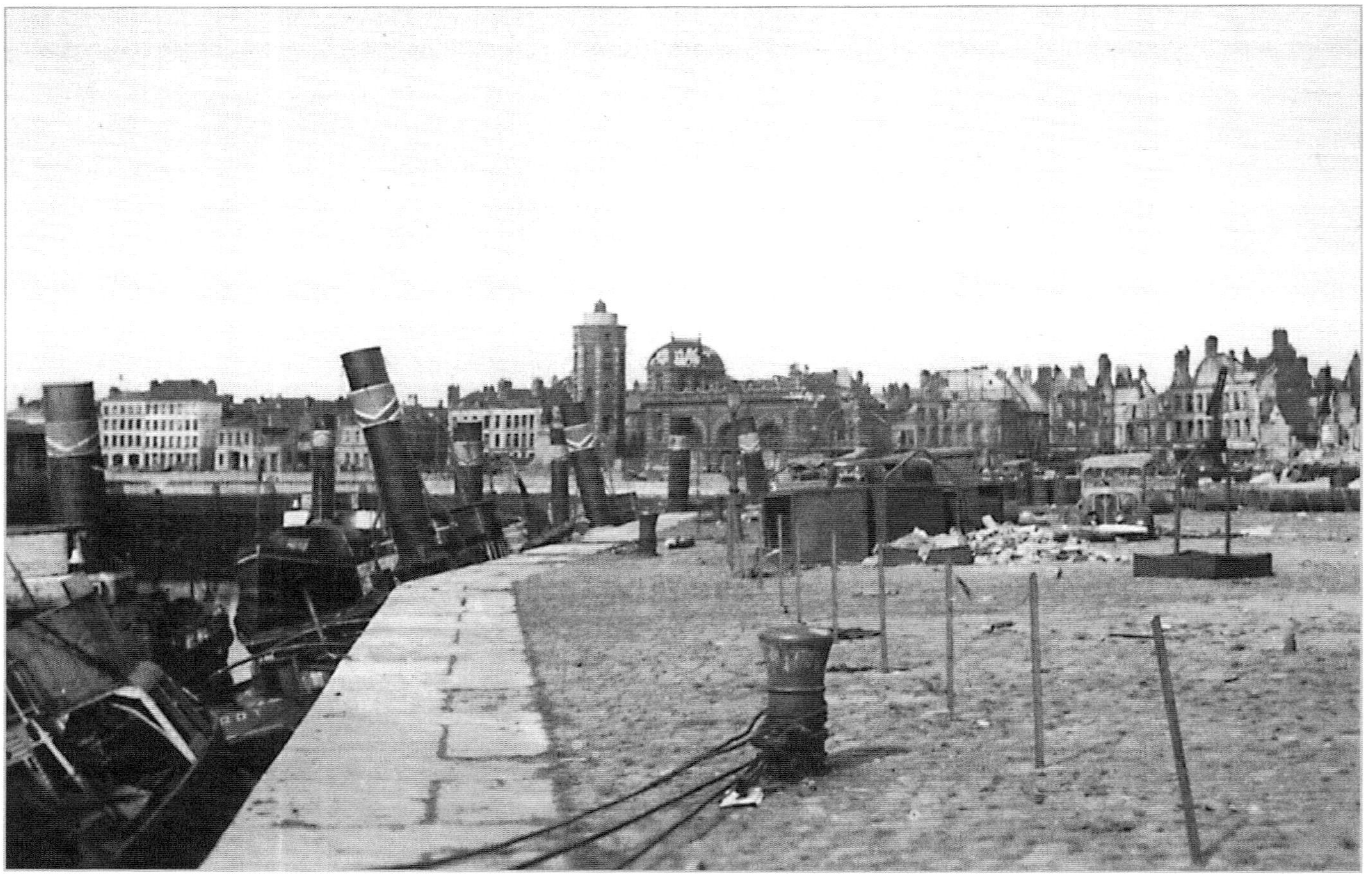

The main trading/loading area of the docks as seen looking over the sunken tug flotilla.

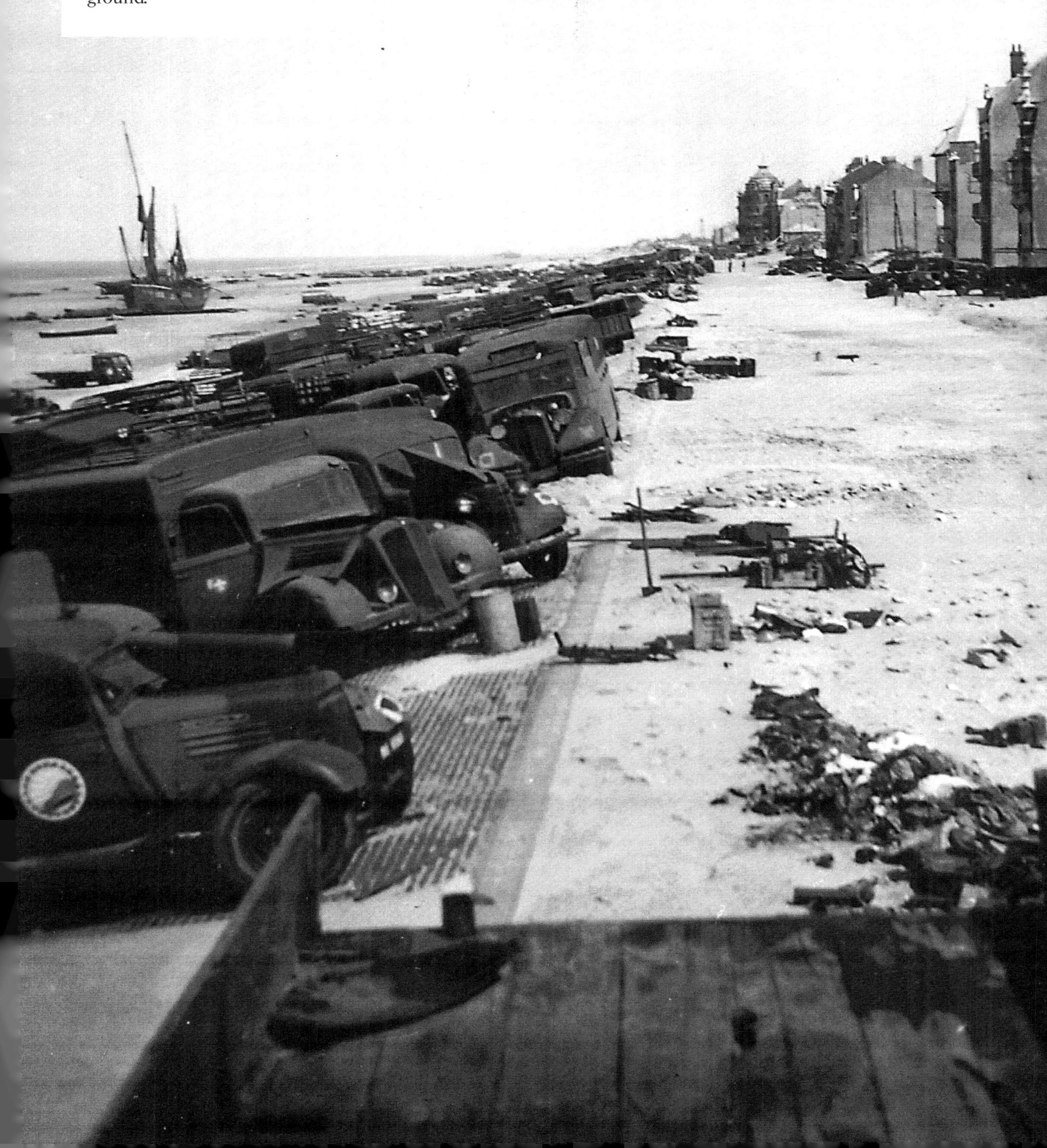

A photograph tak-
en from the back of
a French truck on
the Dunkirk prom-
enade. It shows the
Promenade littered
with both French and
British vehicles of
all shapes and sizes
and the barge *Ethel
Everard* in the back-
ground.

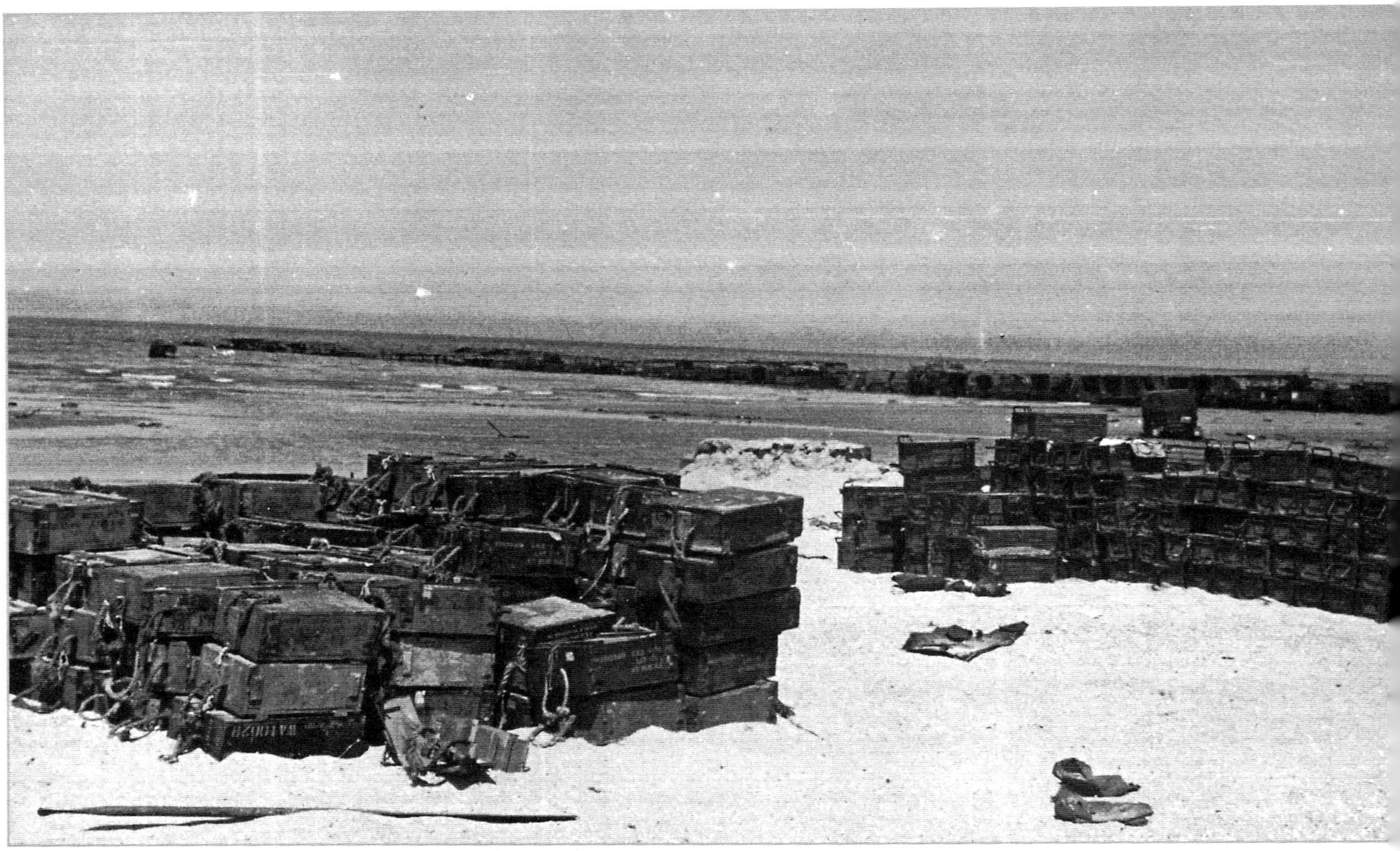

Boxed ammo salvaged from various British trucks littering the area. The Germans put many of the weapons and vehicles recovered following the evacuation back into service.

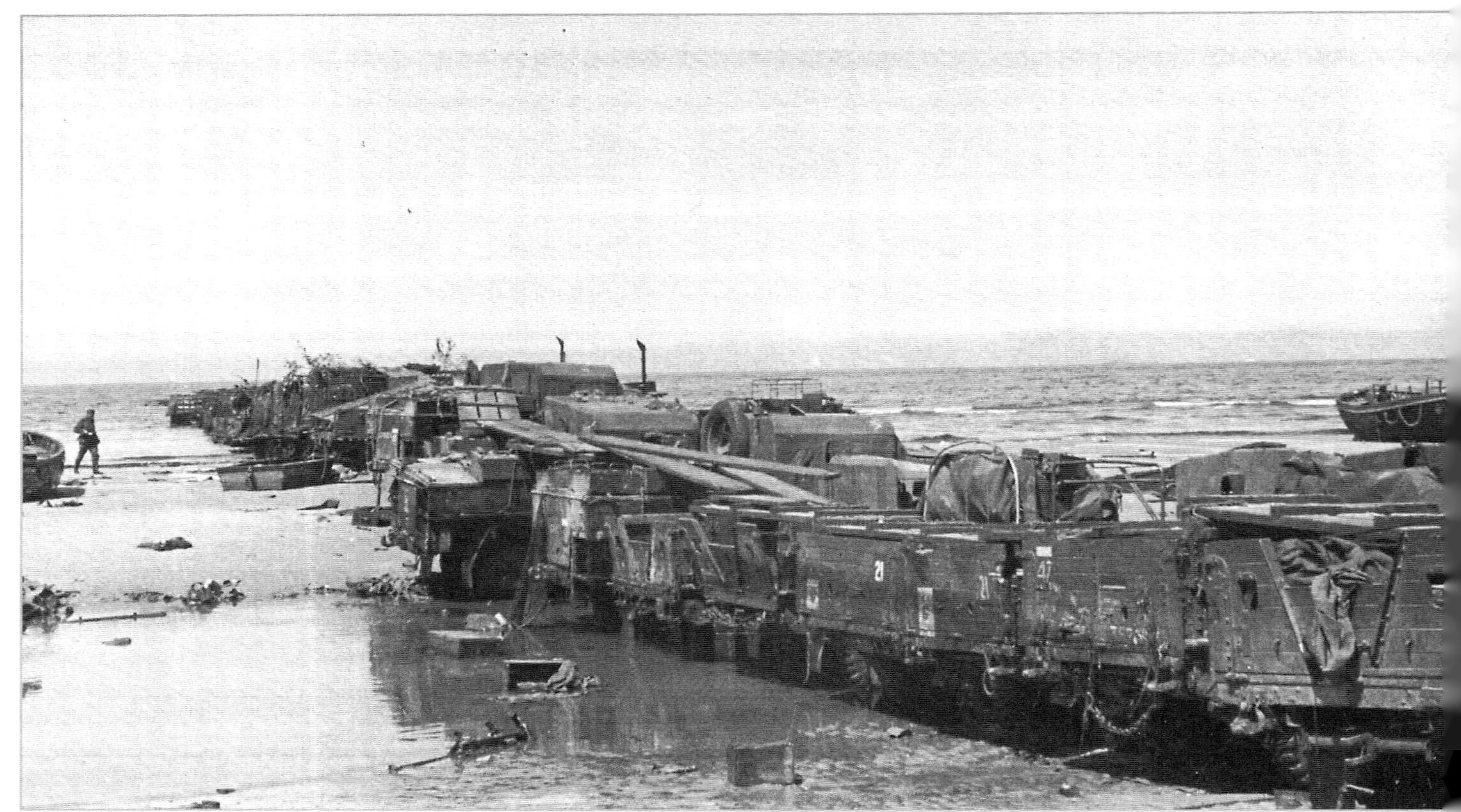

One of the many temporary jetties formed by troops driving trucks into the surf and parking them in line then tying them together. Once assembled these jetties were used as walkways to enable troops to get out into deeper water. This allowed them to board larger boats directly, without waiting to be ferried to them by the small row boats and other shallow draft craft of the 'little ship' fleet.

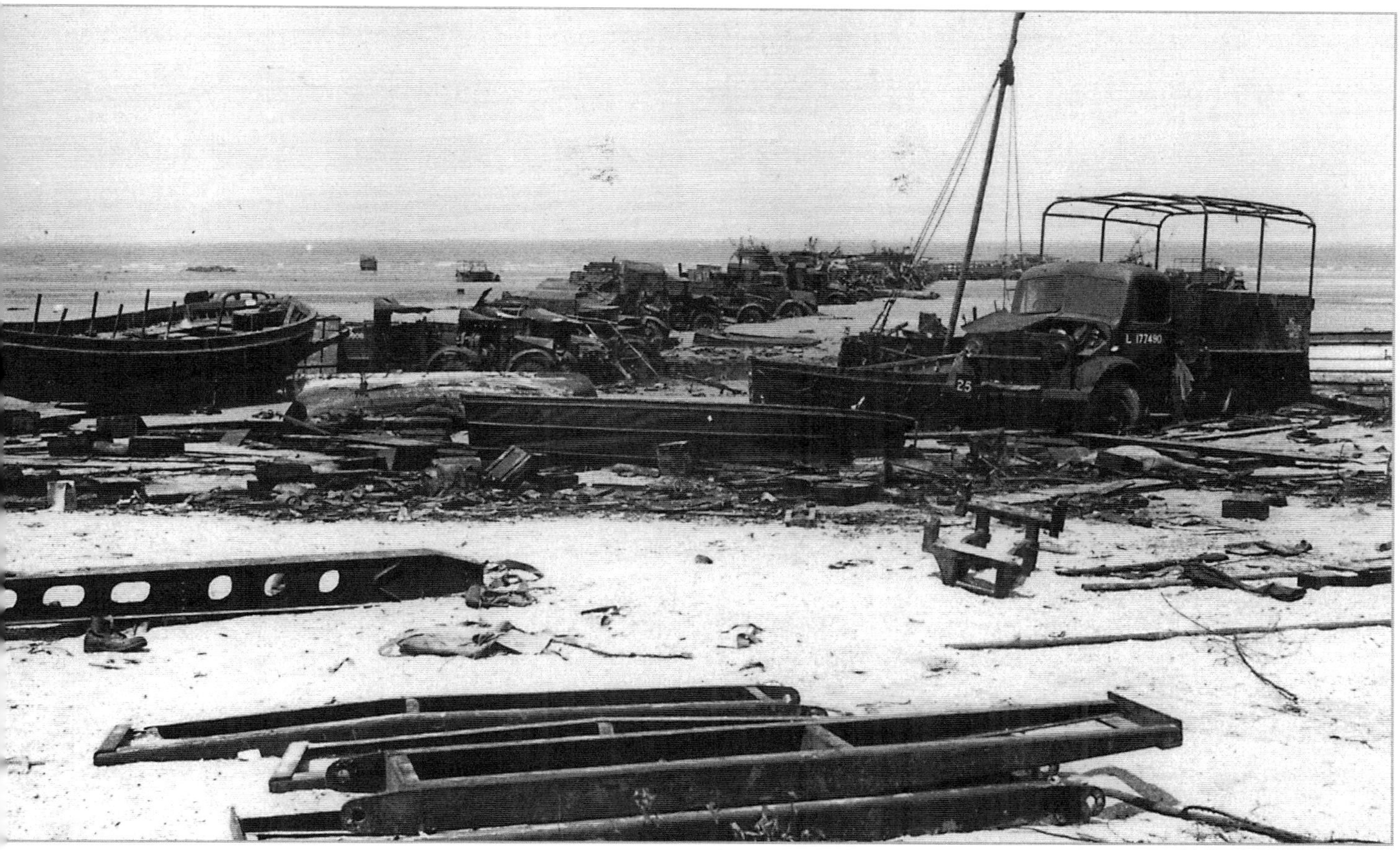

Another photograph of the temporary jetty showing the number of small craft damaged and abandoned whilst attempting to get as many troops as possible out to the larger ships for evacuation back to England.

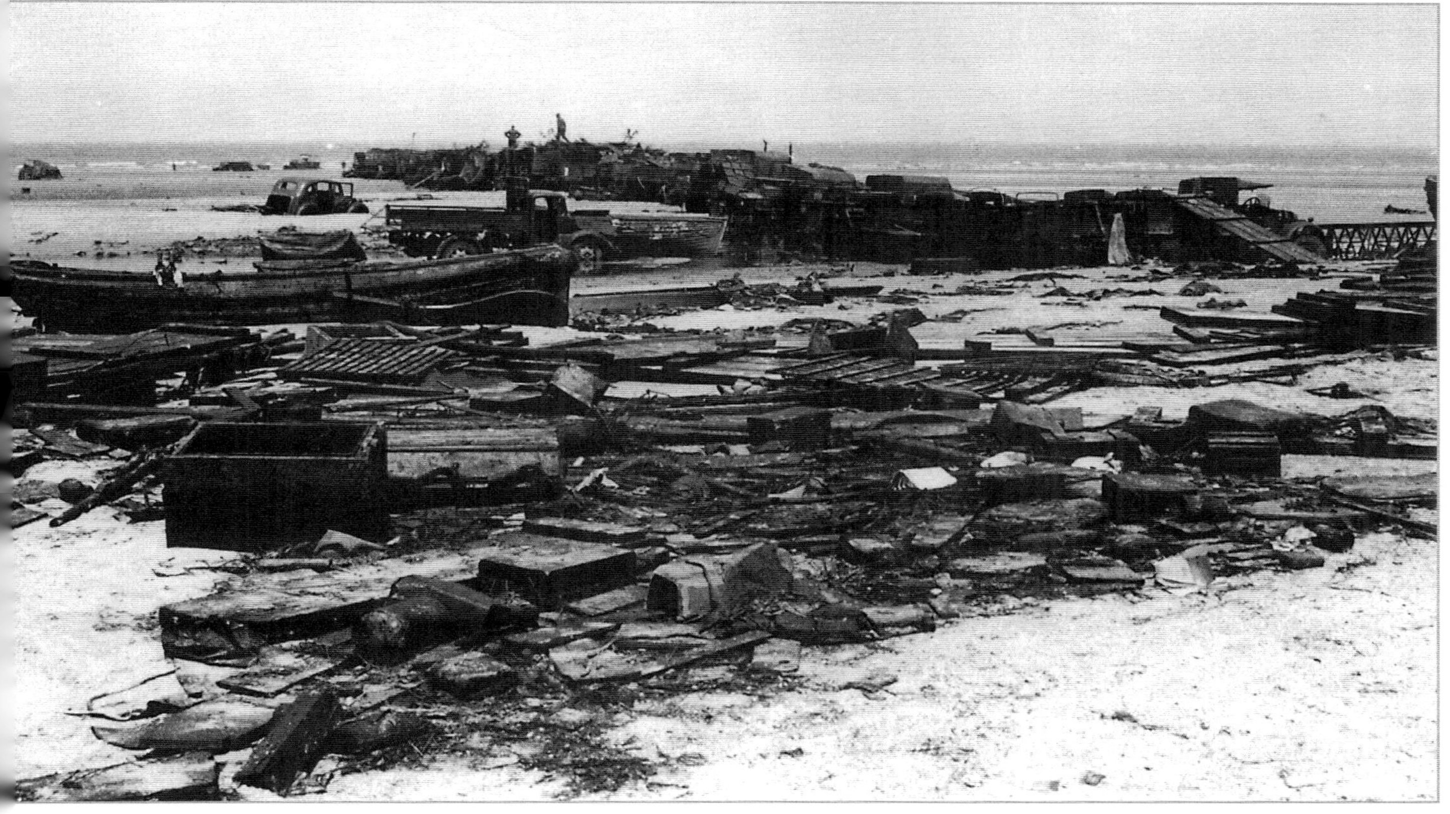

More photographs of the temporary jetties assembled from trucks of all shapes and sizes. As can be seen, some thought was given to the type of truck to be used with larger trucks being driven as far out from the high tide mark as possible so that the jetty could still be used at high tide.

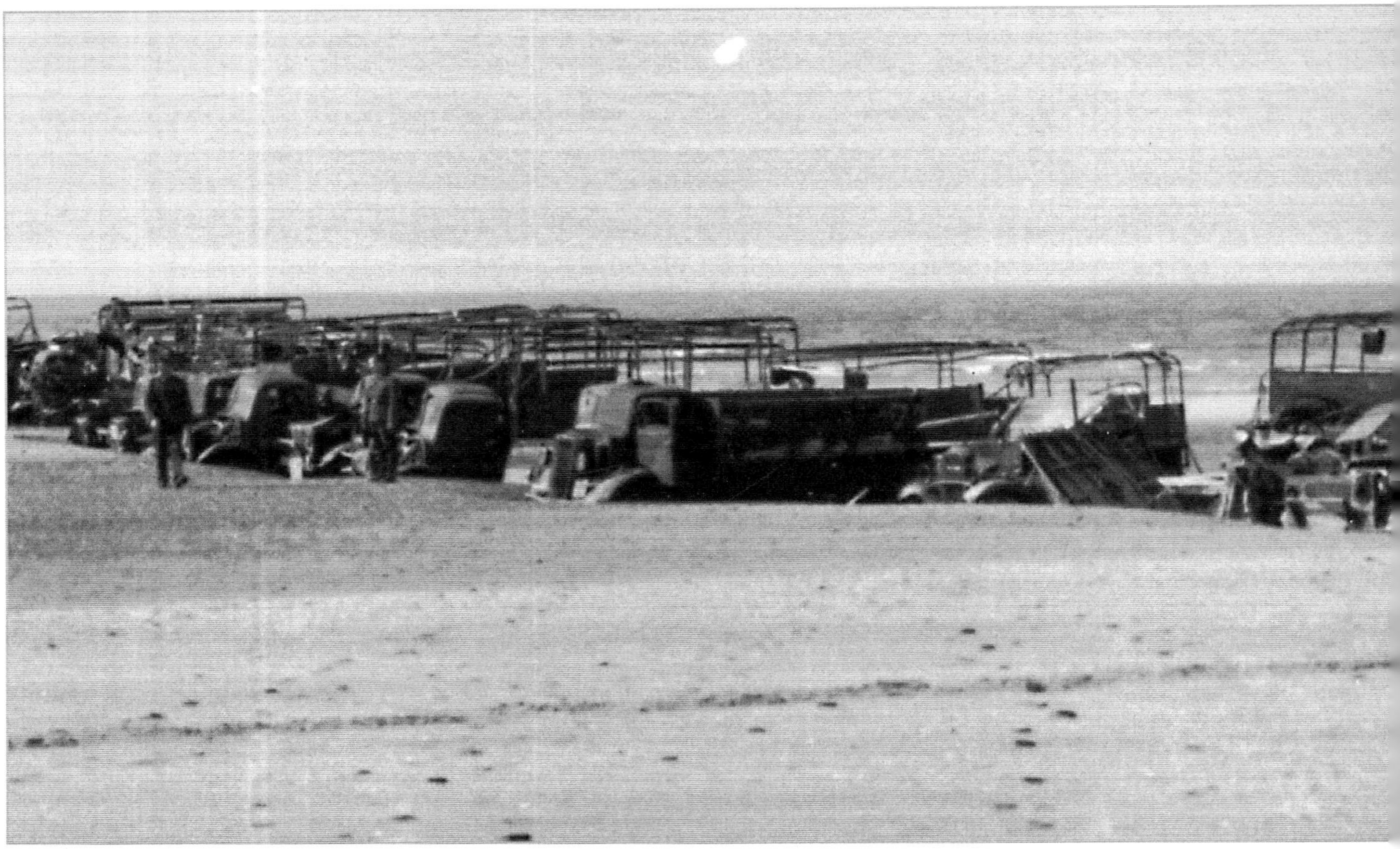

More of the temporary jetties.

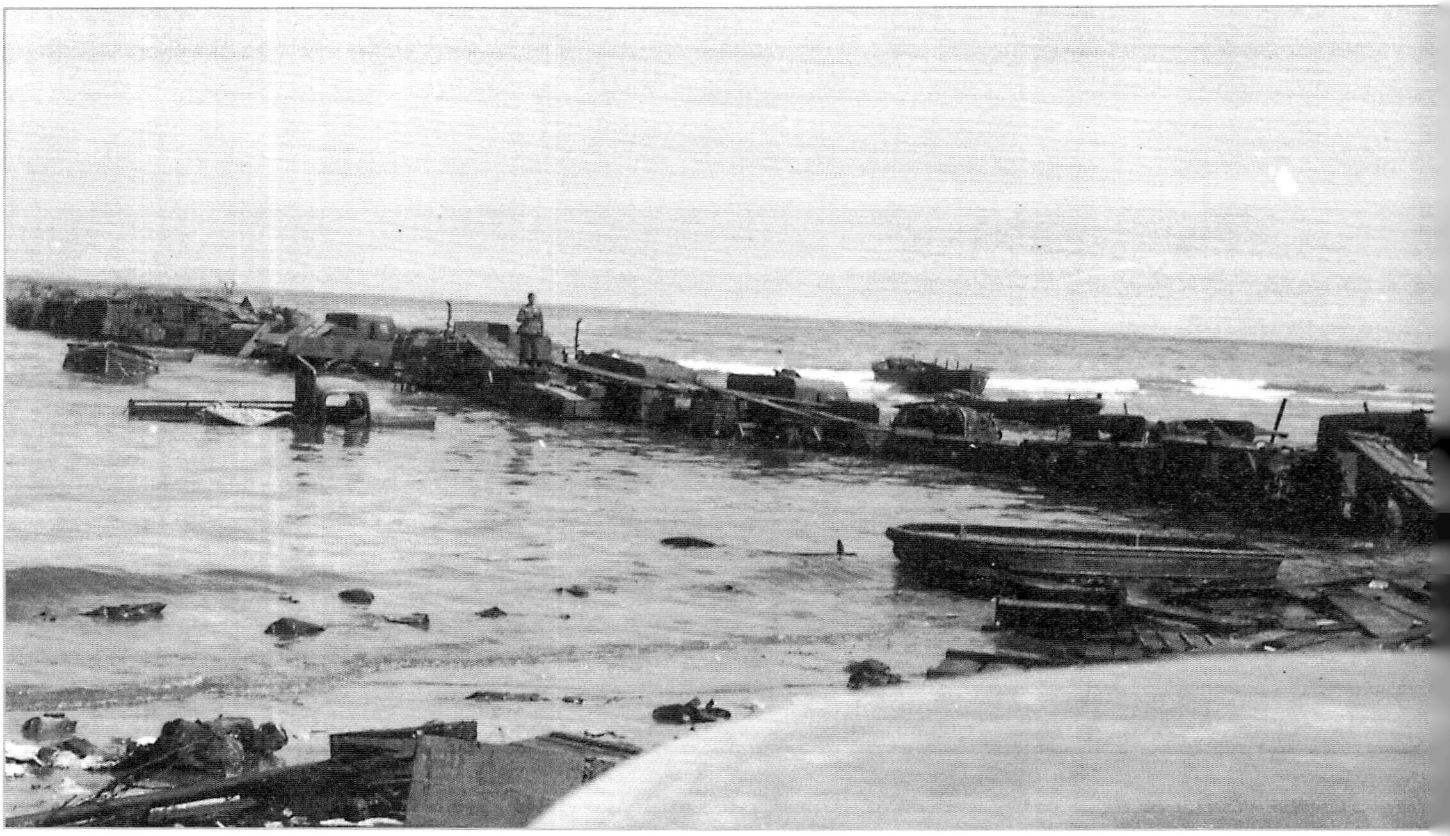

A German soldier poses halfway along one of the temporary jetties demonstrating the perilous nature of the task of moving large numbers of troops along the unstable jetties.

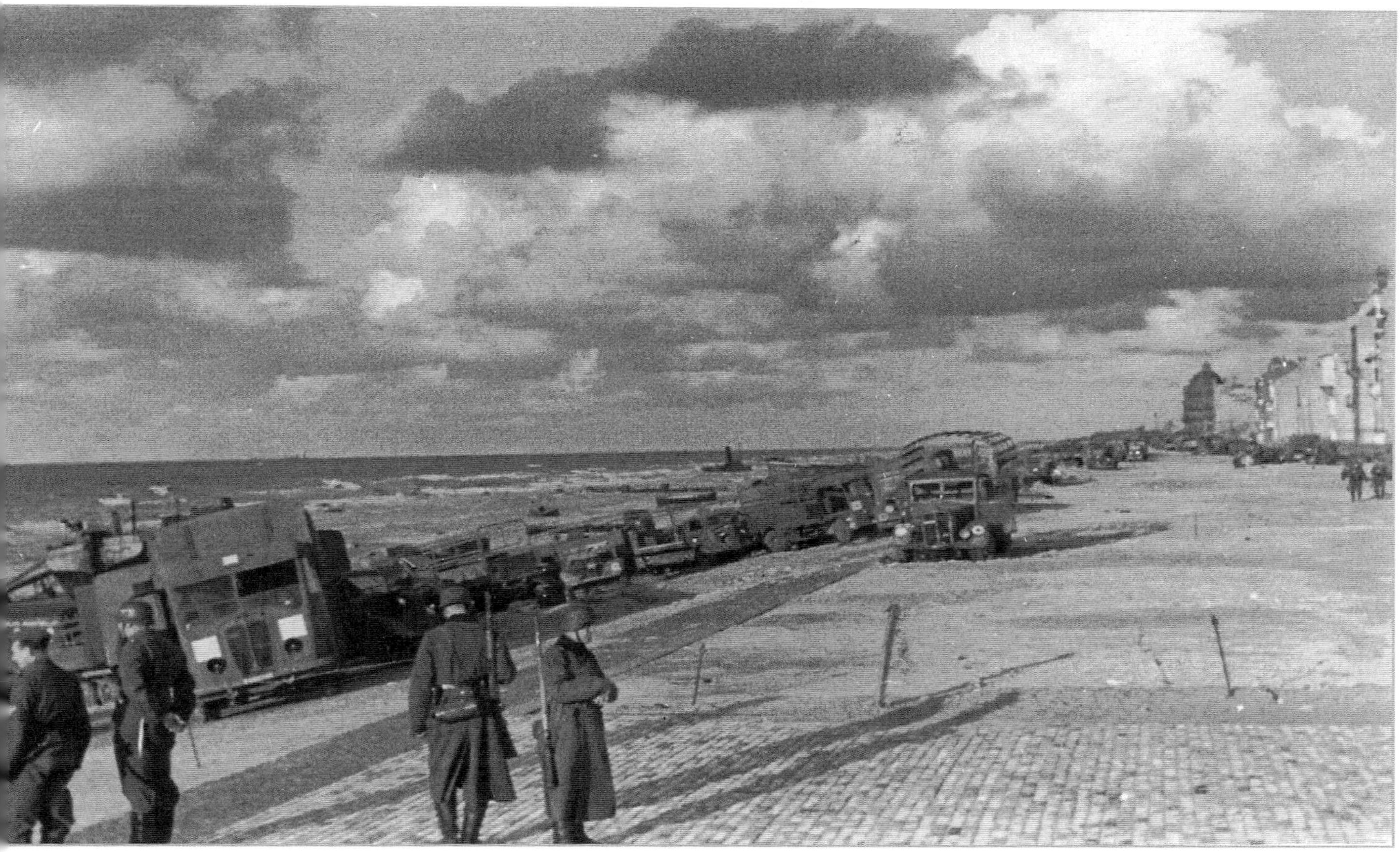

This page has two great views of Dunkirk's promenade both taken from the same place at the same time but together covering the scene of devastation and abandonment.

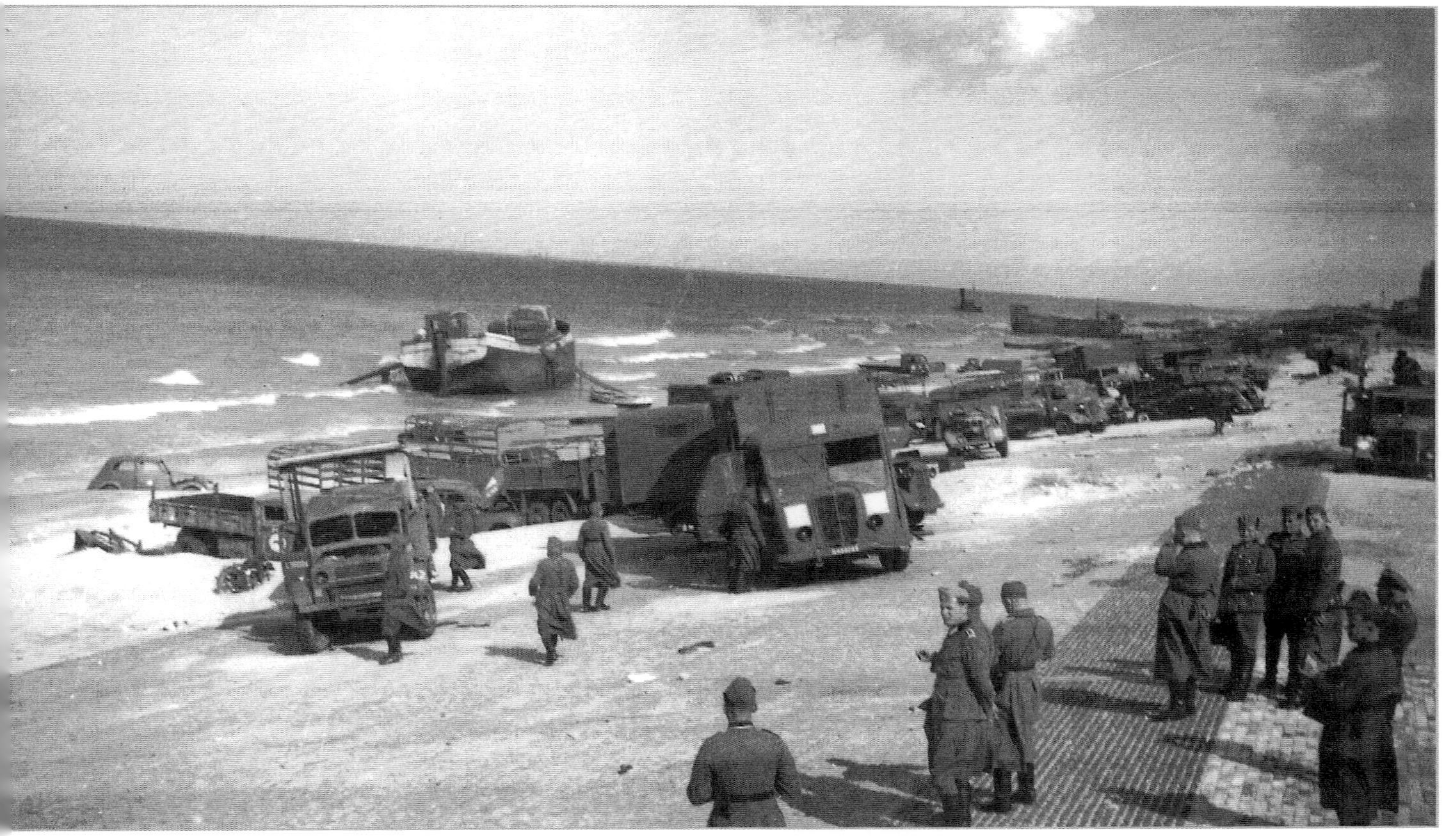

Note the days since the evacuation. Now the masts have gone from the Thames barges and although many of the vehicles were recovered in running order, the sheer number of abandoned vehicles that obviously require work to move is still amazing.

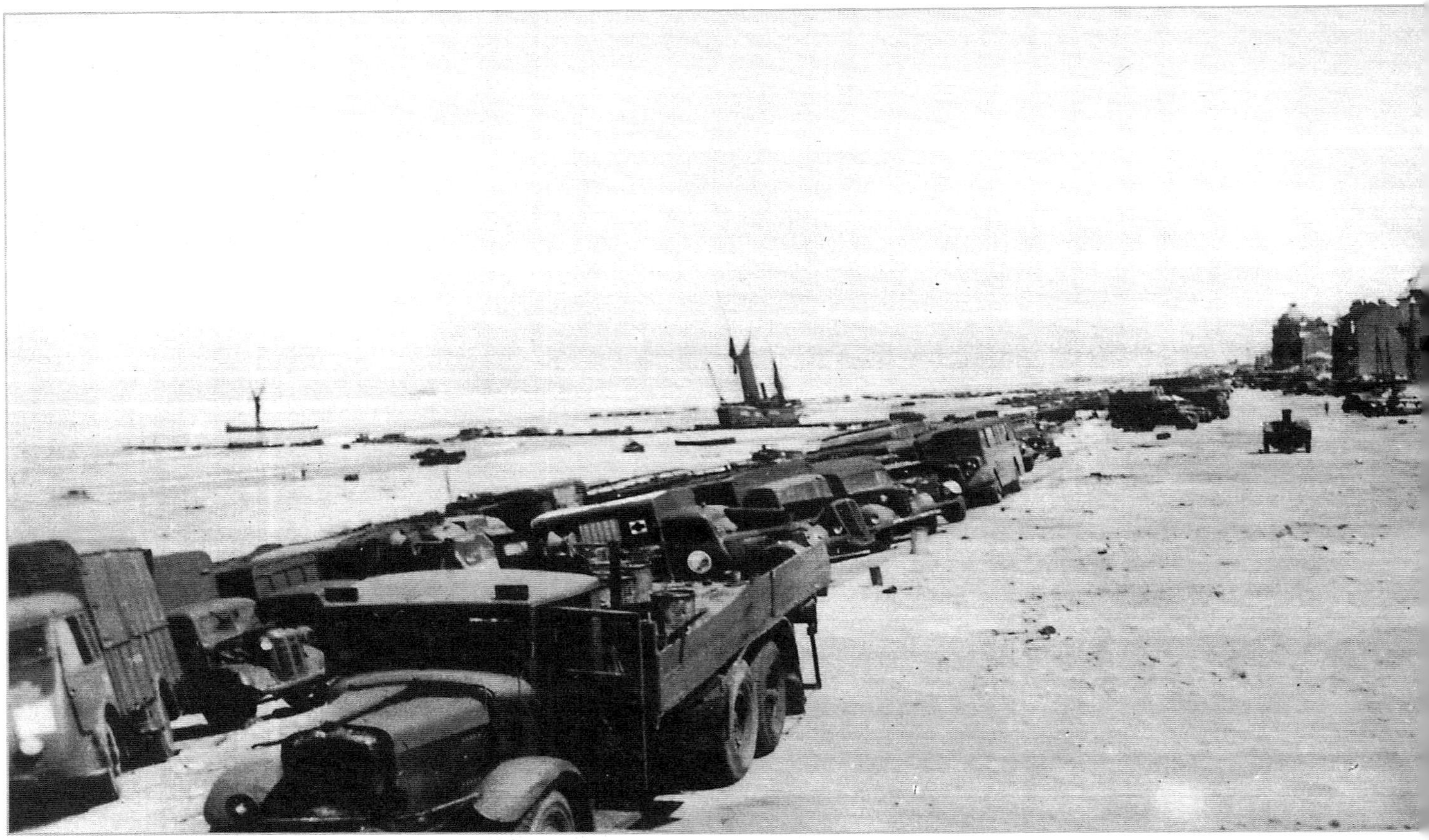

This photo taken only two days after the evacuation (6th June 1940), is in contrast to the ones on the preceding page. The promenade is awash with abandoned French and British equipment, trucks, cars, ambulances and even a few troop buses. In the only open area of the promenade is a forlorn French field kitchen.

Taken from behind the sand dunes of Bray beach, Dunkirk, is an example of orders being followed. The abandoned vehicles left here have been thoroughly destroyed by fire and thus denied to the enemy for future use. Note: the two trucks in the foreground are 1938 Citroën 3 tonners.

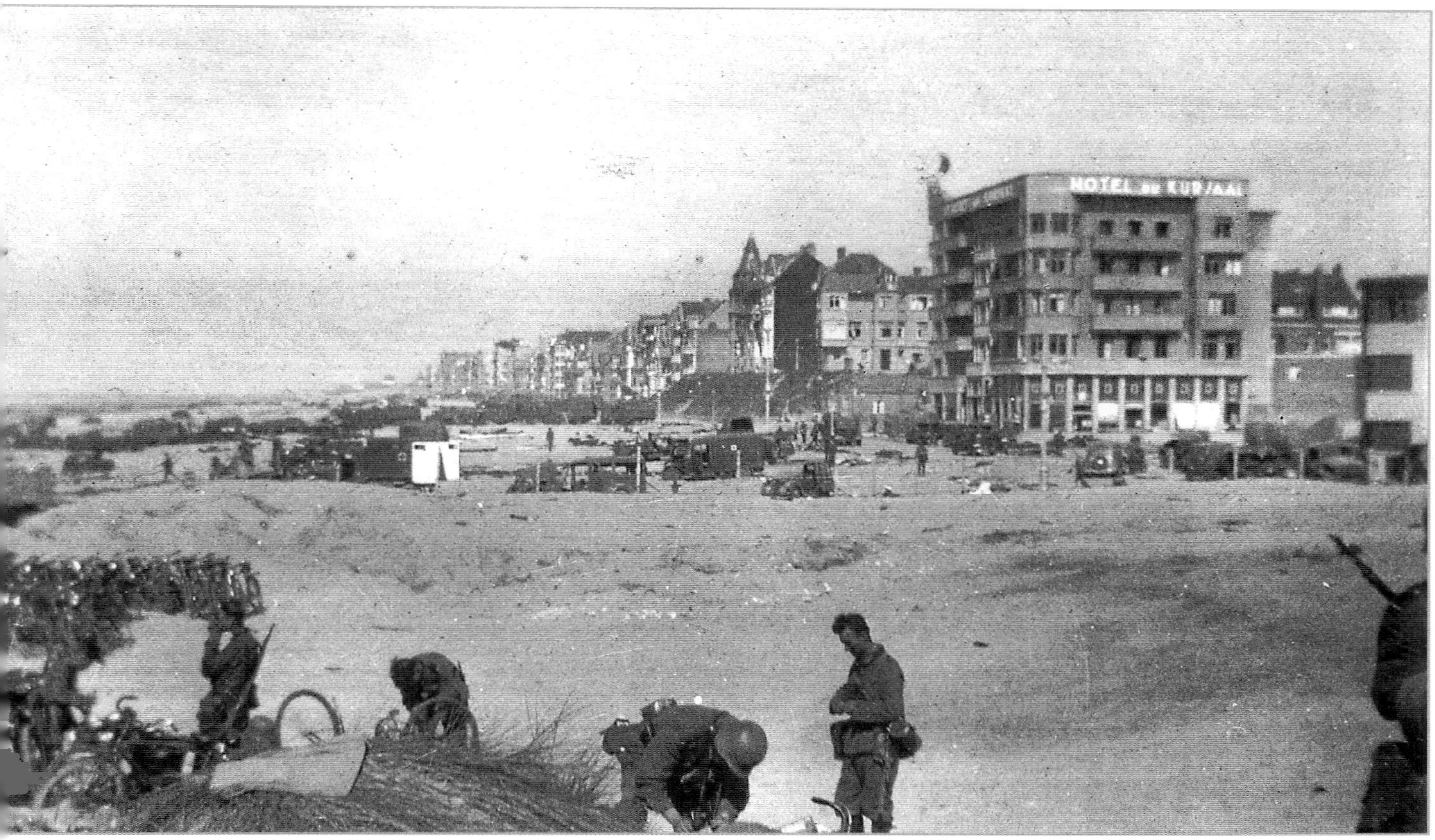

This page shows two photographs of a German infantry unit arriving in Dunkirk and making their way to the beach at the centre of the Promenade close to the hotel 'Hotel De AUR/AAL'. Note as was more common in the German army of this time they are not a motorised unit, transport for this unit is the bicycle.

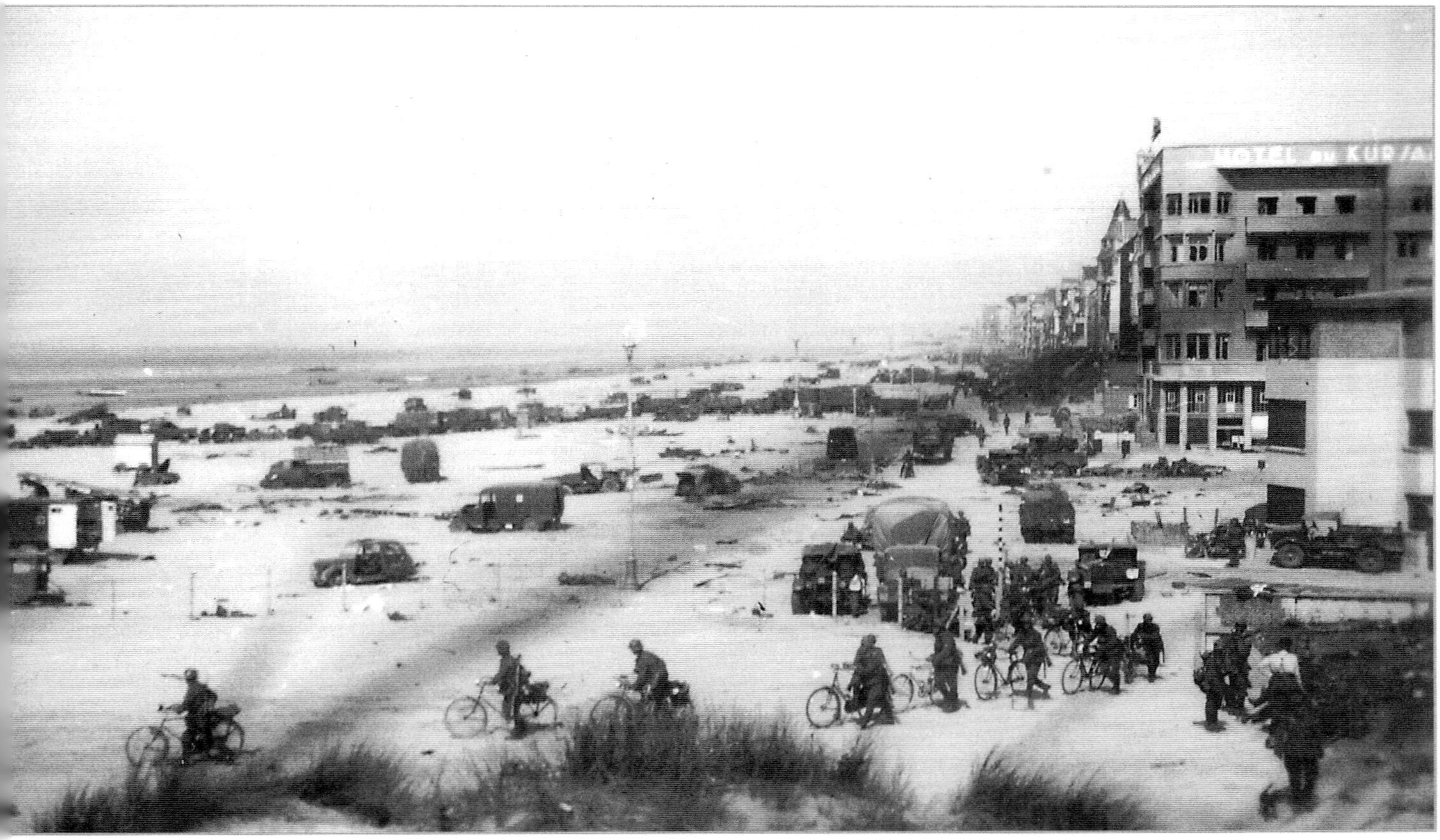

A number of German infantry units were diverted to Dunkirk following the evacuation where in only a few days they became motorised units. They were assigned transport from the vast pool of captured and repaired equipment being reclaimed from the mass of abandoned allied motorised vehicles.

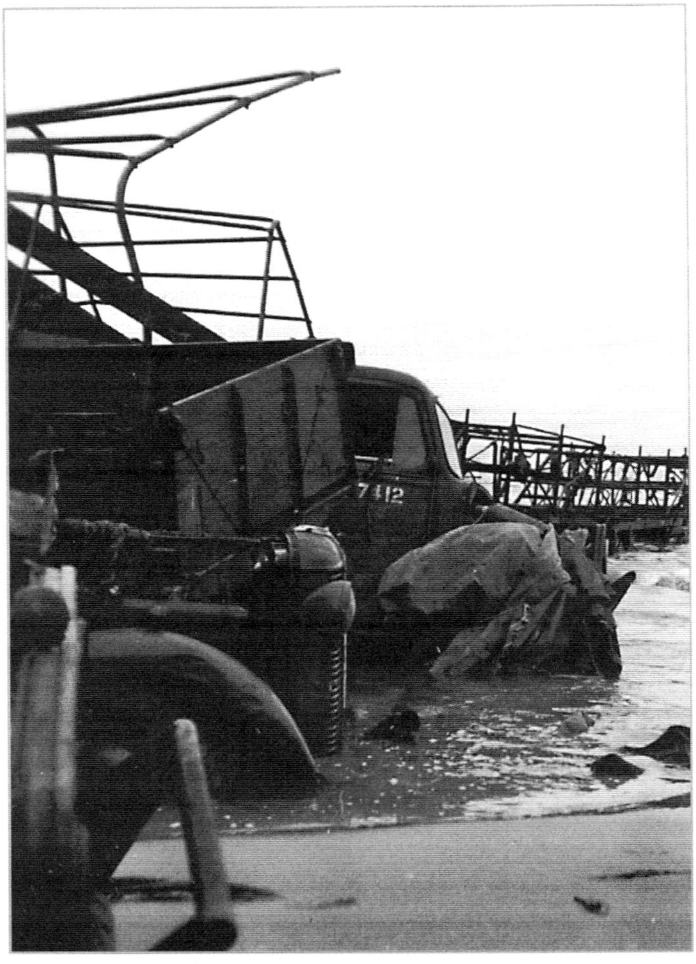

One of the many temporary jetties slowly being claimed by the tides as the trucks are both torn apart and sinking into the sand.

Another view along the promenade showing the vast array of vehicles abandoned following the evacuation. As is clear many are still in good condition no doubt many have been subjected to attempted sabotage by their previous owners, but ultimately so many vehicles and indeed supplies were left behind meant many could be repaired for reuse.

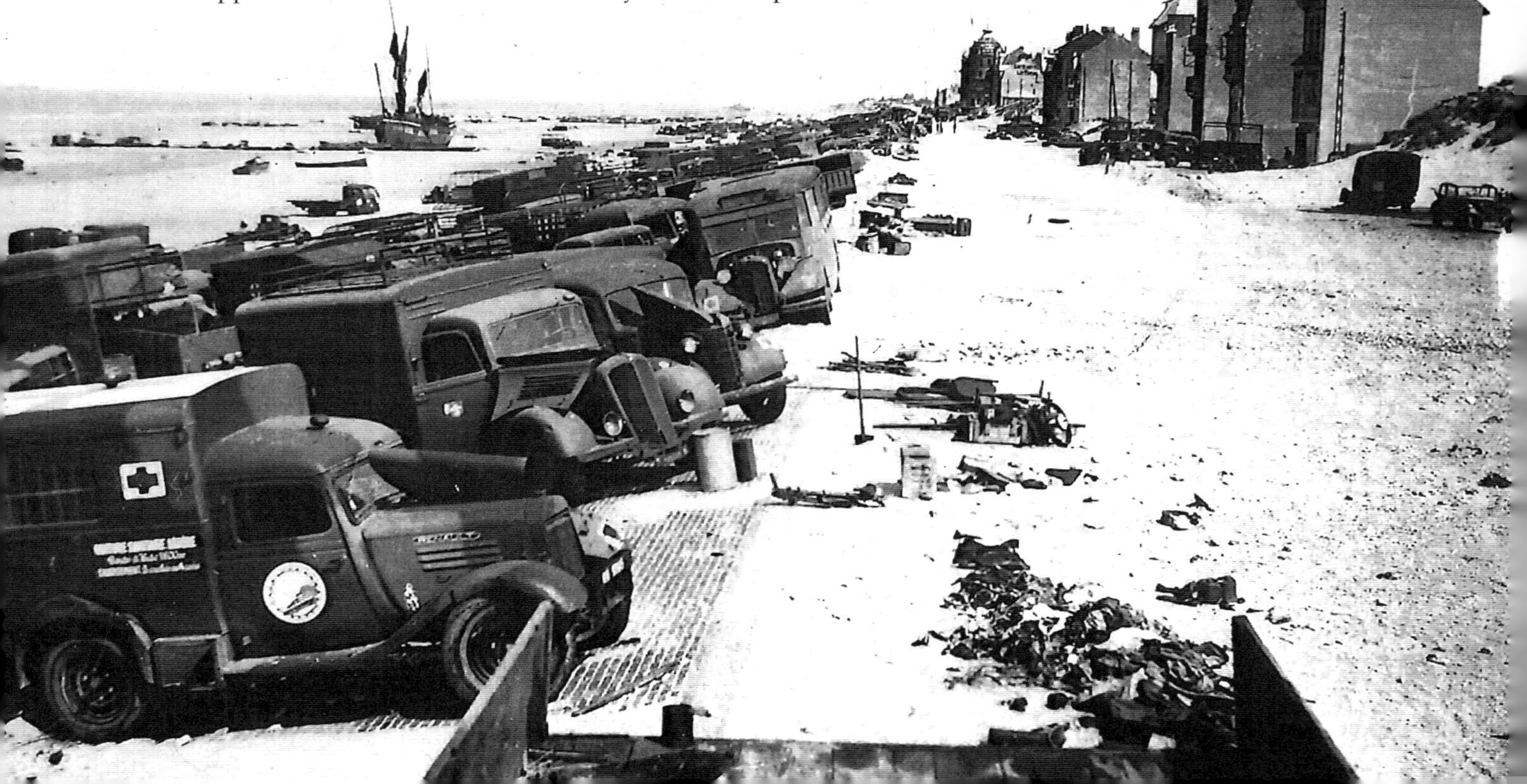

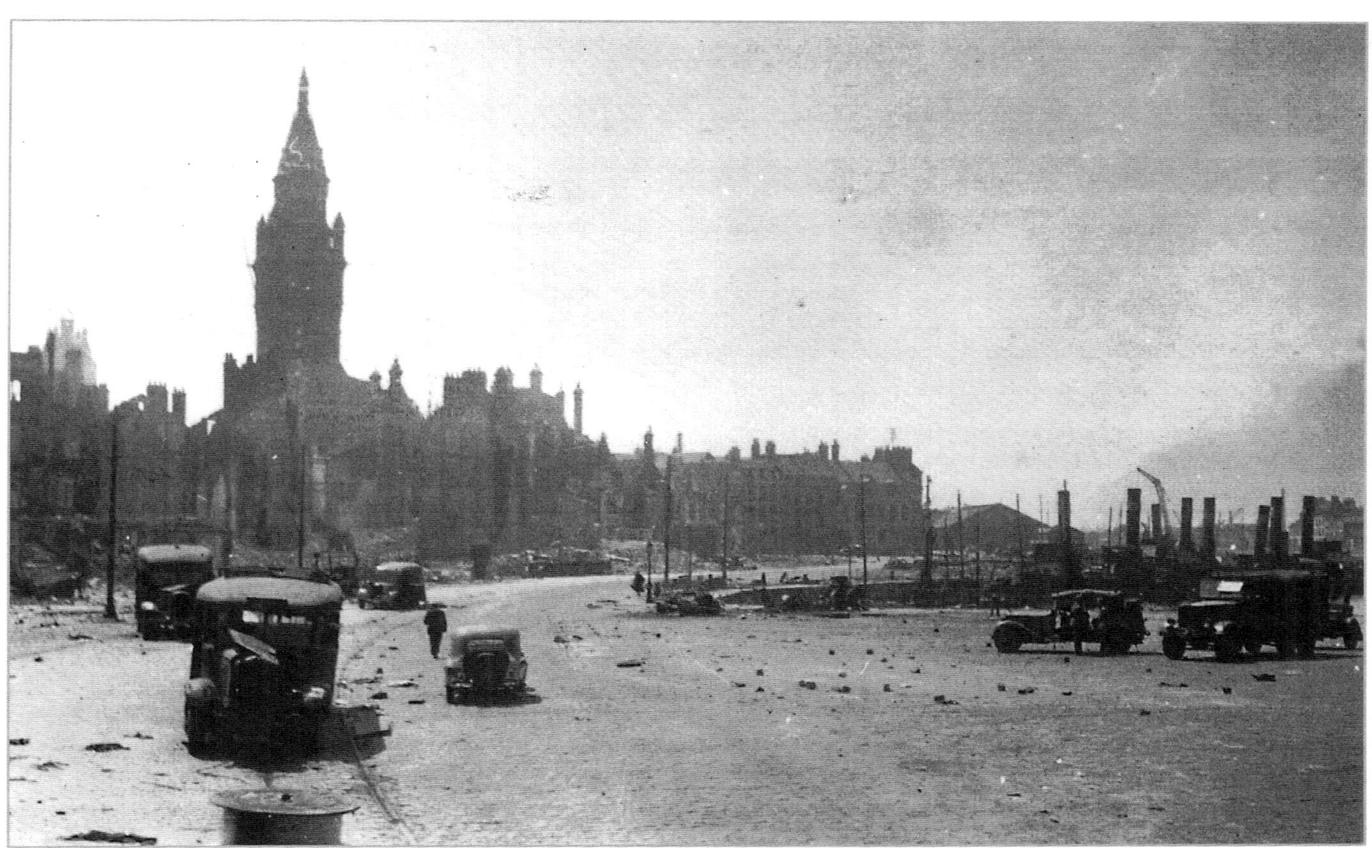

A view of the main trading area of Dunkirk docks with the wrecked tug flotilla in shot off to the right with the docks mostly cleared of abandoned vehicles. All that can be seen are two civilian French buses as well as a German Adler staff car and Universal Diesel truck.

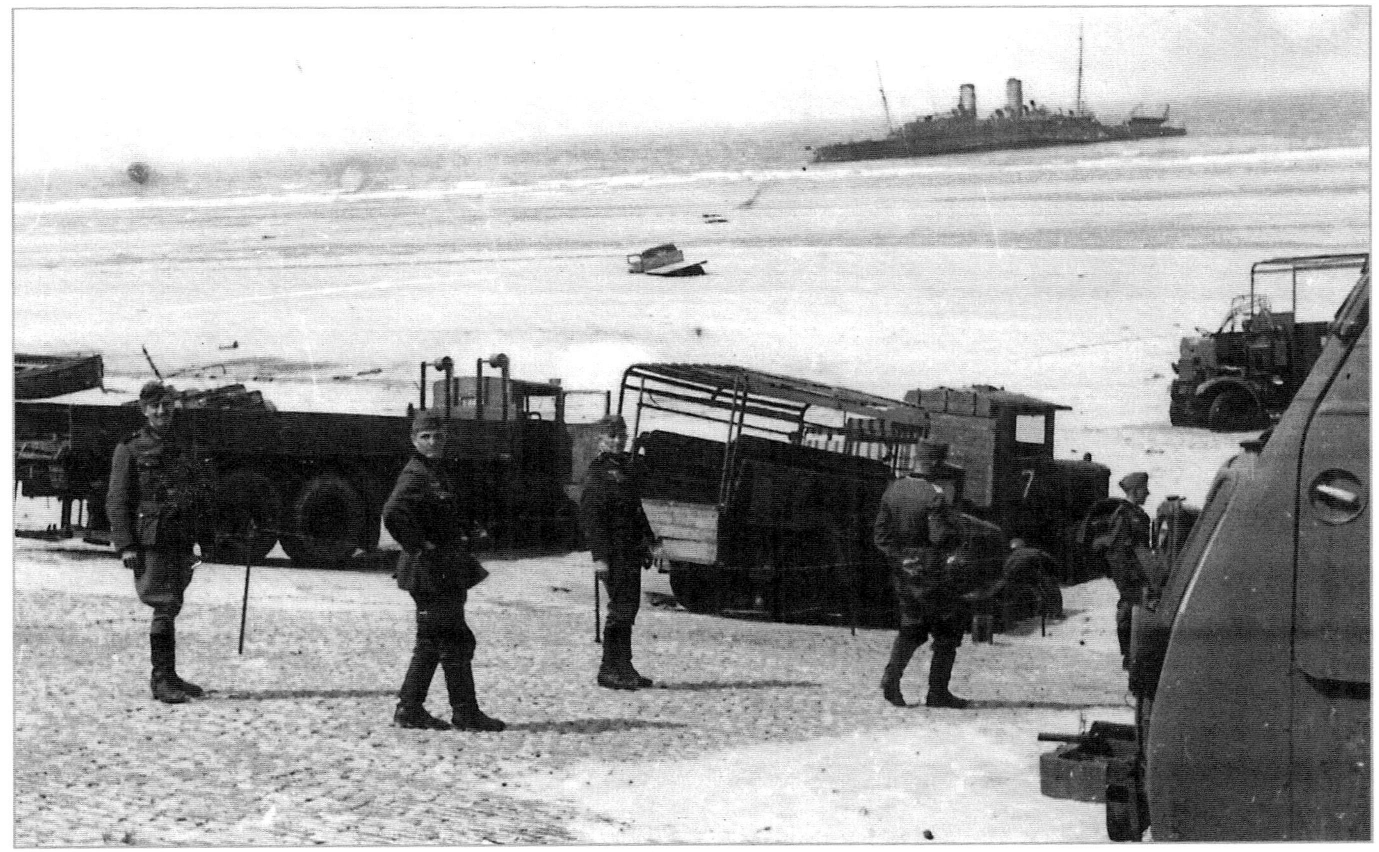

The beach at Le Panne at the far east of the defensive perimeter, photographed 10 days after the evacuation. This beach was predominantly in the French section and a quantity of French abandoned equipment is still in evidence on site.

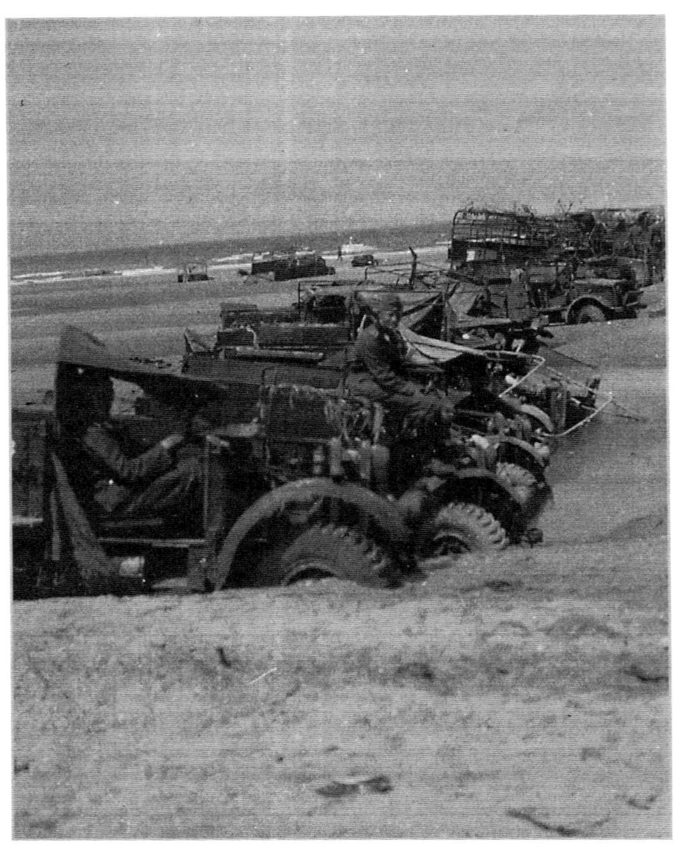

Another view of the temporary boarding jetties made by driving trucks into the surf at low tide, this one seems to be made up of mainly Bedford 15cwts

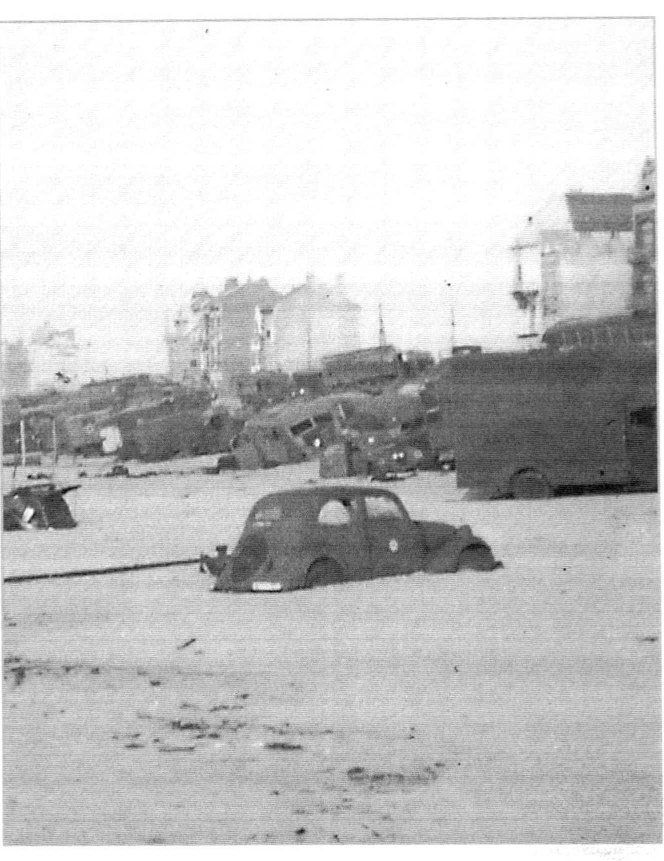

A rare photograph from the beach looking up towards the promenade showing mostly abandoned French vehicles in this view.

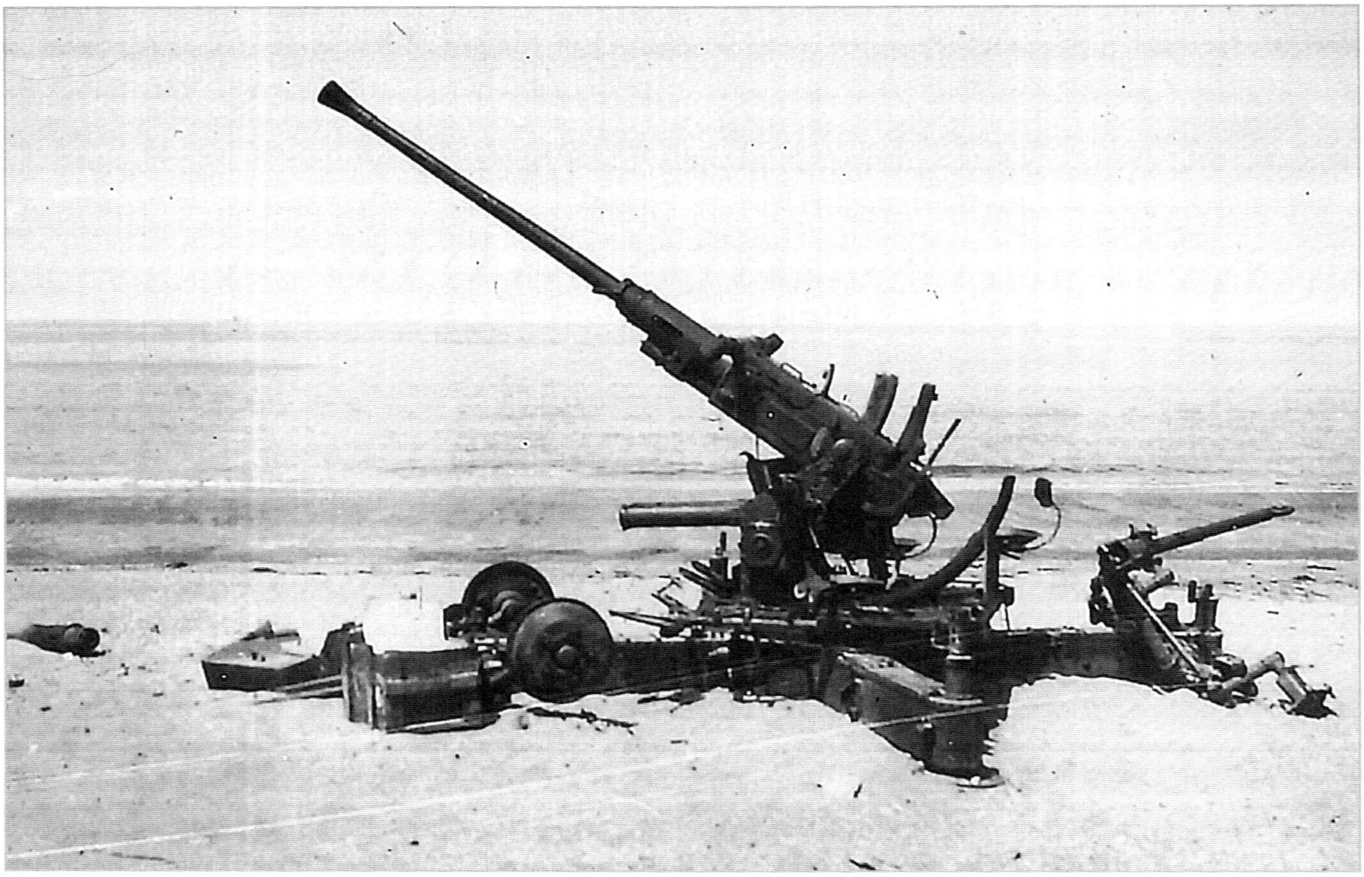

An abandoned and stripped 40 mm Bofors Gun. Locals probably made off with the wheels for use elsewhere on a homemade cart as was common practice at the time.

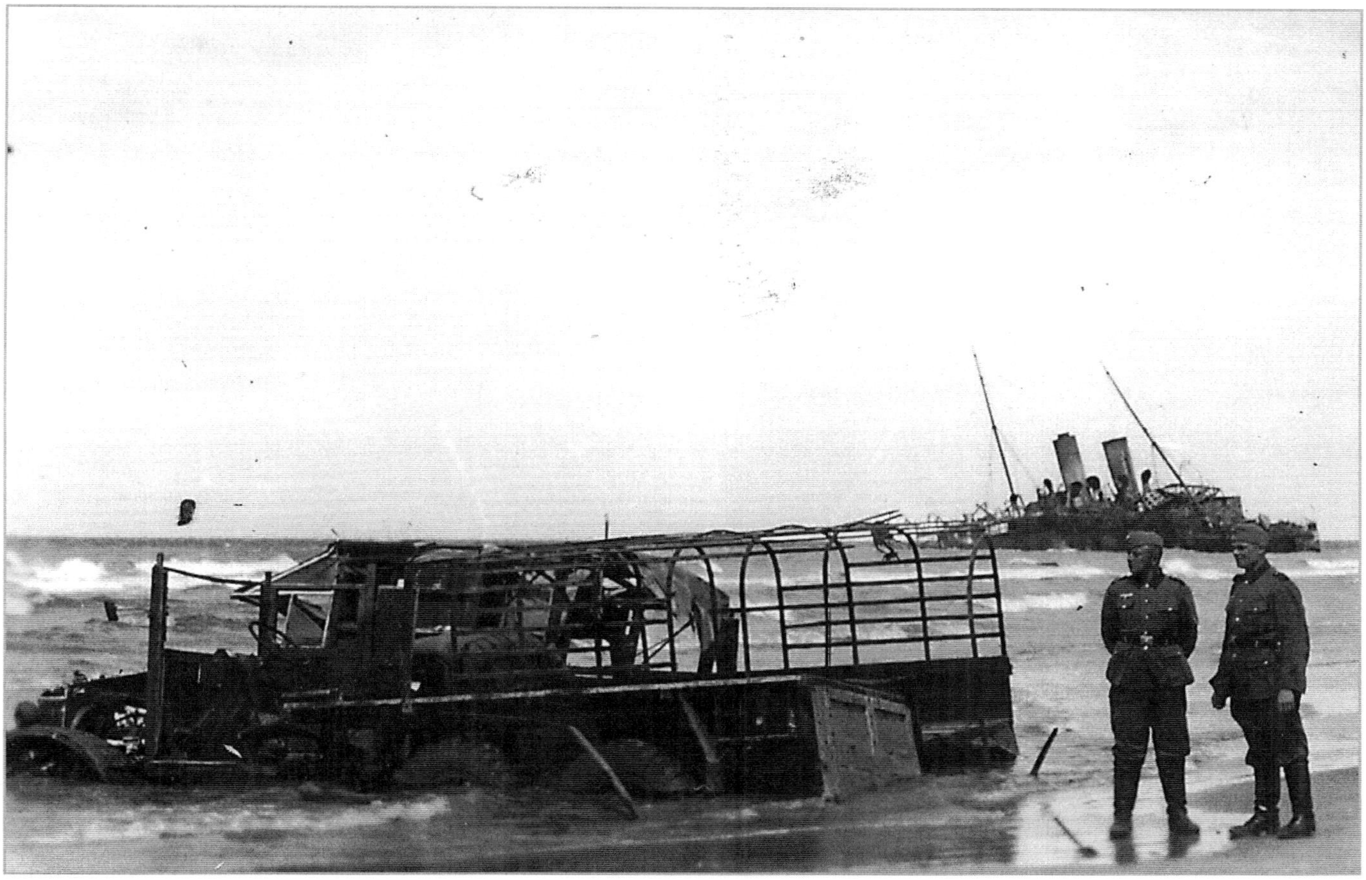

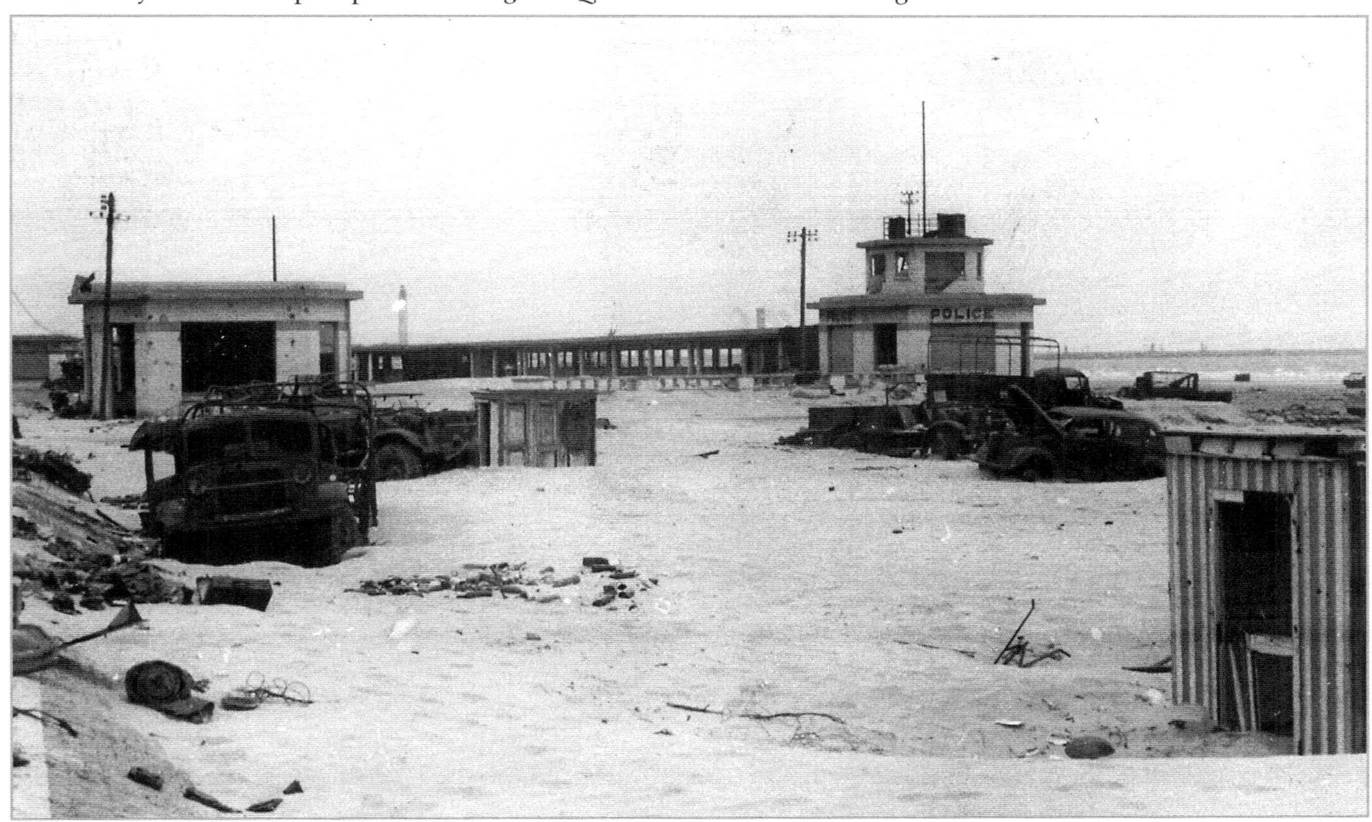

Two German artillerymen posing next to an abandoned truck, slowly being claimed by the sea with the commandeered ferry turned troop ship the *The Brighten Queen* wrecked in the background.

The private closed off area of beach outside the Malo Les Bains Casino showing the police office and ice-cream parlour which were both used as control offices by the beach commanders during the evacuation. The covered cloisters behind were used as part of the First Aid set up and many casualties were taken there for first aid and triage assessment.

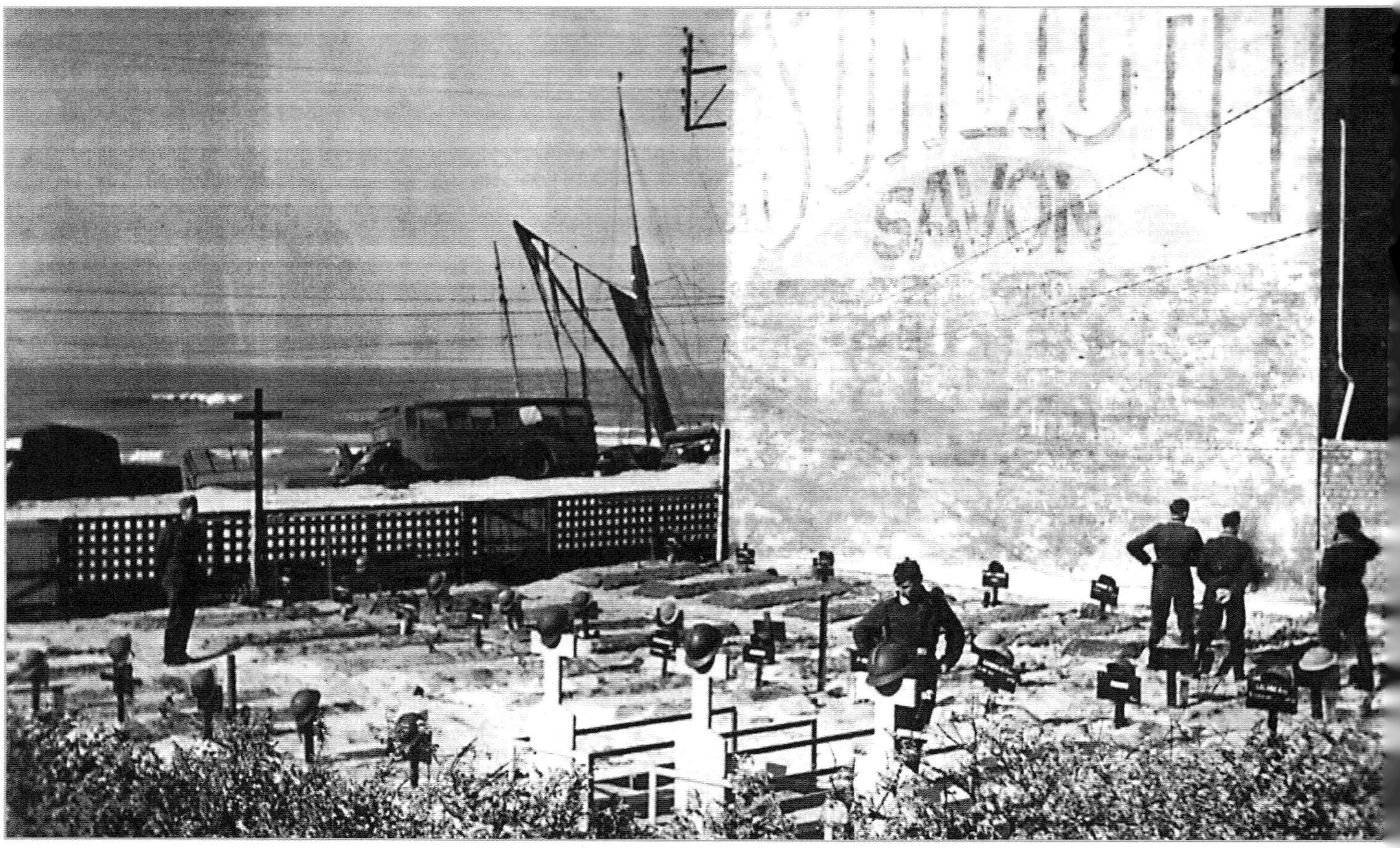

A temporary burial ground located in the plot of land next to the Malo Les Bains Casino on its east side. Before the evacuation was completed many such plots would be needed.

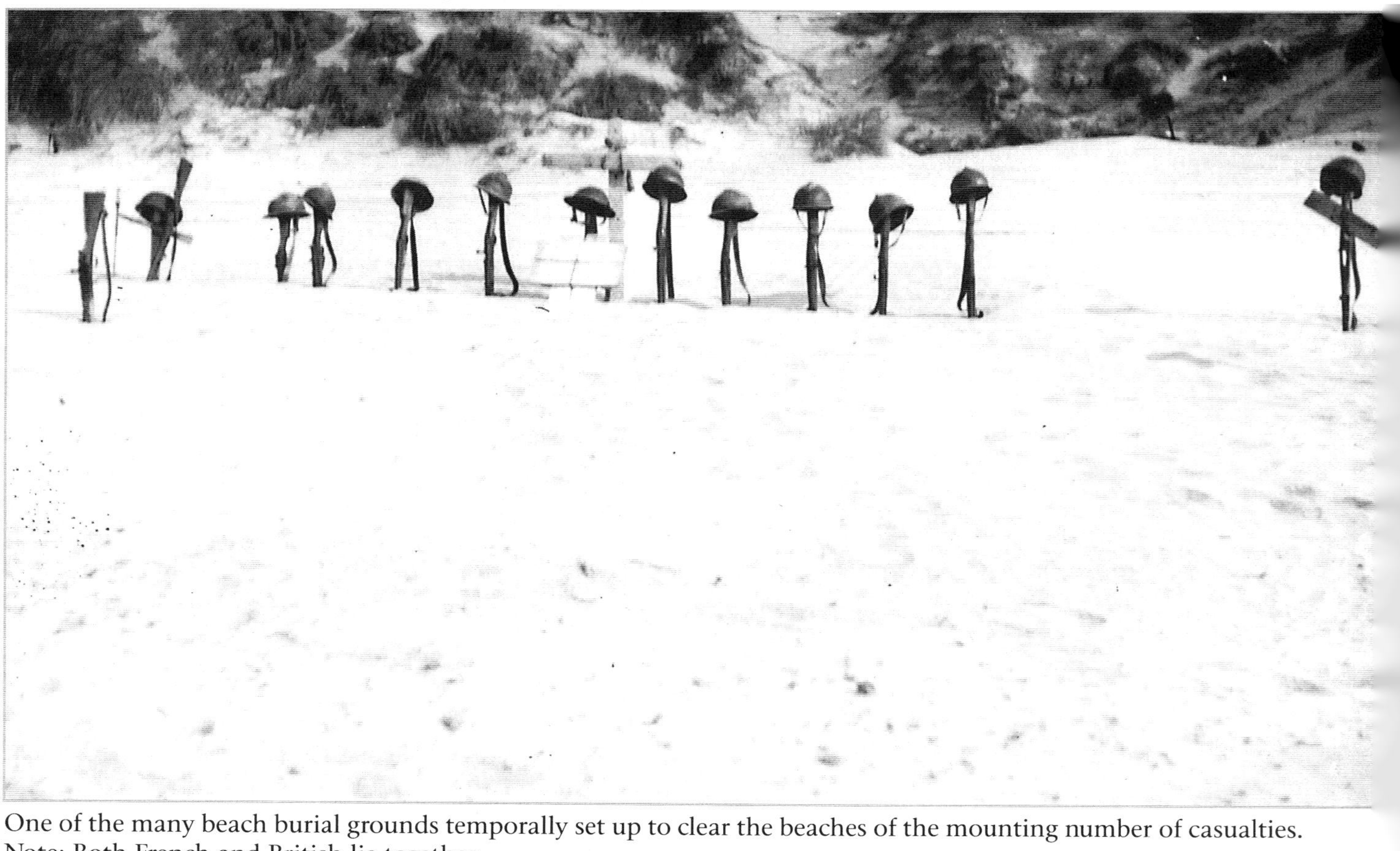

One of the many beach burial grounds temporally set up to clear the beaches of the mounting number of casualties. Note: Both French and British lie together.

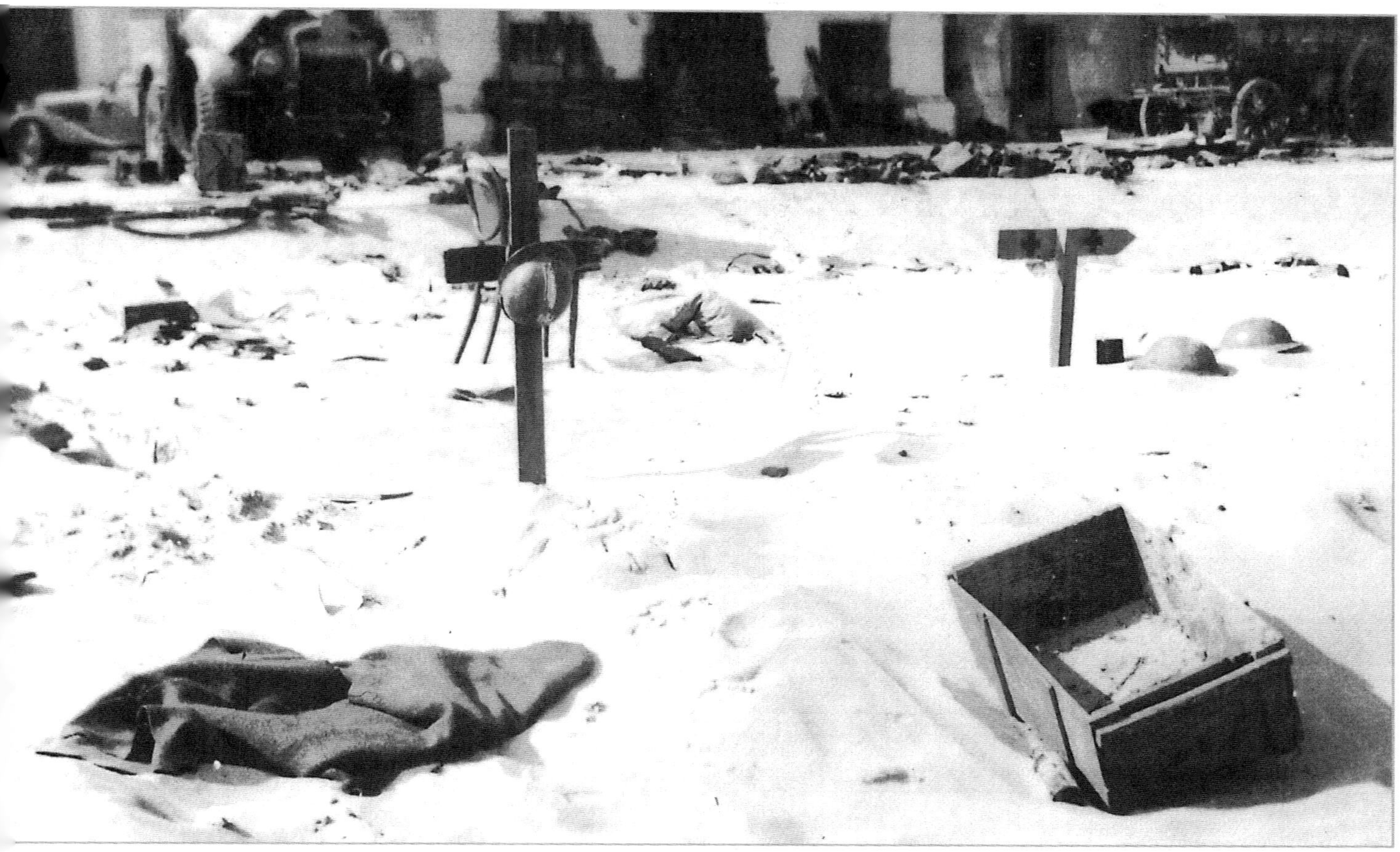

Only days after the evacuation the dried loose sand and weather made some of the beach burial grounds hard to locate. Sadly many of the buried dead had been lost to time.

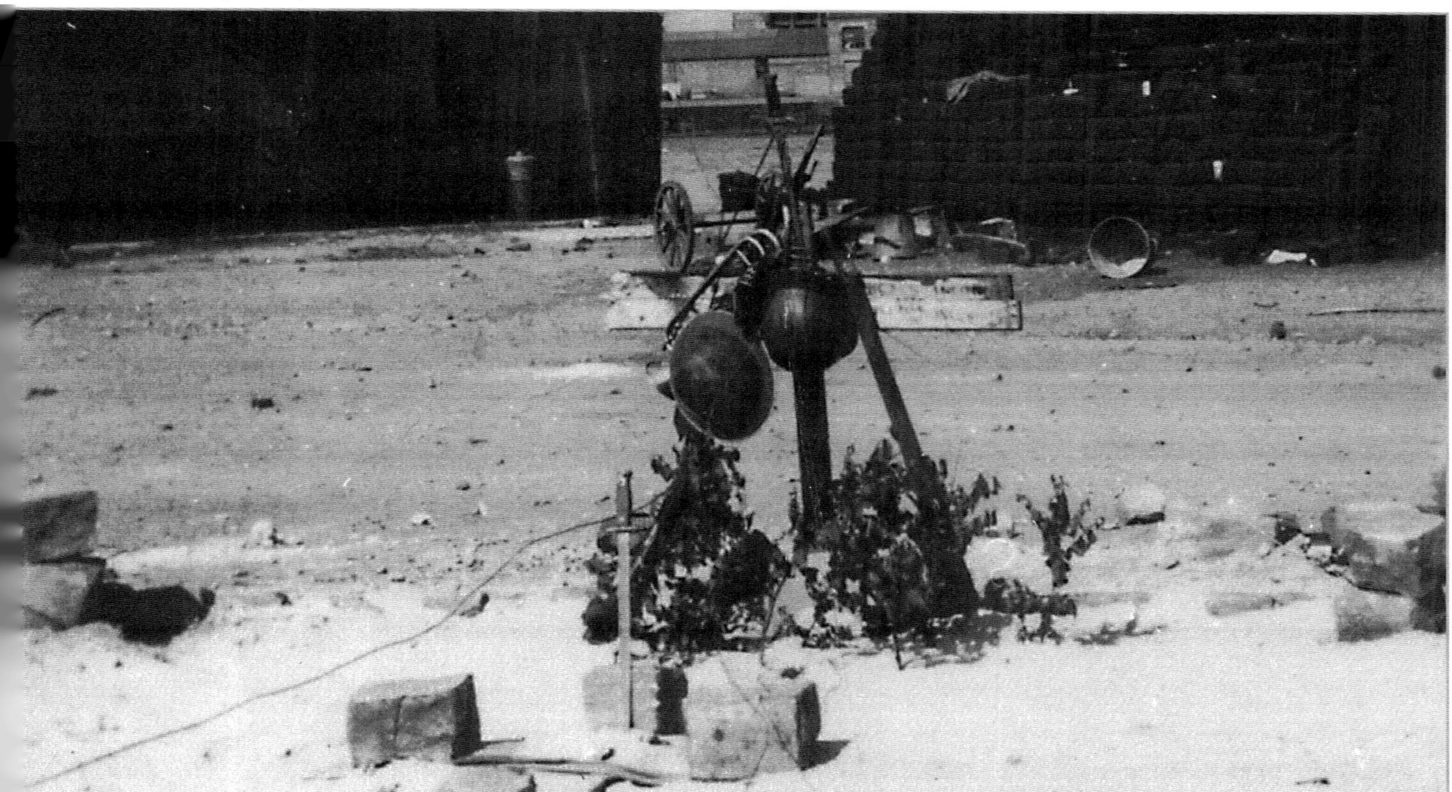

A poignant shot of the site of the temporary altar made for the church service that took place on the last morning of the evacuation to the west side of the main docks. Although in a partially sheltered area, the gathering of a mass of troops was spotted from the air and was strafed by a German aircraft. Sadly more casualties was the result.

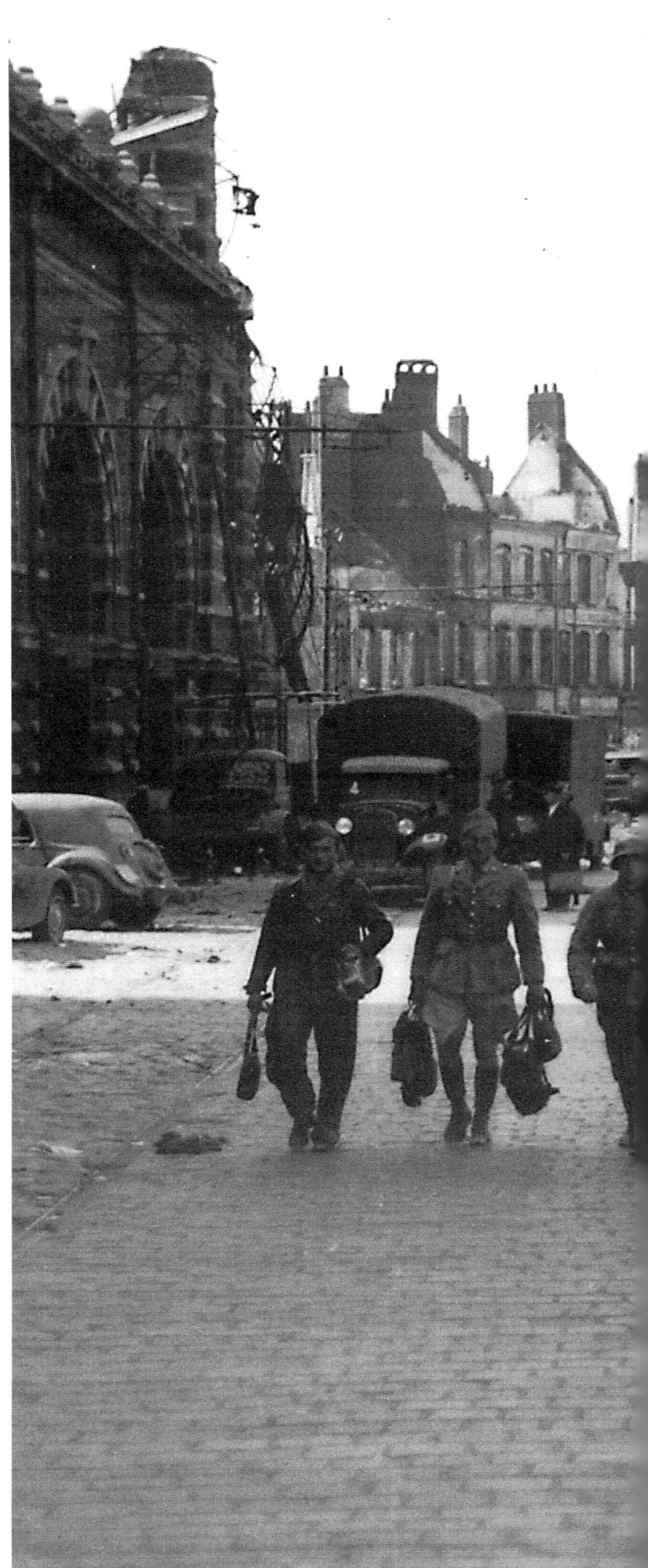

Dunkirk dock's main trading/loading area only a days after the evacuation, note the German troops in the foreground have a captive French officer they found hiding in the remains of the town.

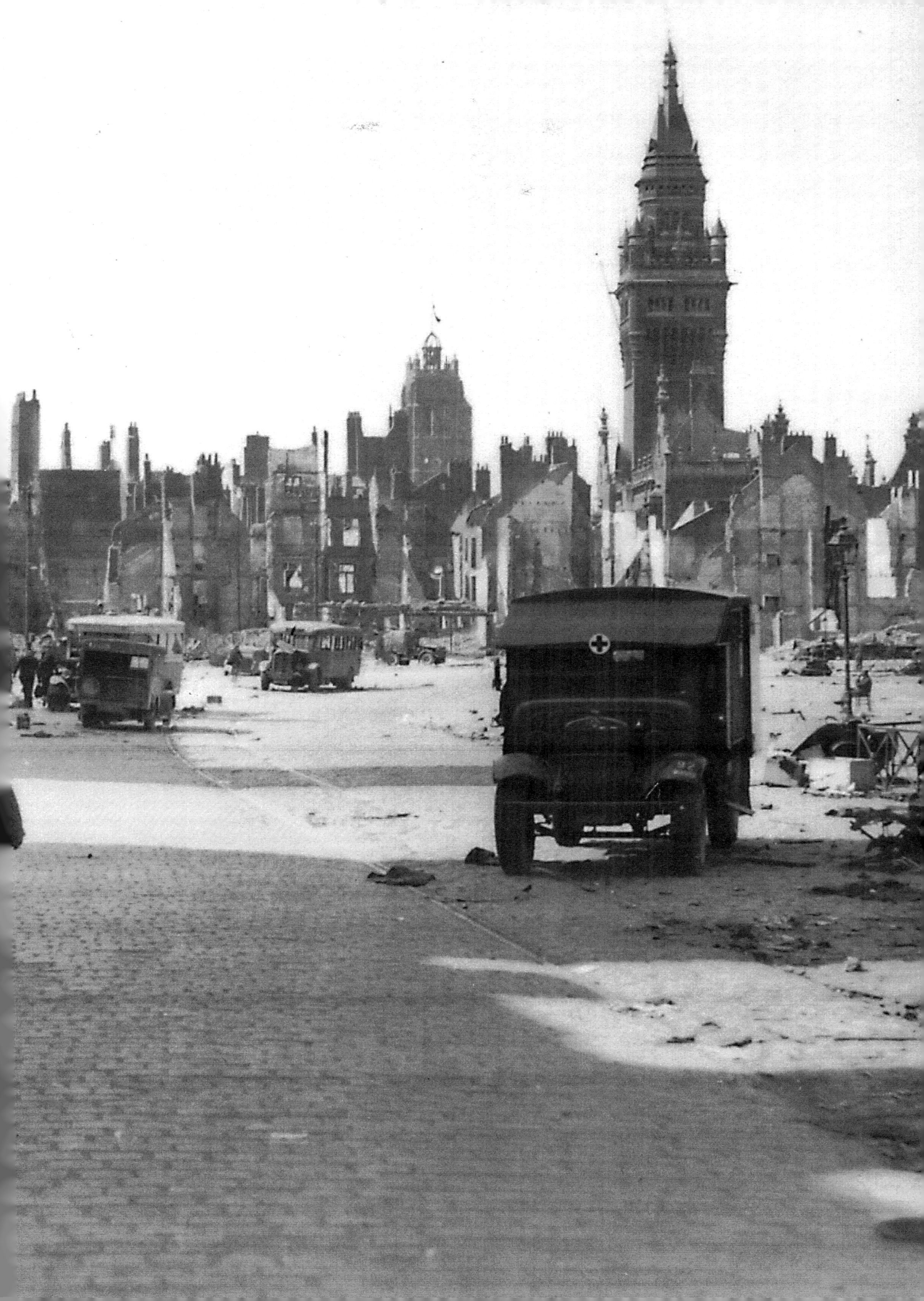

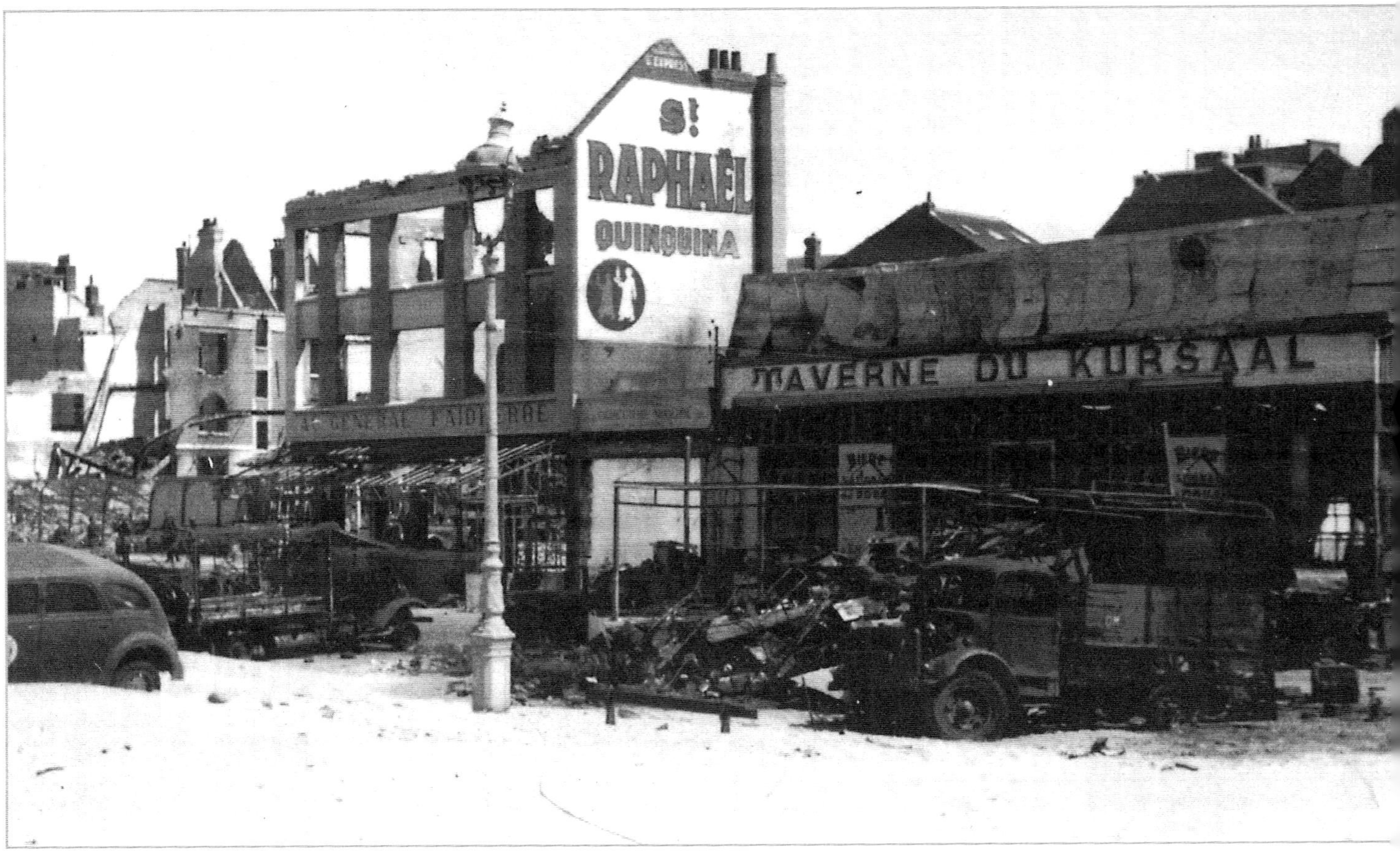

A rare photograph as it is taken of the mostly missed inland side of the promenade and also was taken on the morning of the 6th only hours after the evacuation was completed. Note the road is still blocked by abandoned vehicles.

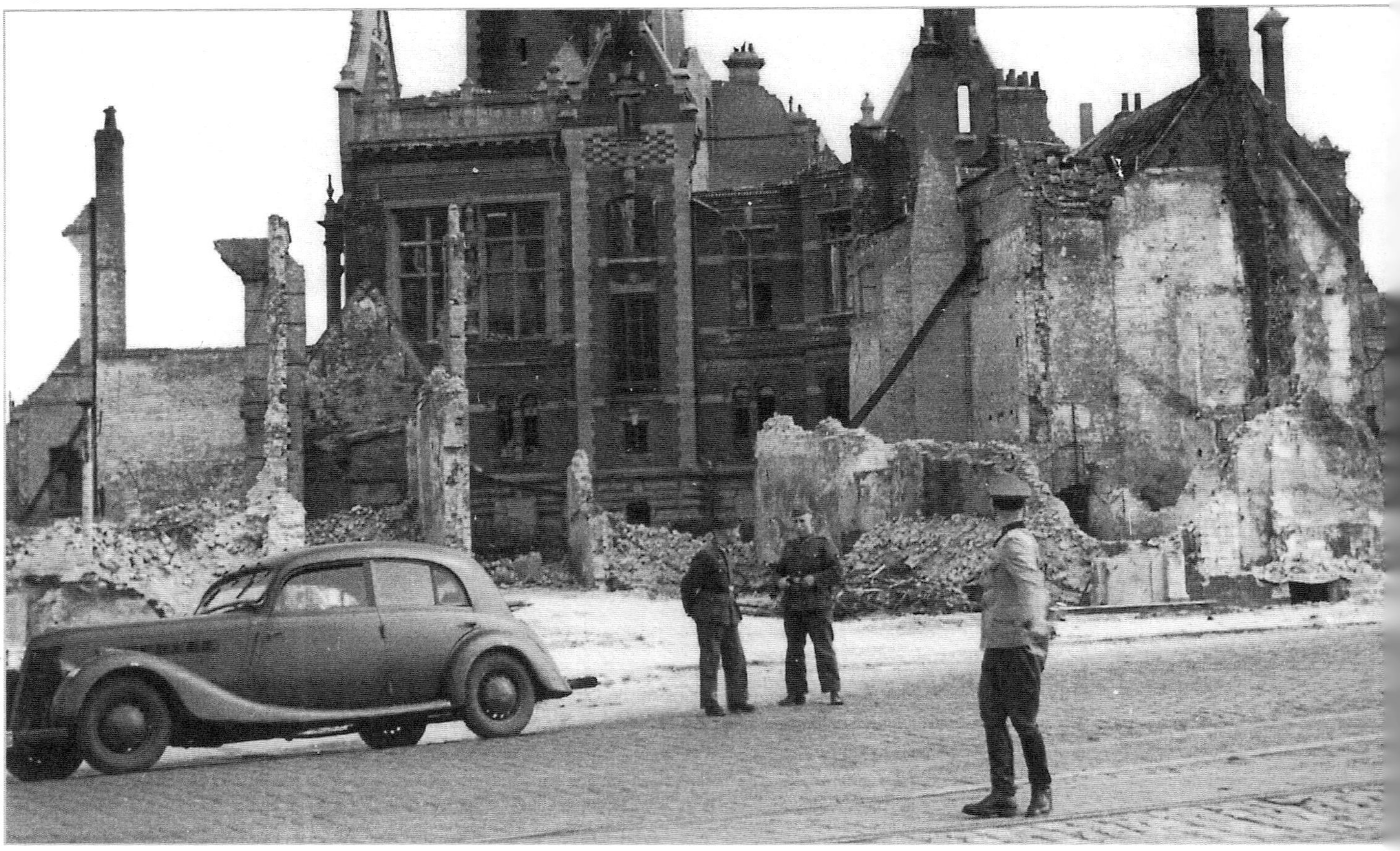

The wreckage of the town now slowly being cleaned up. Here is a view of the rear of the town hall with a German officer and his Audi Staff car in the foreground.

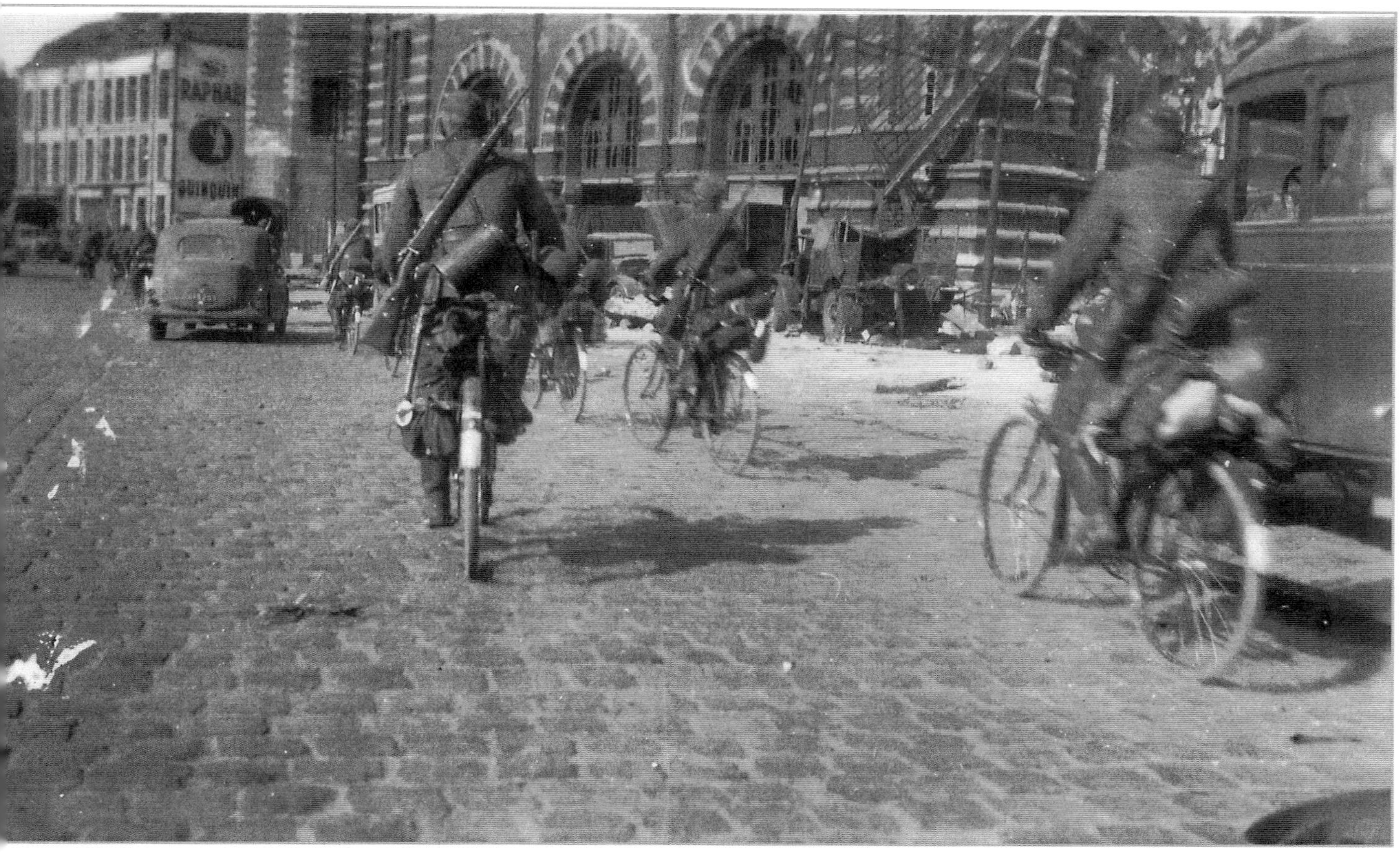

An atmospheric shot of German troops arriving in the town for a 'quick recce'. The whole area became a 'must see' for the victorious Germans in the region.

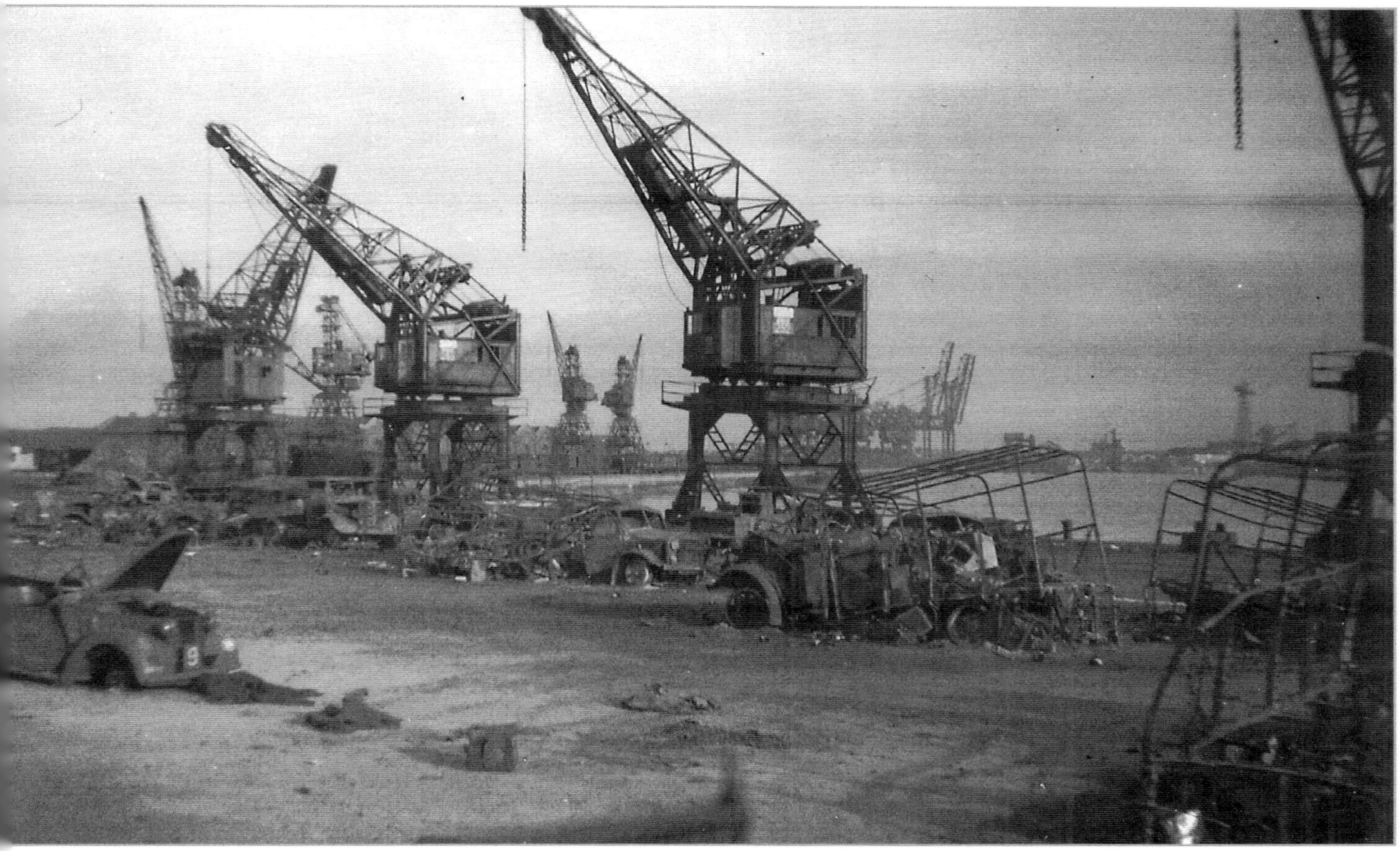

A shot of the main docks only 24 hours after the evacuation – the devastation is both immense and obvious.

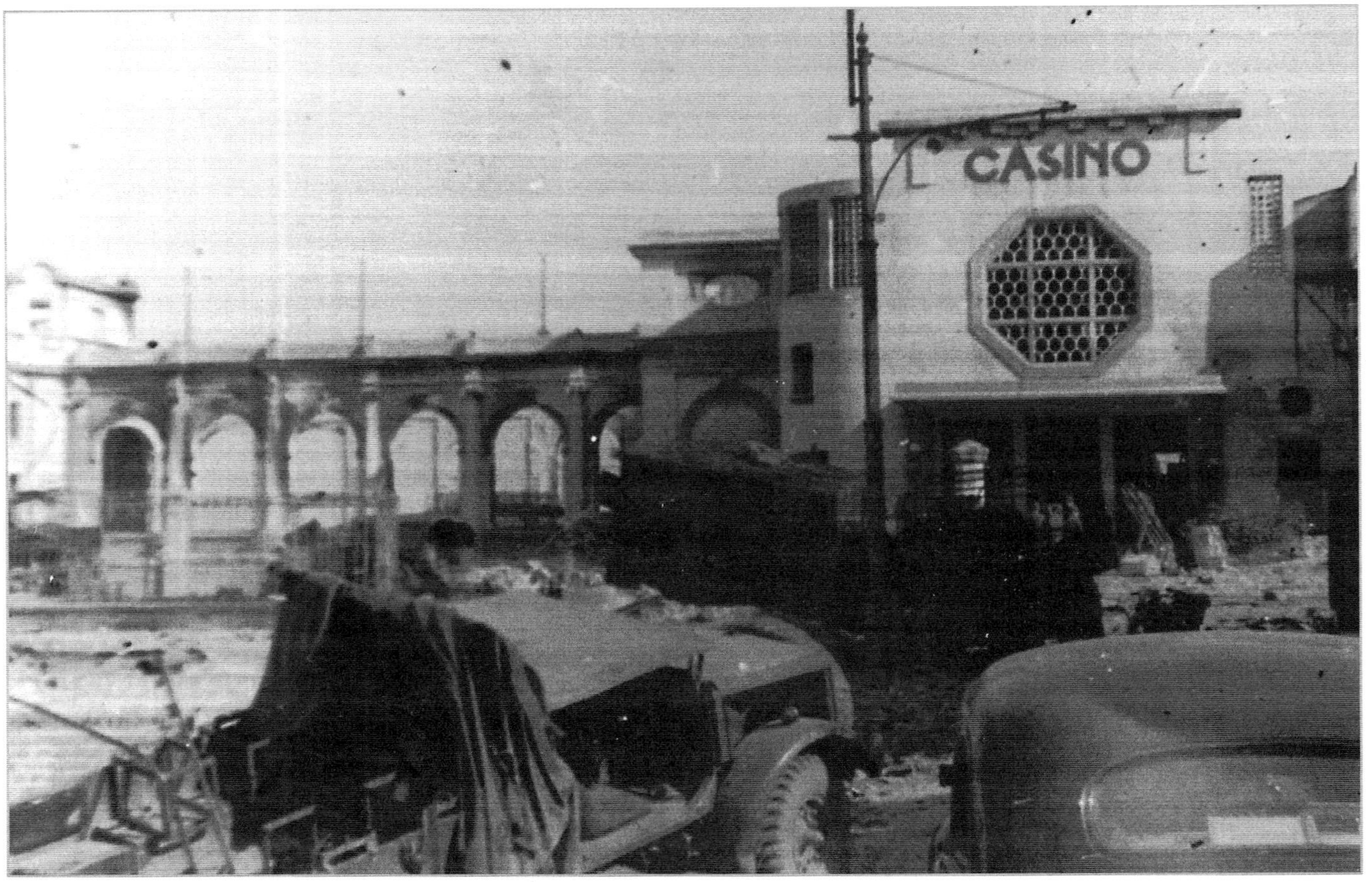

This is the frontage of Malo Les Bains Casino which was a key building to the allies during the defence of the Dunkirk pocket, as it was used as the main hospital and casualty gathering centre during those few hectic days.

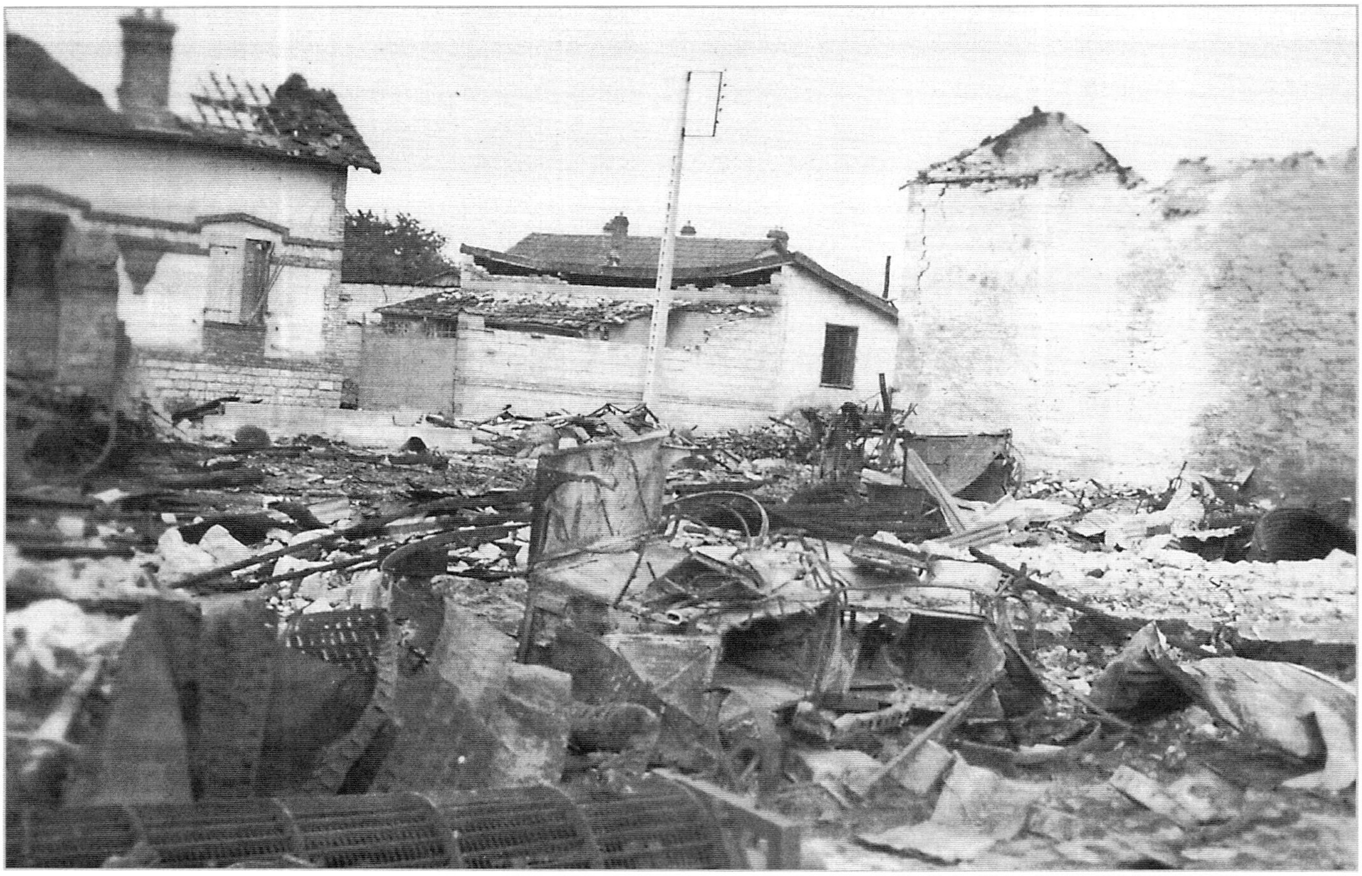

Another photograph of the town in general and like so many others in my collection it shows the devastation to the town. It is said that not one single building was left undamaged, some clearly more than others.

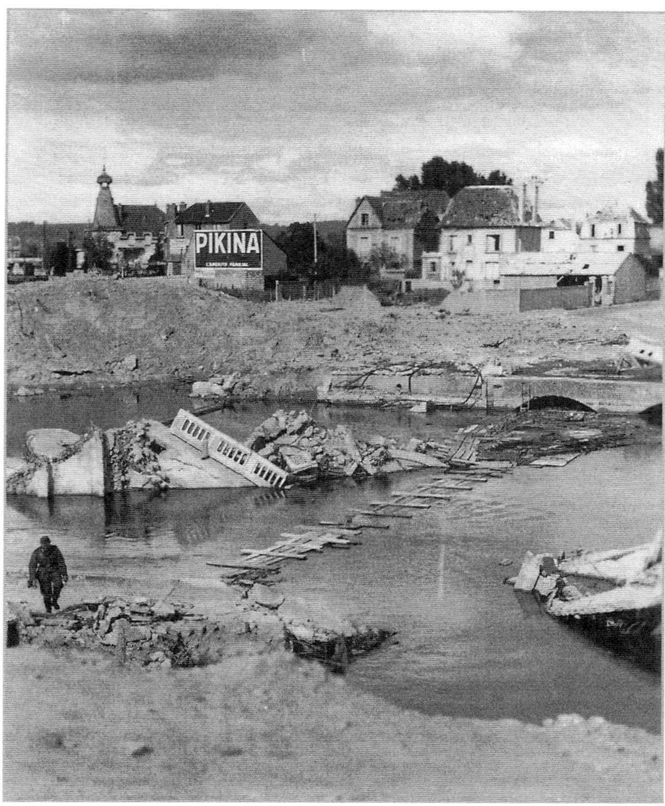

One of the many canals that lace their way through the town, with the main road bridge blown down the remains of a temporary footbridge can be seen.

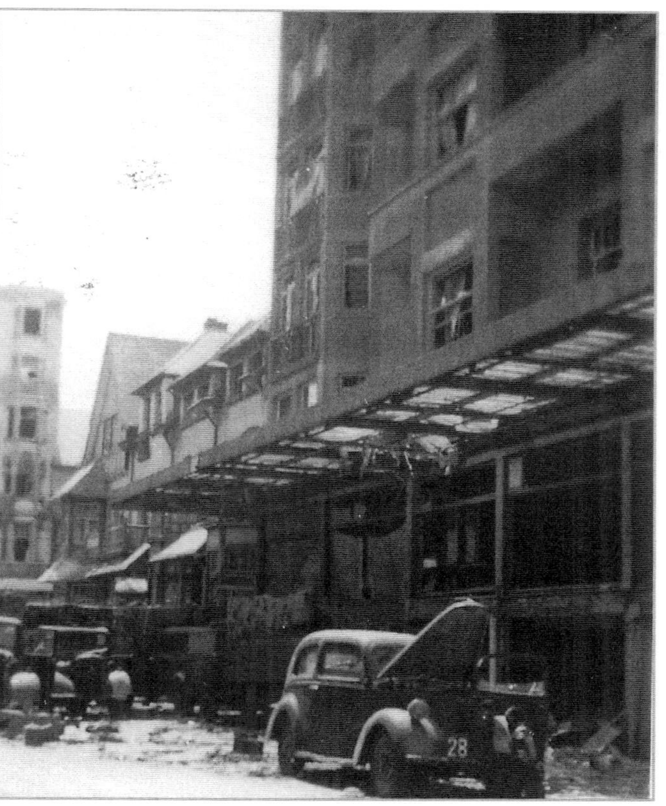

The inland frontage to one of the many multi-story hotel buildings located along the promenade, not only does it look worse for the experience so does the little British Austin Staff car left outside the main door.

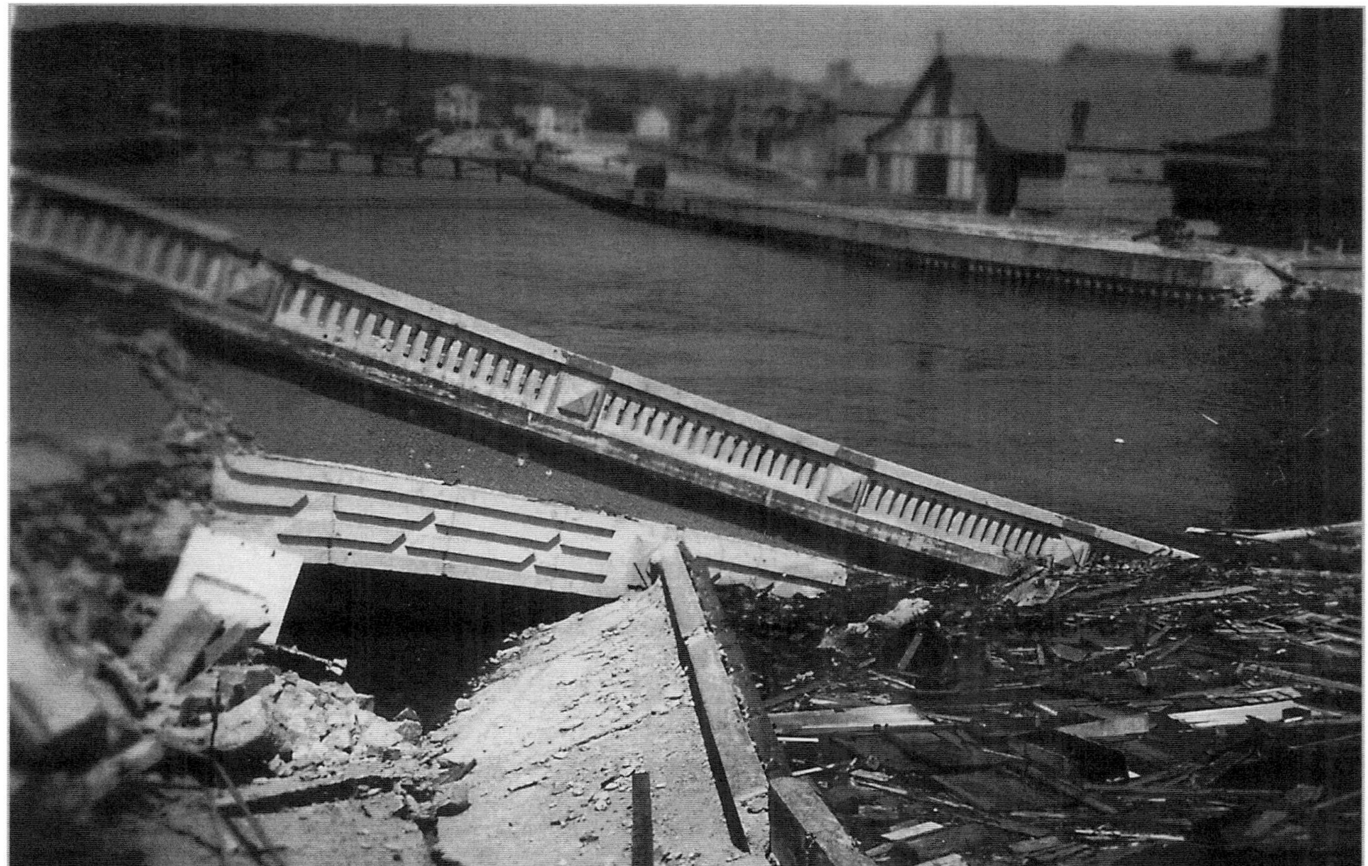

Another view of a destroyed road bridge across one of canals in the area with a lighter bridge that survived in the background.

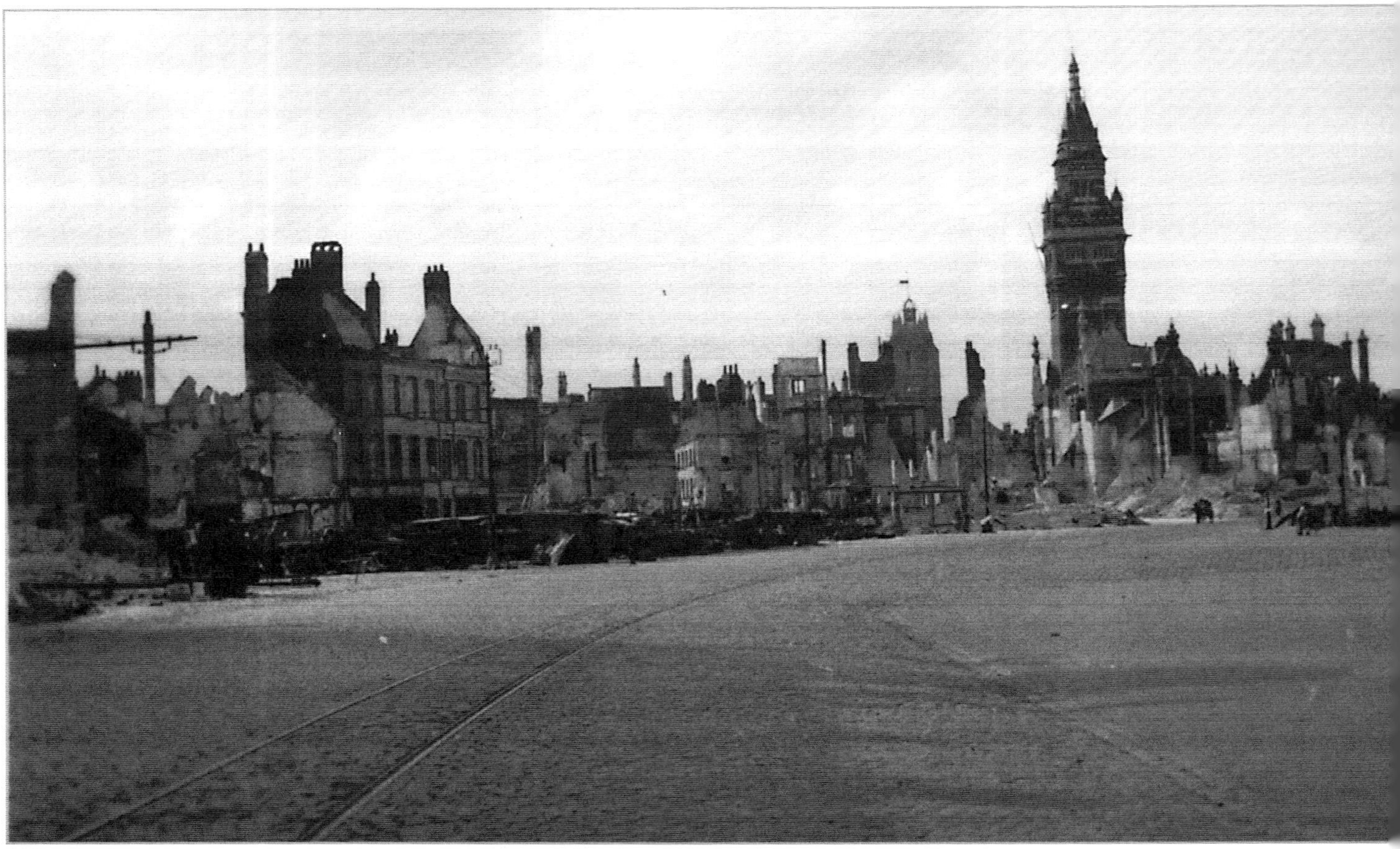

These two views of the main trading/loading area of the docks show roughly the same view. This one shows the area after the initial clean up with a vehicle gathering point in the south western most corner.

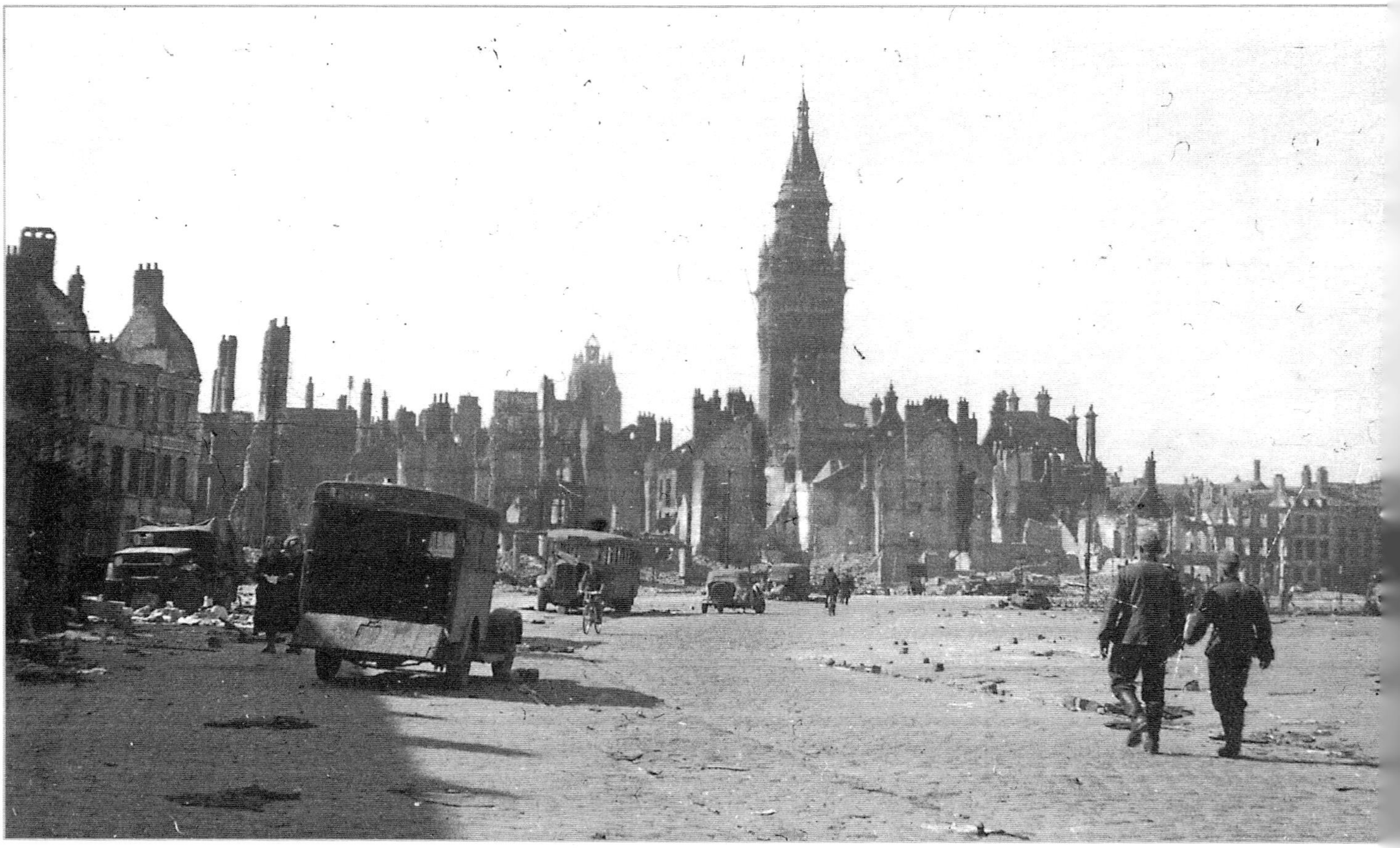

In this photo the area is shown as the Germans found it upon their arrival. Both French and British trucks are to be seen abandoned here, with a Bedford 15cwt seen on the far left.

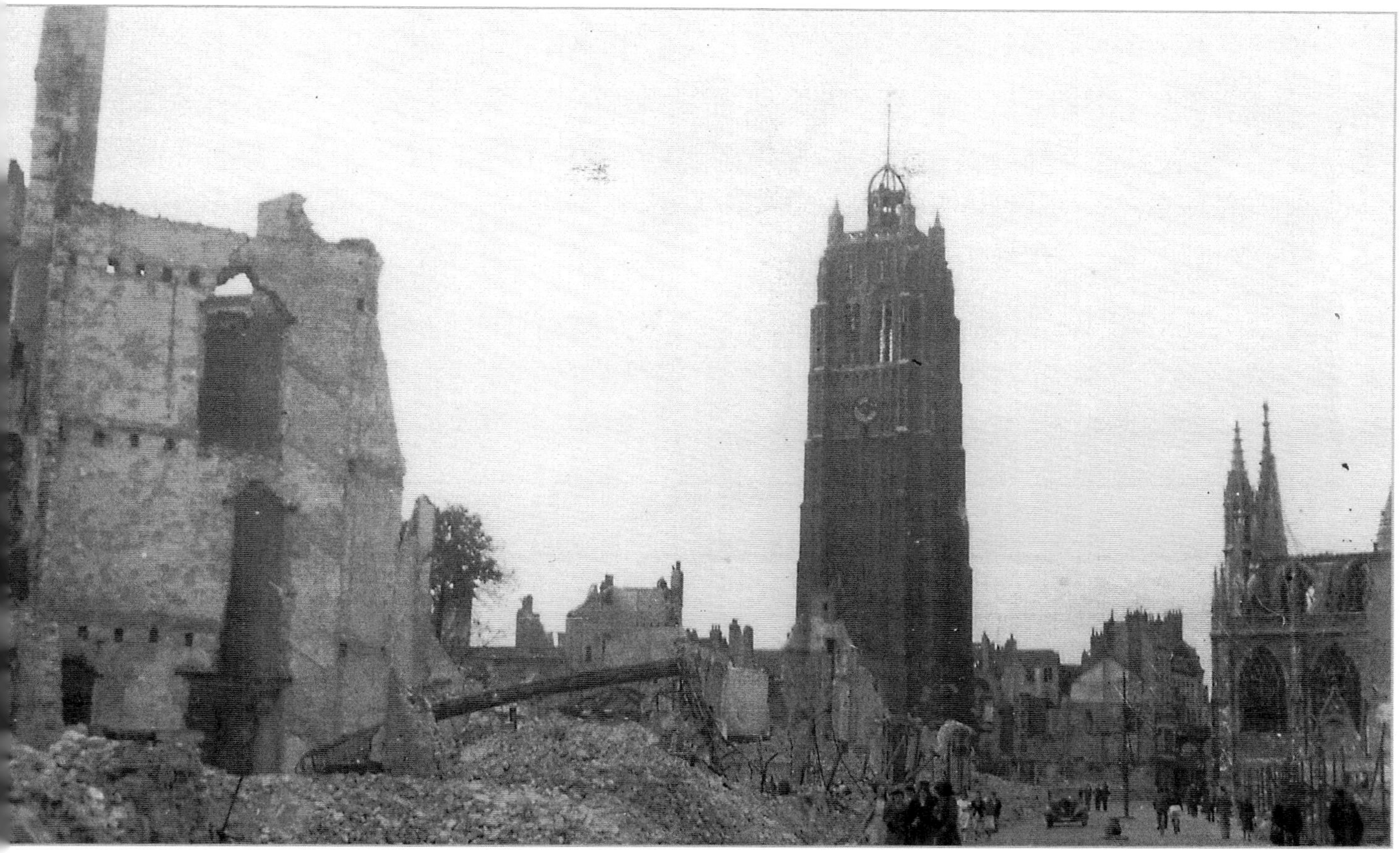

On this page we have two photographs of the town square. Here we see the north-western corner of it and the devastation to the housing around its edge.

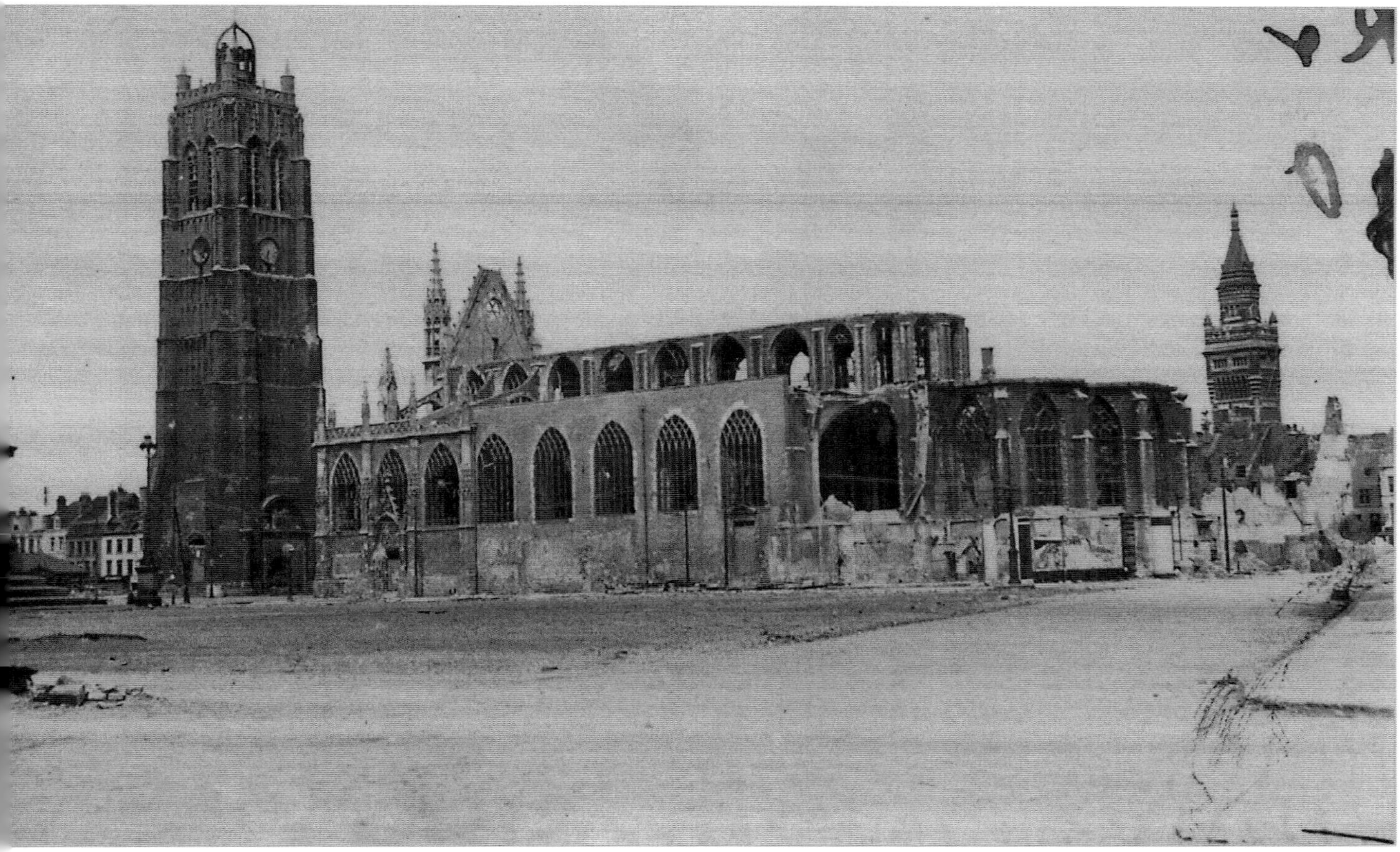

In this photograph also looking to the north-western corner of the town square but from the far eastern edge of it, we can see all the main civic buildings the bell tower, the Cathedral and the Town Hall in the background.

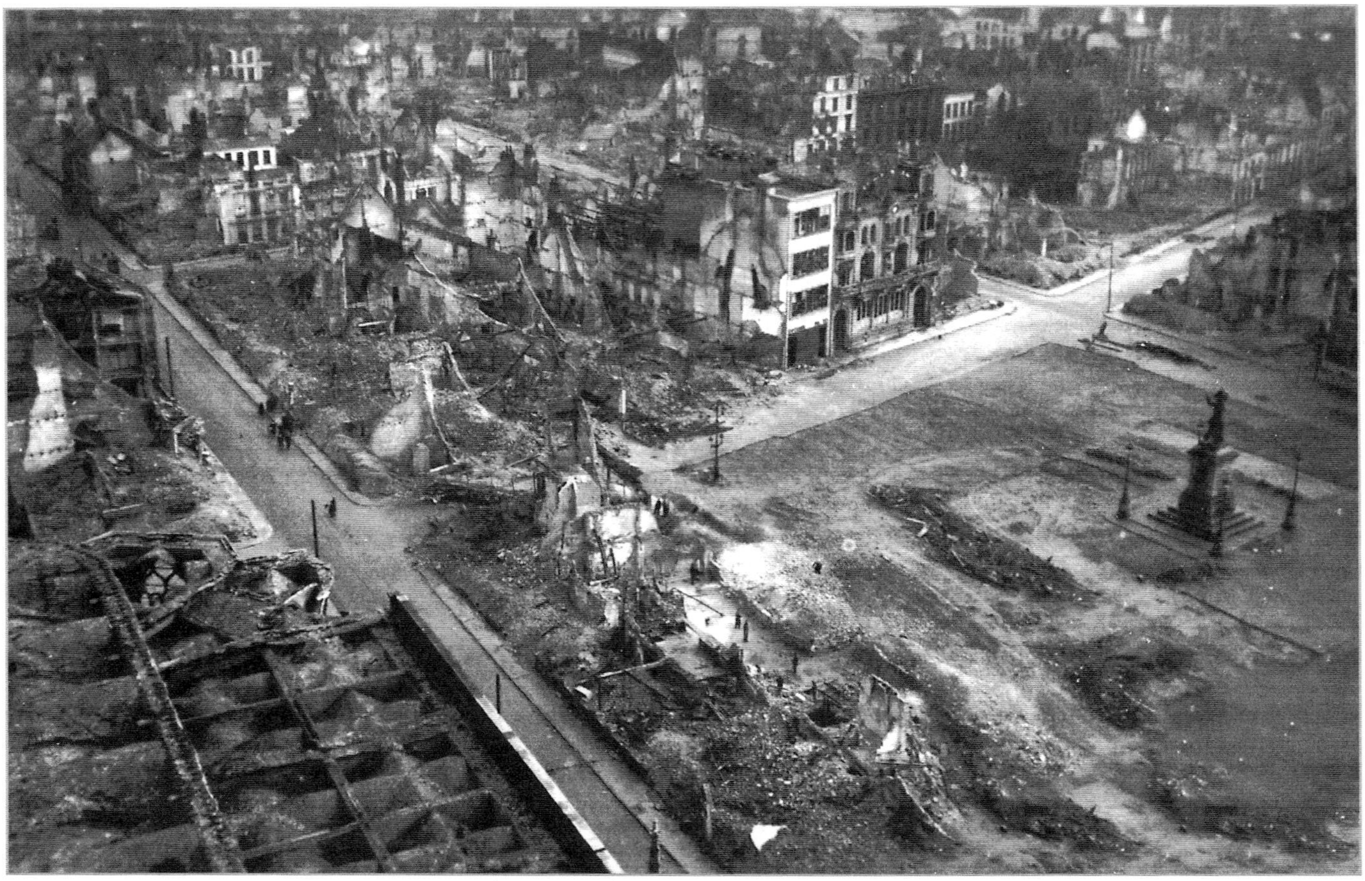

The Town square (The Jean Bart square) from the bell tower of the cathedral. Note the slate roof has totally collapsed but the gothic arch forms that cover the Nave have survived.

A view from the town square looking to the north-eastern corner where
a pharmacy was located.

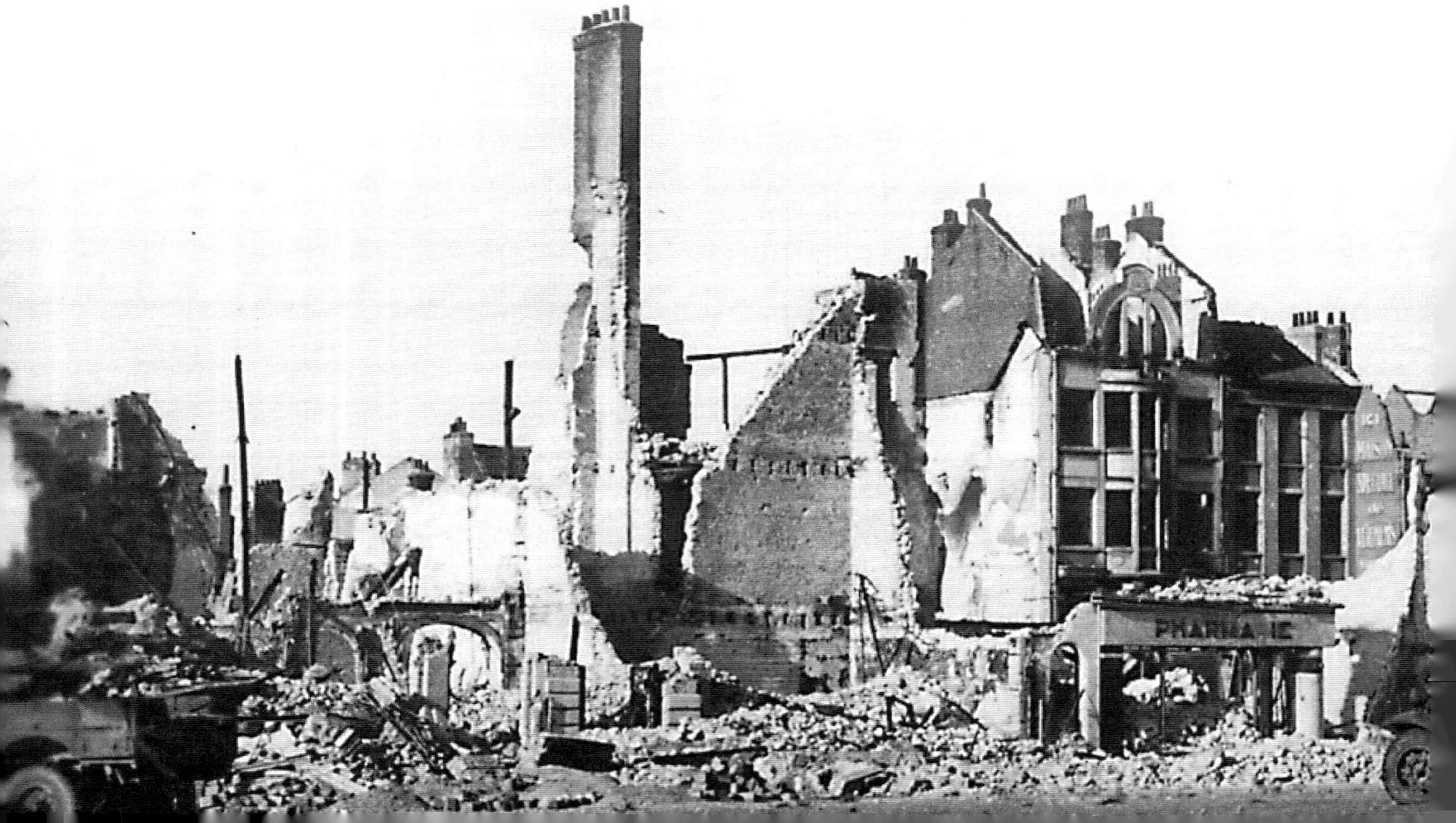

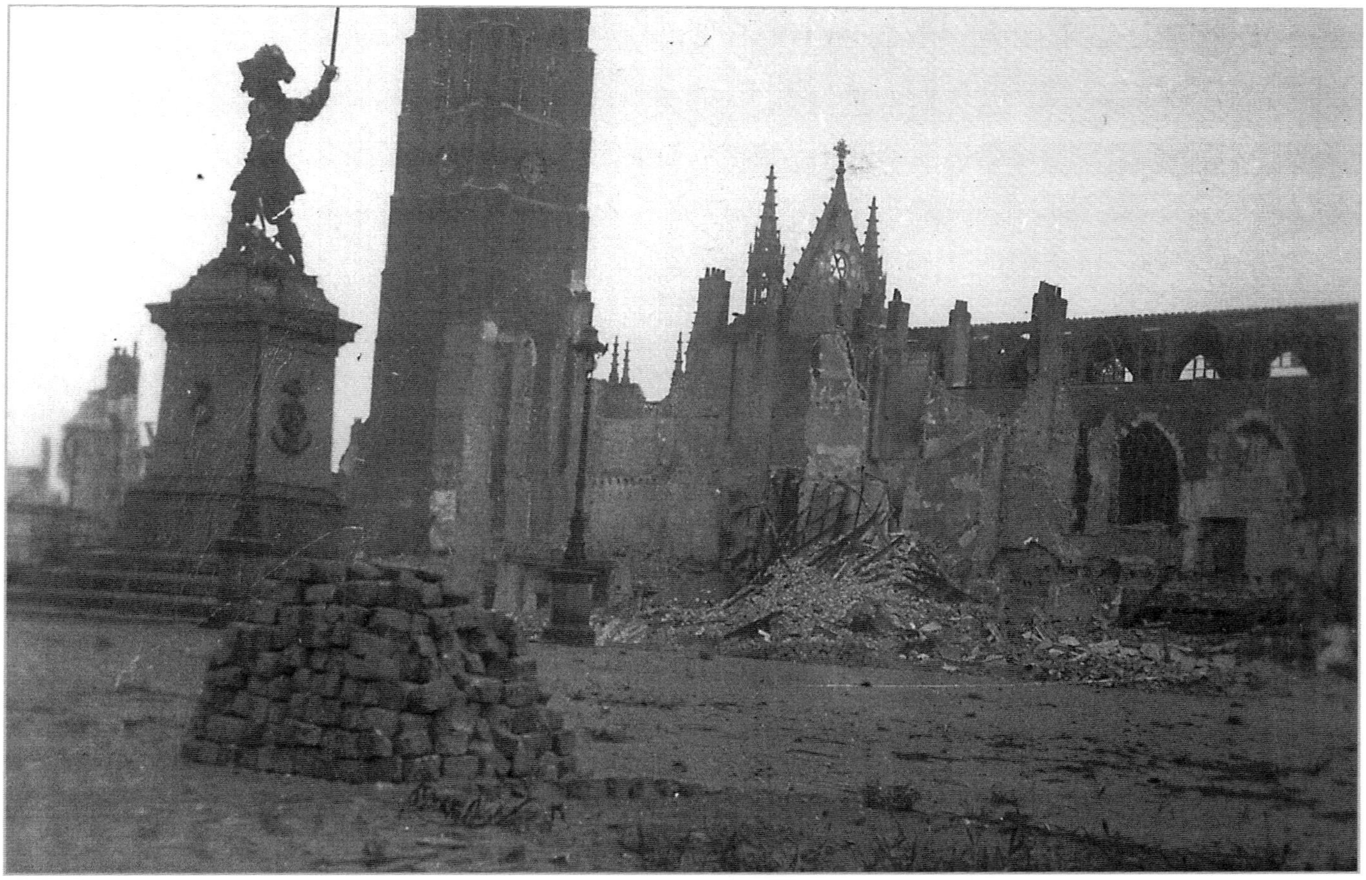

Another view of the Town Square looking towards the north-western corner at the remains of the cathedral and in the foreground the statue of Jean Bart.

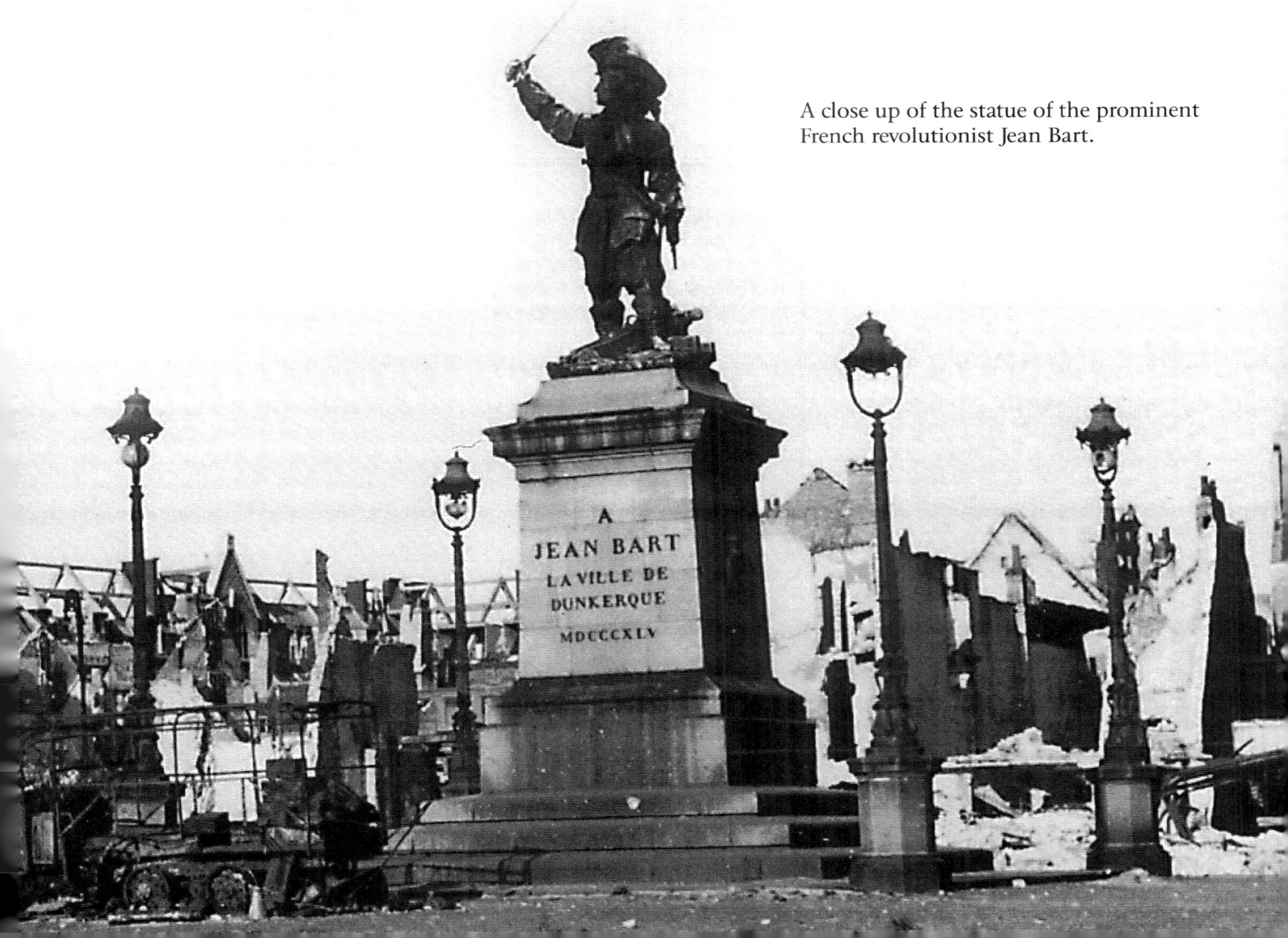

A close up of the statue of the prominent French revolutionist Jean Bart.

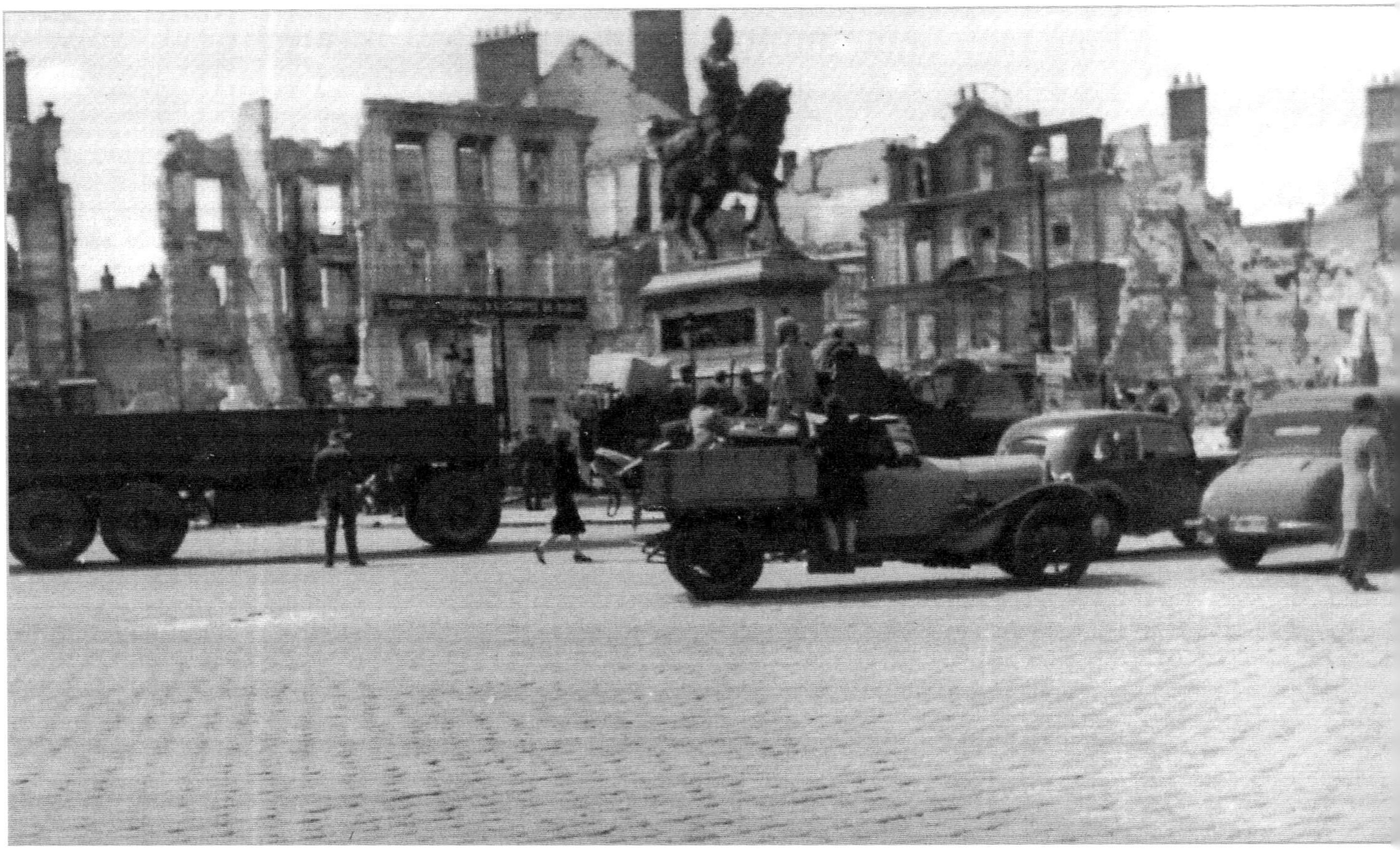

A view of the large paved area in front of the southernmost quayside of Dunkirk's inner harbour. Seen here on the far left of the photograph is a German heavy trailer this one is of note as it has been commandeered for military use from the German Railways.

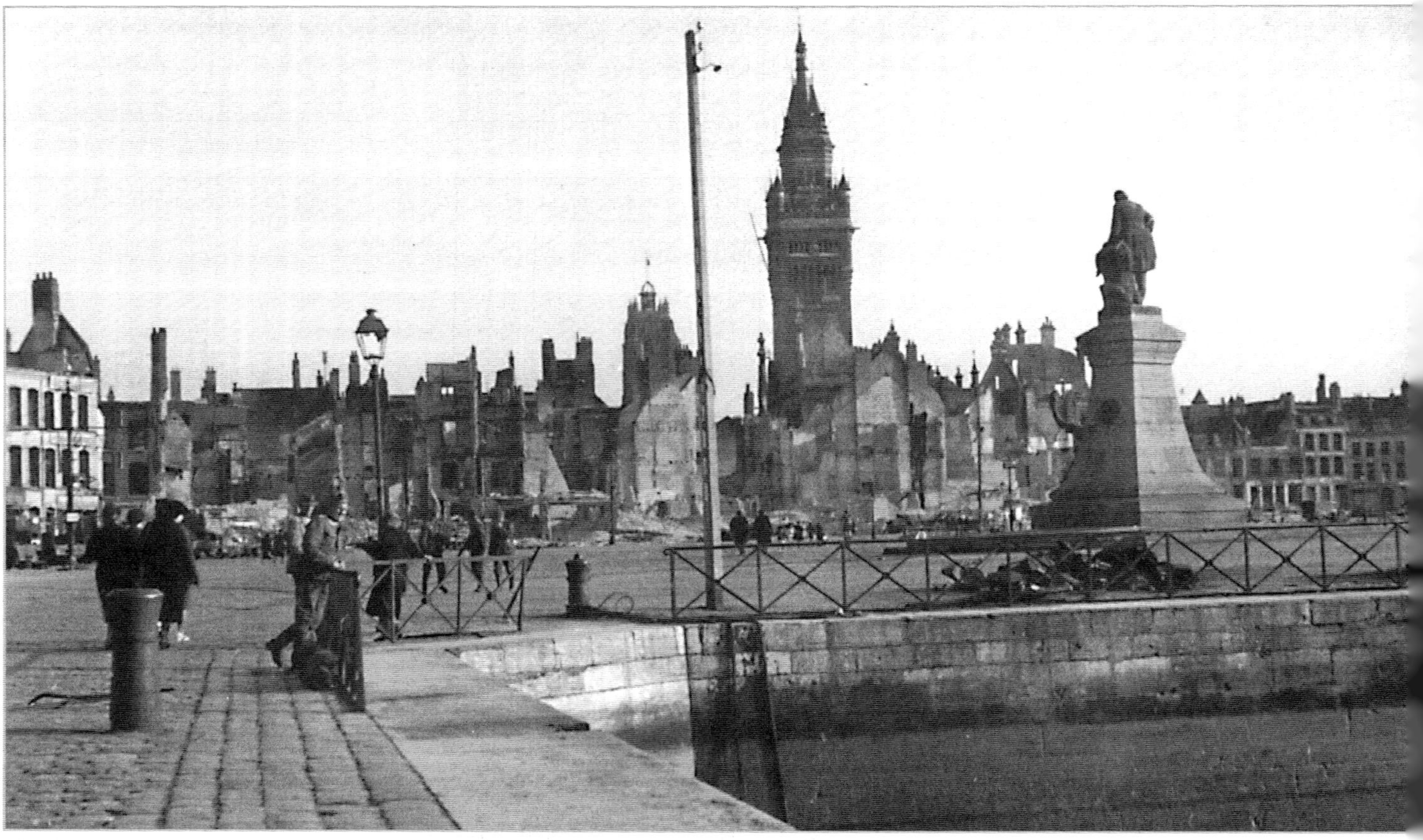

Shown here only a week or two after the evacuation the remaining towns folk are getting on with life and even German soldiers reviewing the sights unarmed.

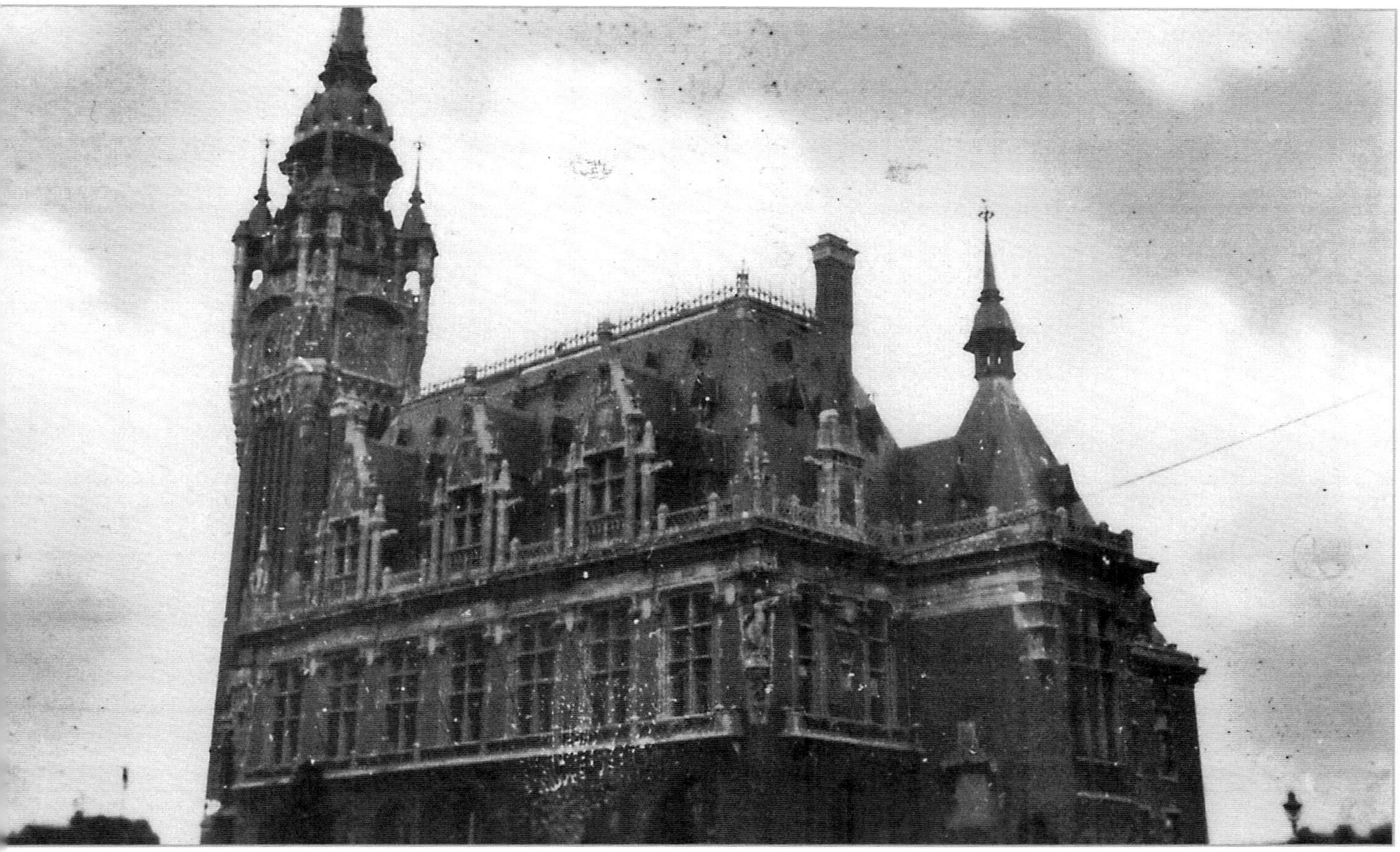

A close up of the Town Hall.

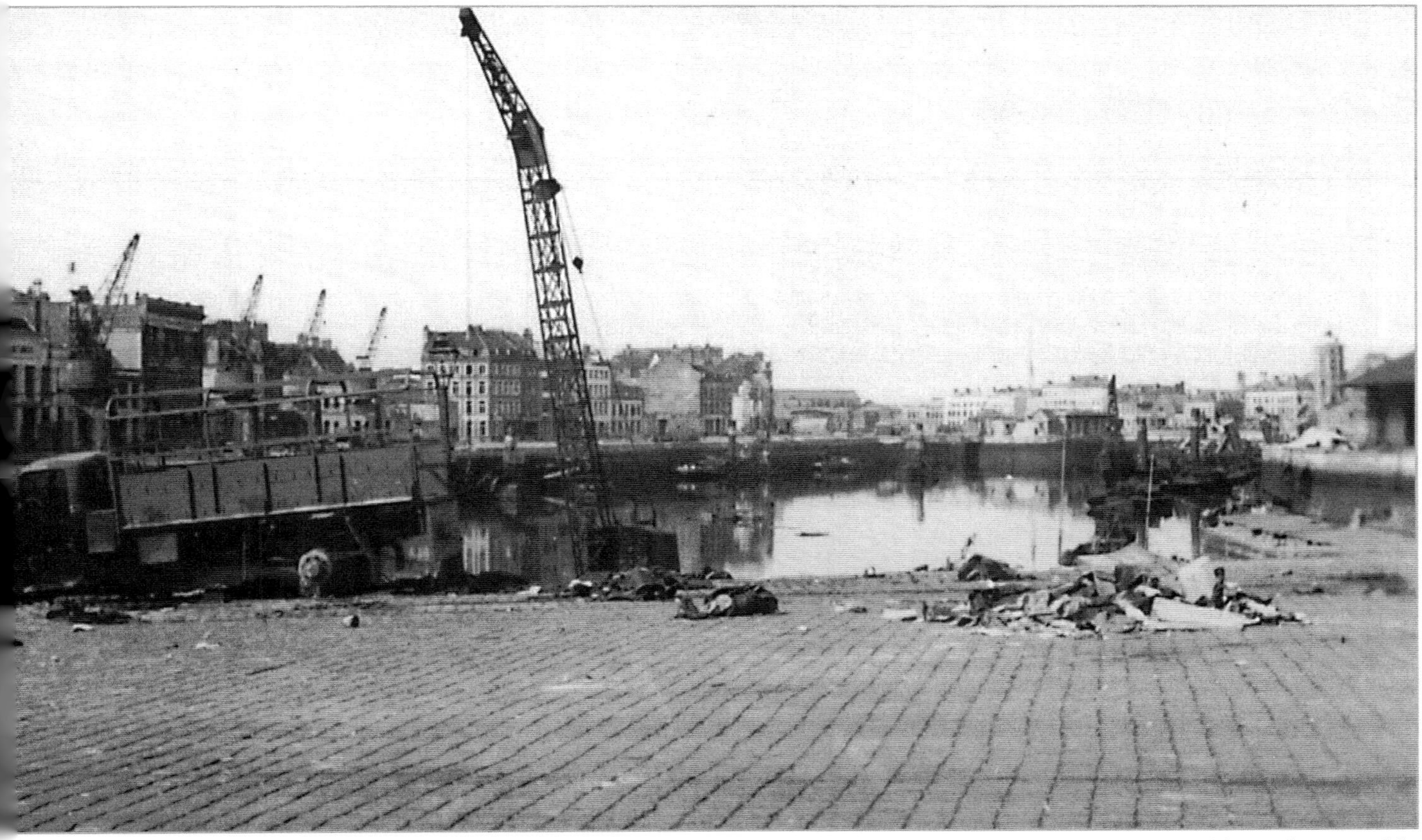

The southern most of the inner harbour shown after the initial clean up; now with all serviceable and repairable vehicles removed, only write-offs remain to be cleared away.

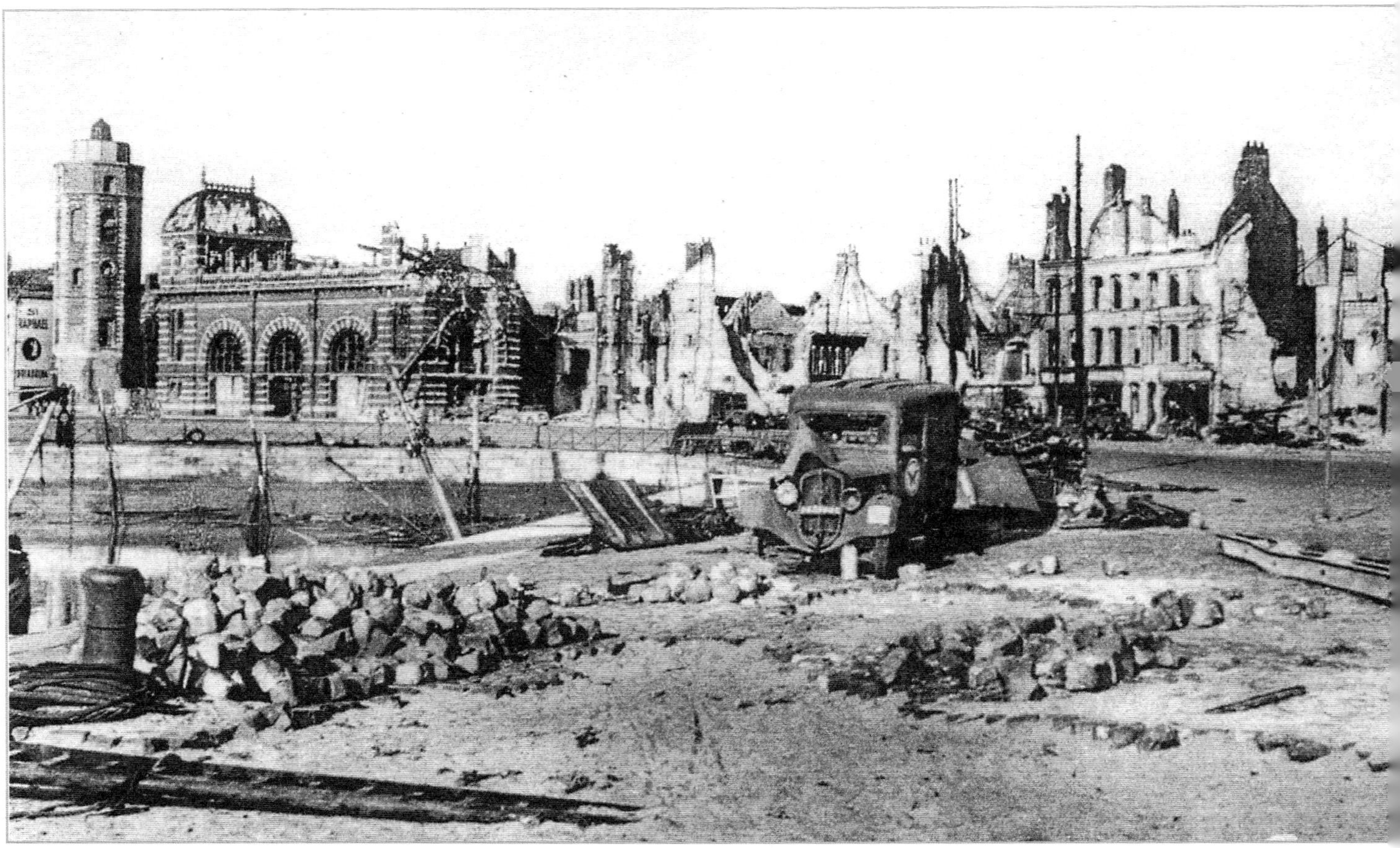

Here at the main inner harbour again after the initial clean up only a disabled French ambulance and other military associated but unidentified scrap remains.

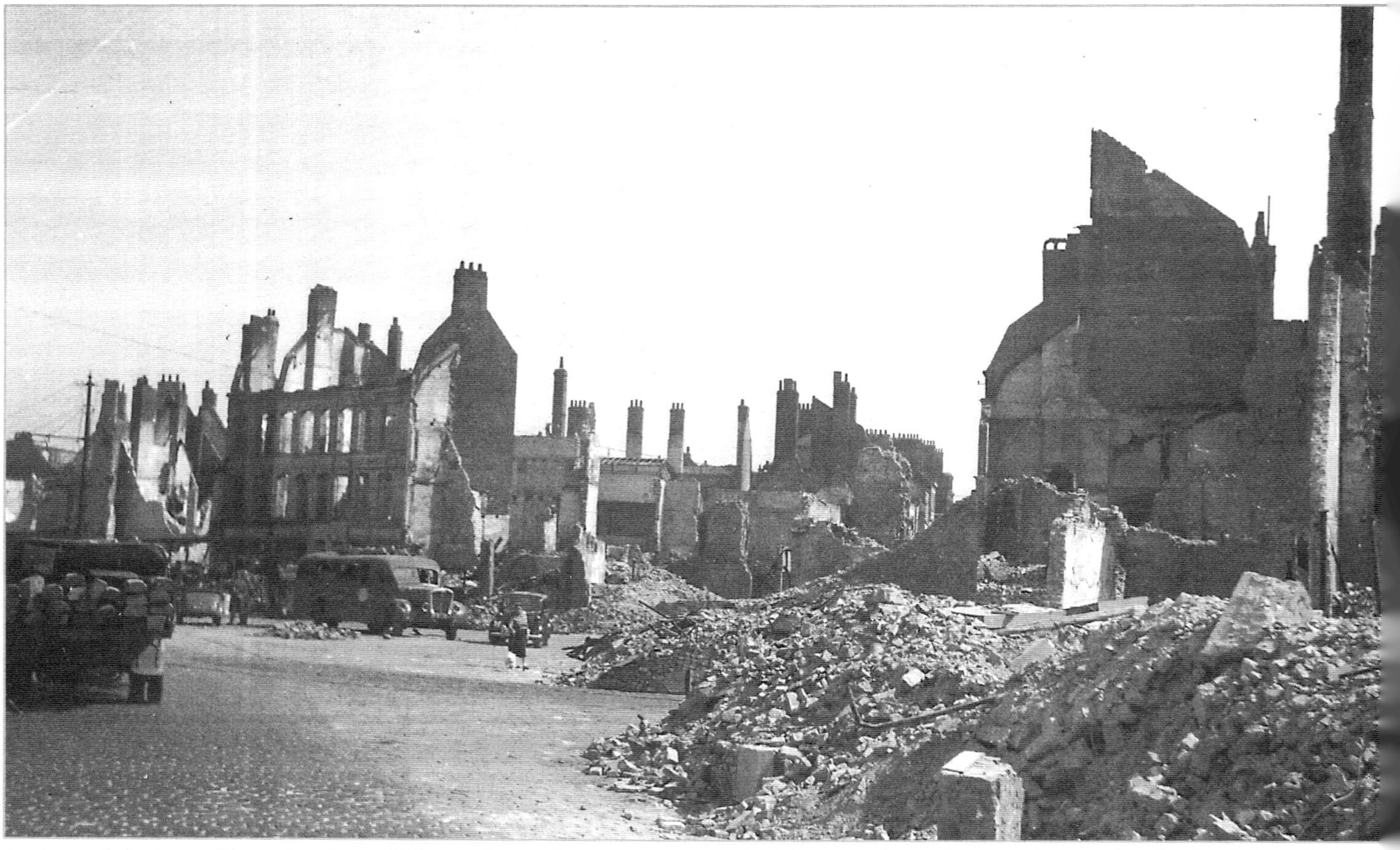

A view of destroyed housing just off from the main town square, the clean-up is underway. A truck load of reclaimed timber can be seen on the move and an Opel troop bus in the background.

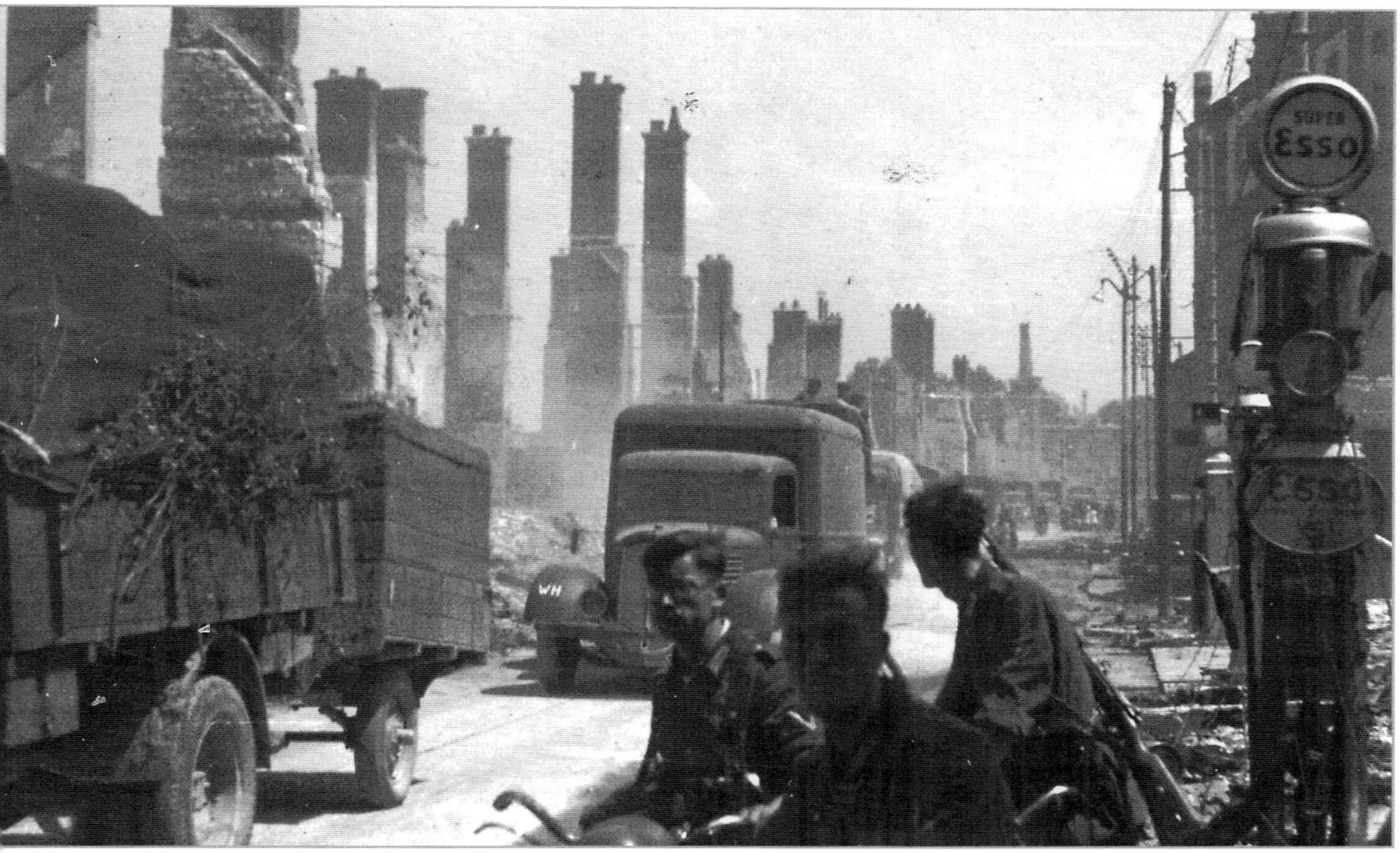

German troops on the move through the town. Note the petrol garage in the foreground, as was usual practice for the German army all available fuel was immediately 'requisitioned'.

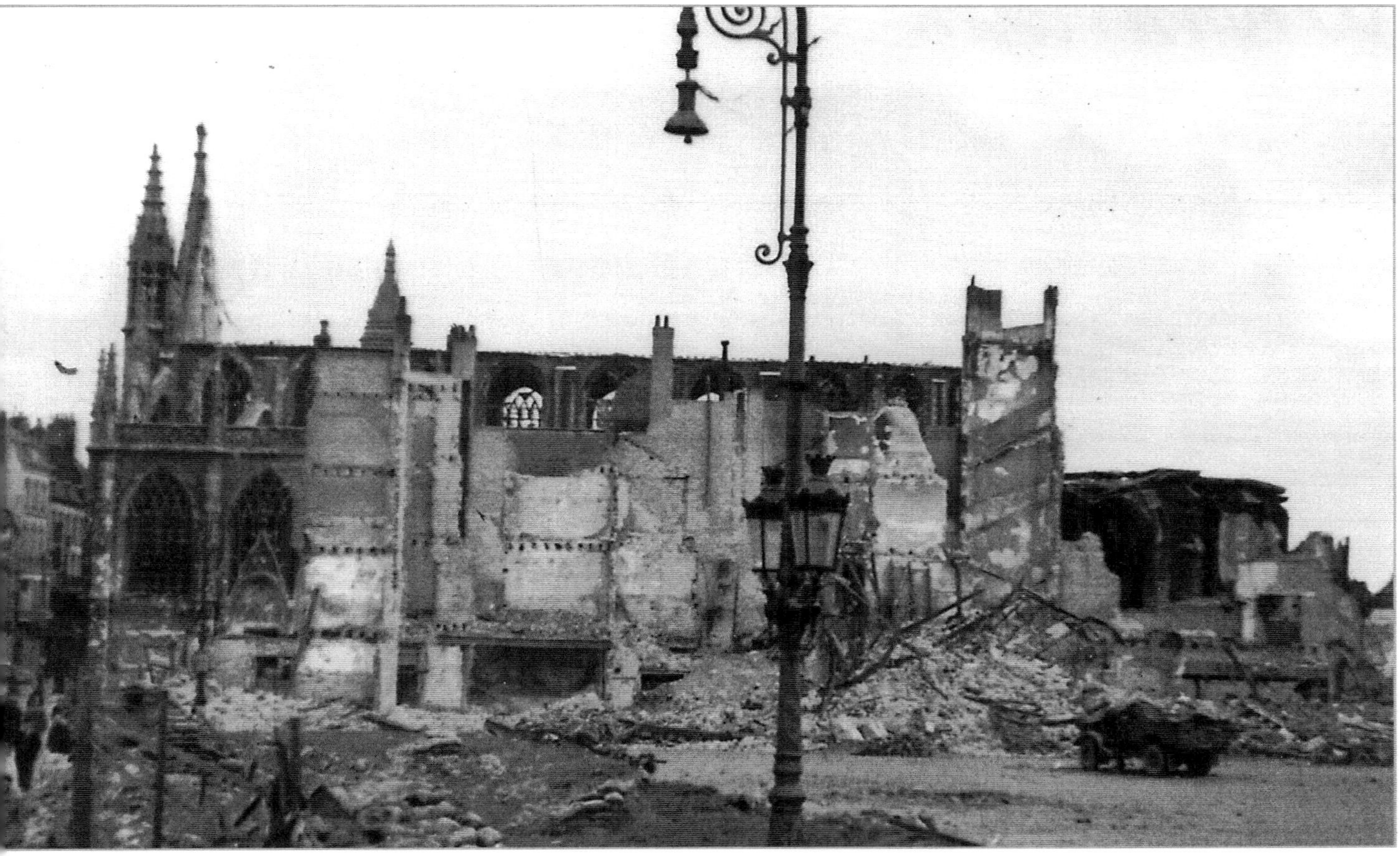

A look at the southern wall of the Cathedral from the town square with yet another abandoned Bedford 15 cwt in the right of photograph.

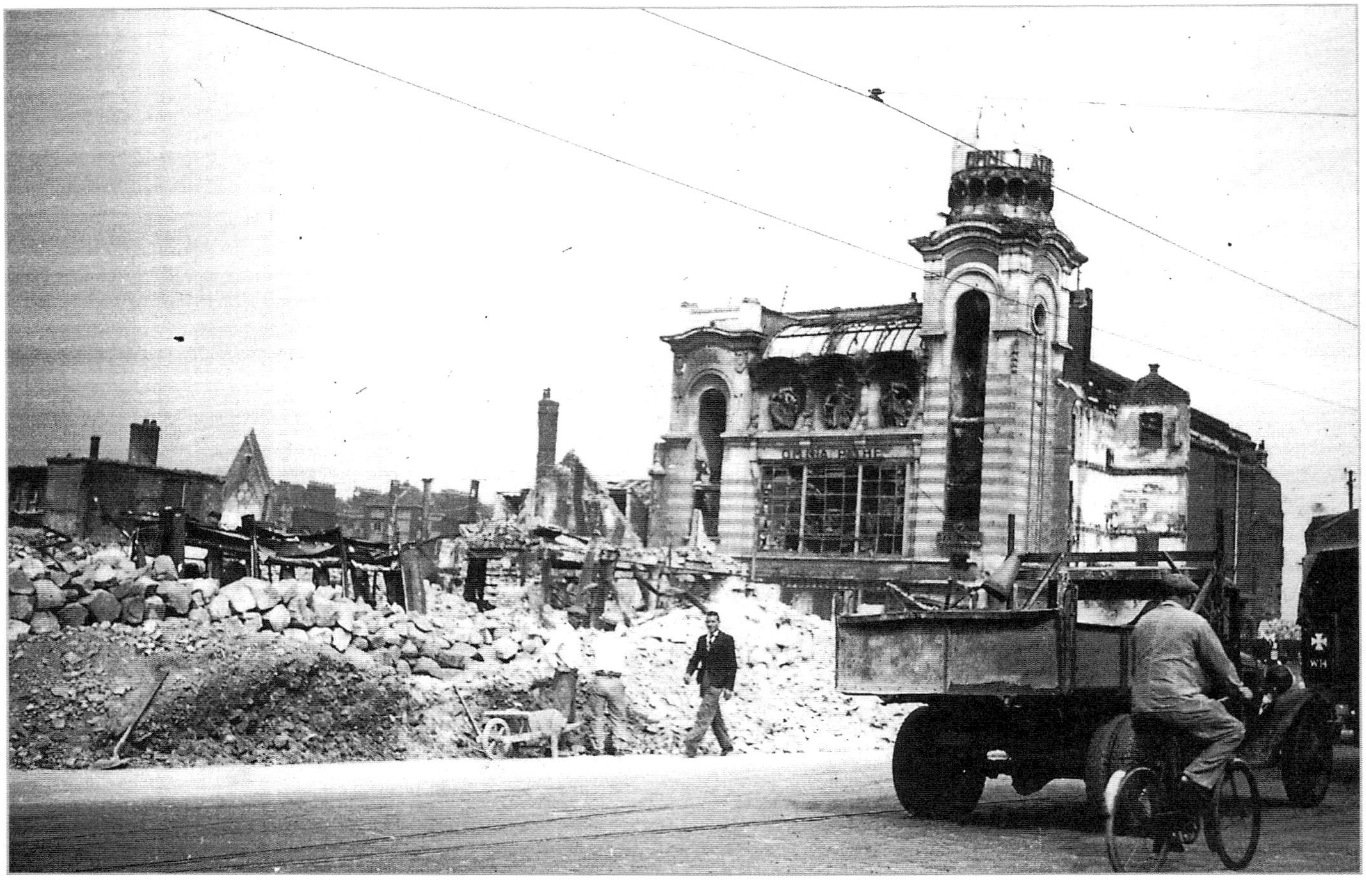

With the clean up well underway here we have two views of the town, in this one we see the town cinema the 'The-atre Pathe' located on the southernmost side of the town square.

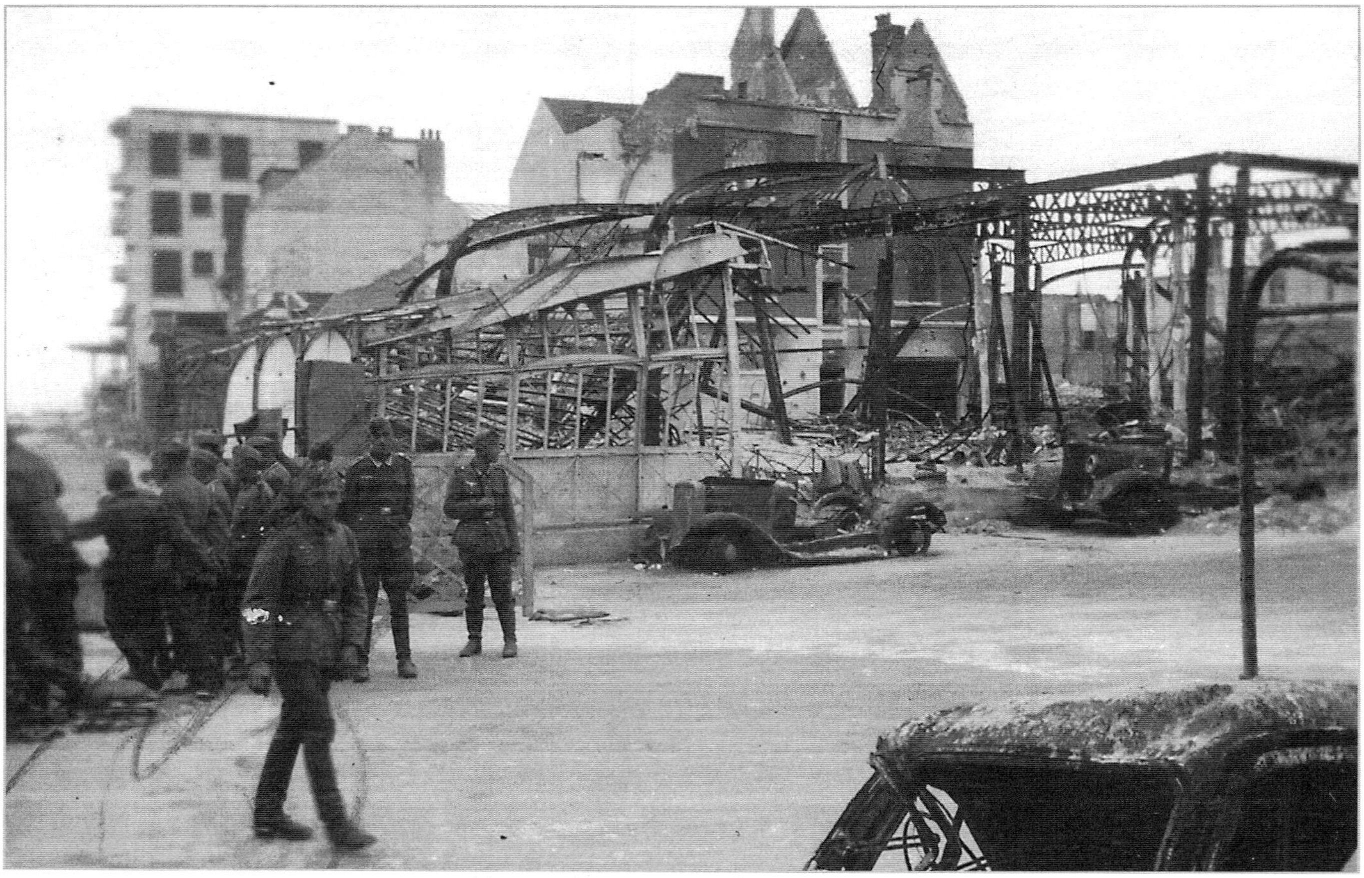

96 Dunkirk's bus station was totally burnt out as were the vehicles left within. Later the site became one of the many not to be missed by the groups of German soldiers 'taking the tour'.

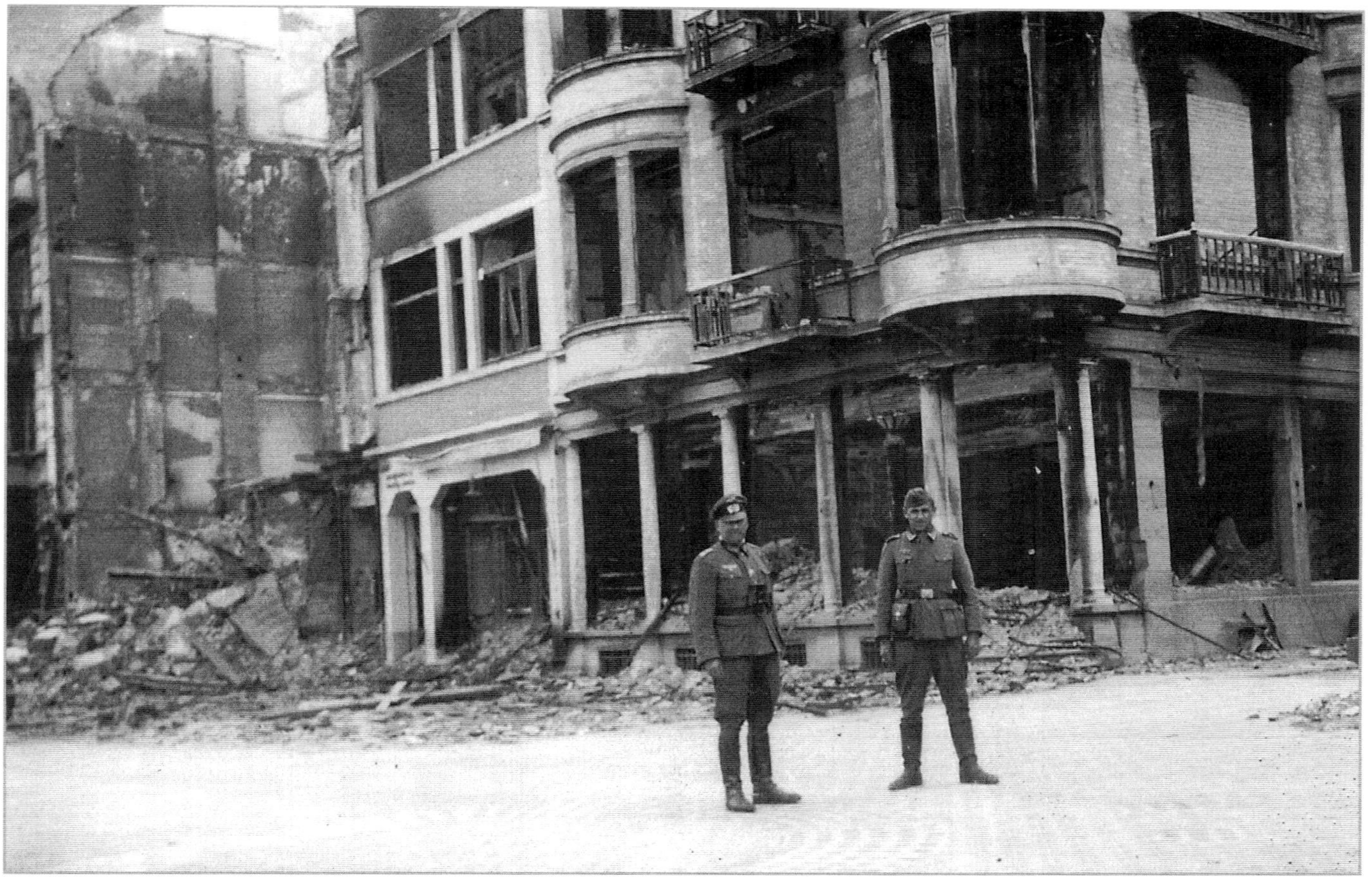

Two German artillery officers pose in front of the wrecked frontage of one of Dunkirk's main hotels situated on the promenade.

A close up of the remains of Dunkirk's bombed out Railway Station.

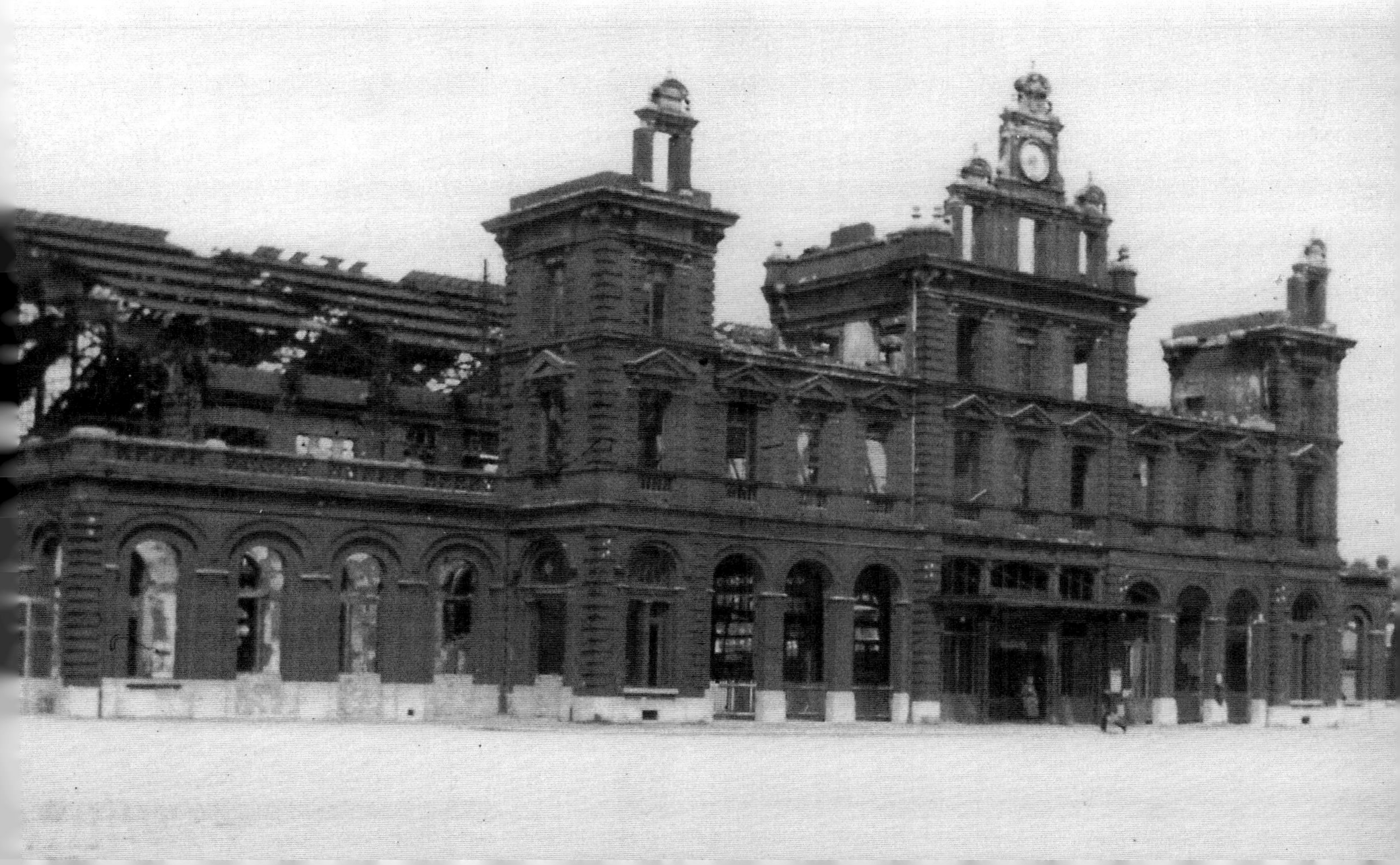

This British A13 Tank has been run into a French Co-op store on the outskirts of Dunkirk, on the Rue Du Canada named in honour of the Canadians who fought in this area during the First World War.

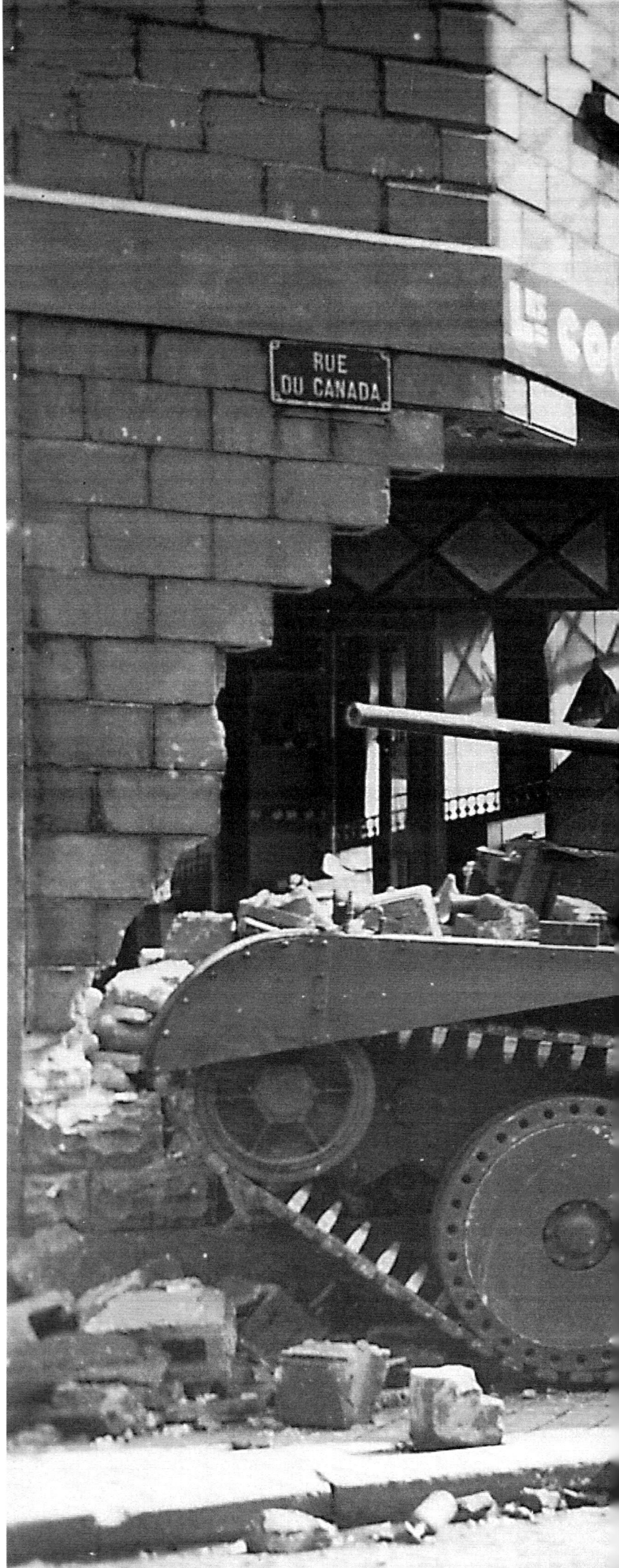

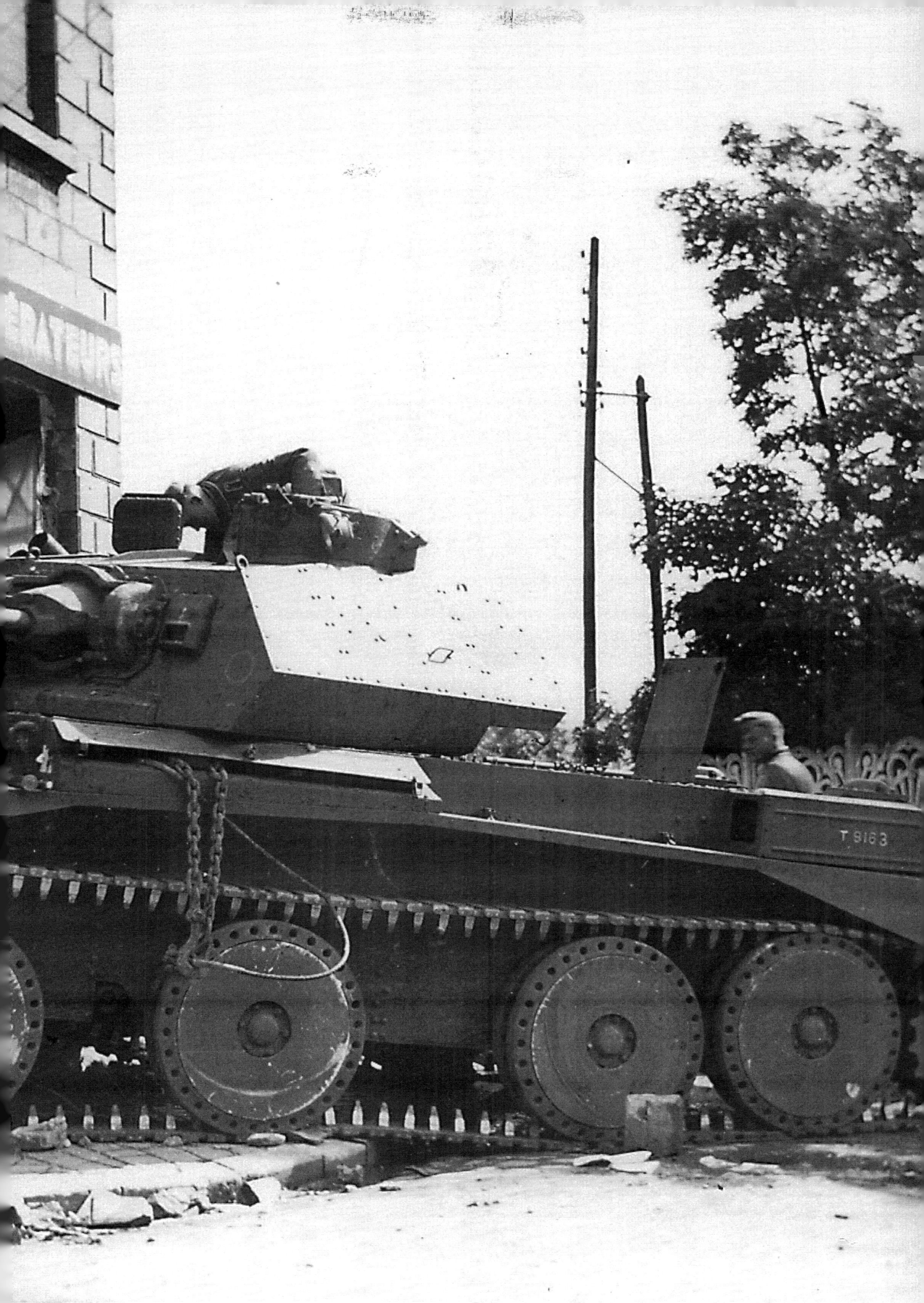

ÉRATEURS
T 9163

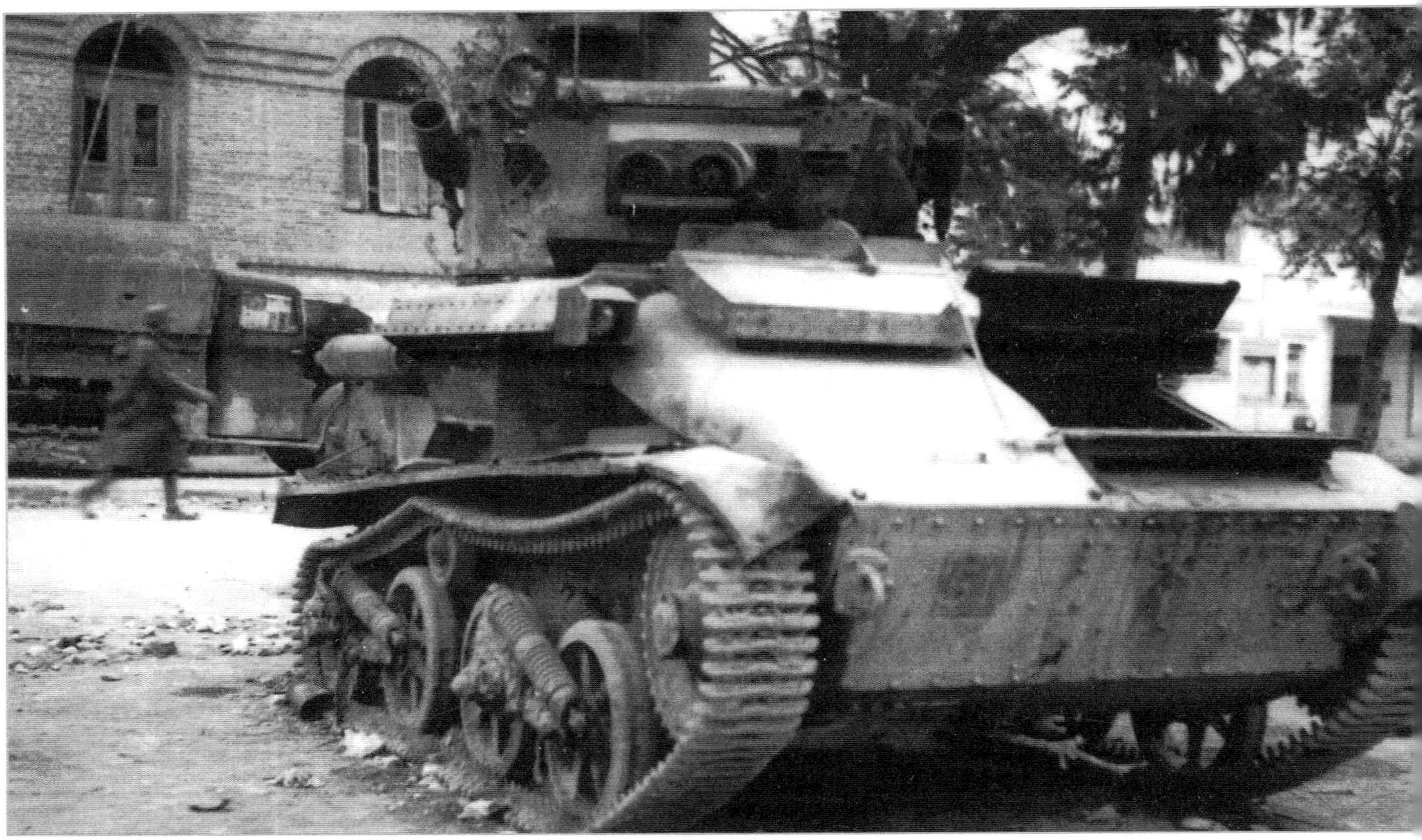

A good photo of an abandoned British Vickers Light Tank Mk. VI B left on the outskirts of Dunkirk town. Many tanks were abandoned on the perimeter, where they served as either road blocks and or strong points in the defence network.

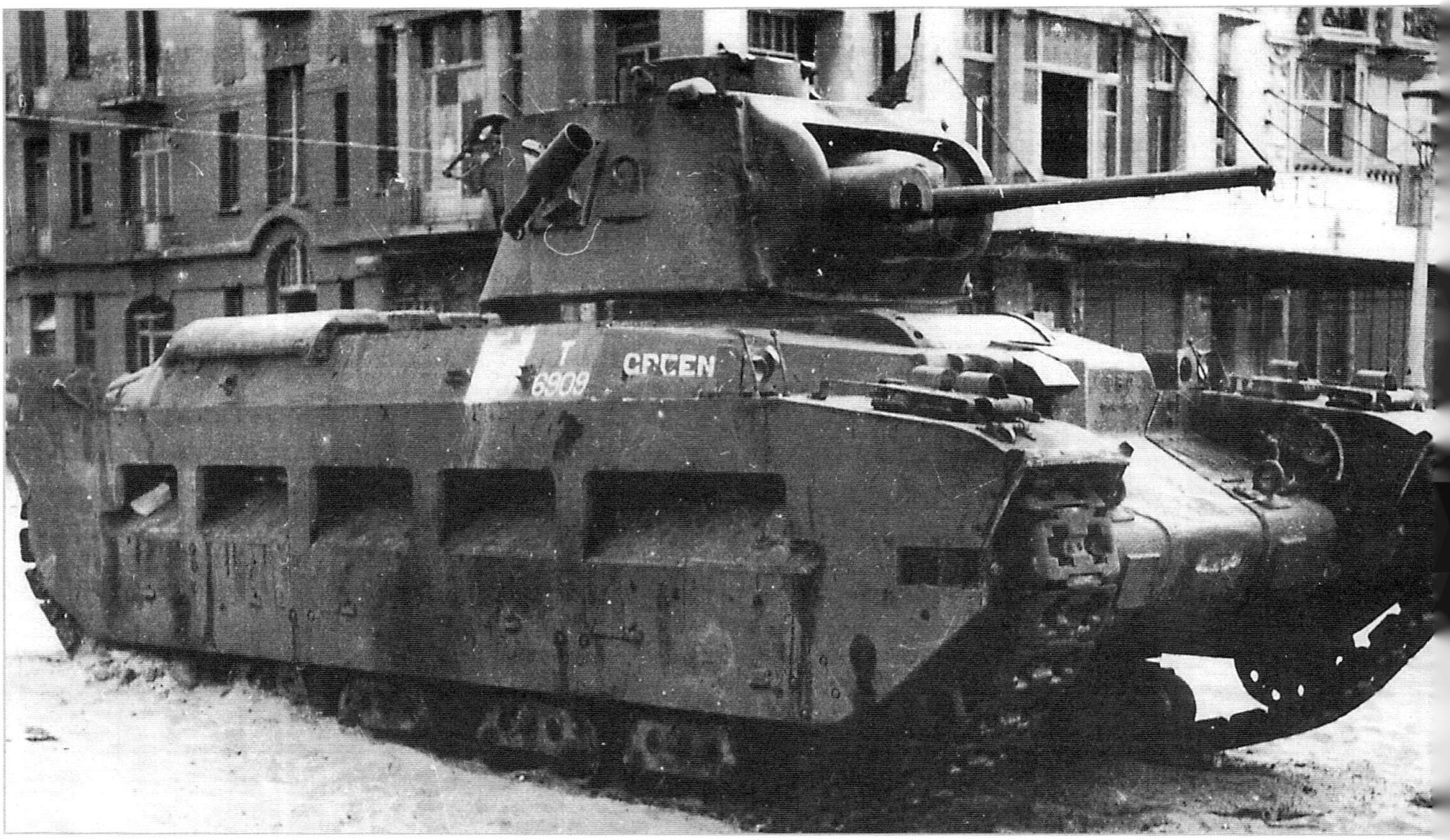

Here a British Matilda Mk. II rests abandoned on the promenade, as is witnessed by the amount of sand on the pavement. Identifiable as an early Mk. II by the hollow cast tracks and the turret mounted Vickers .303 machine gun, later variants had this gun replaced with a Besa machine gun.

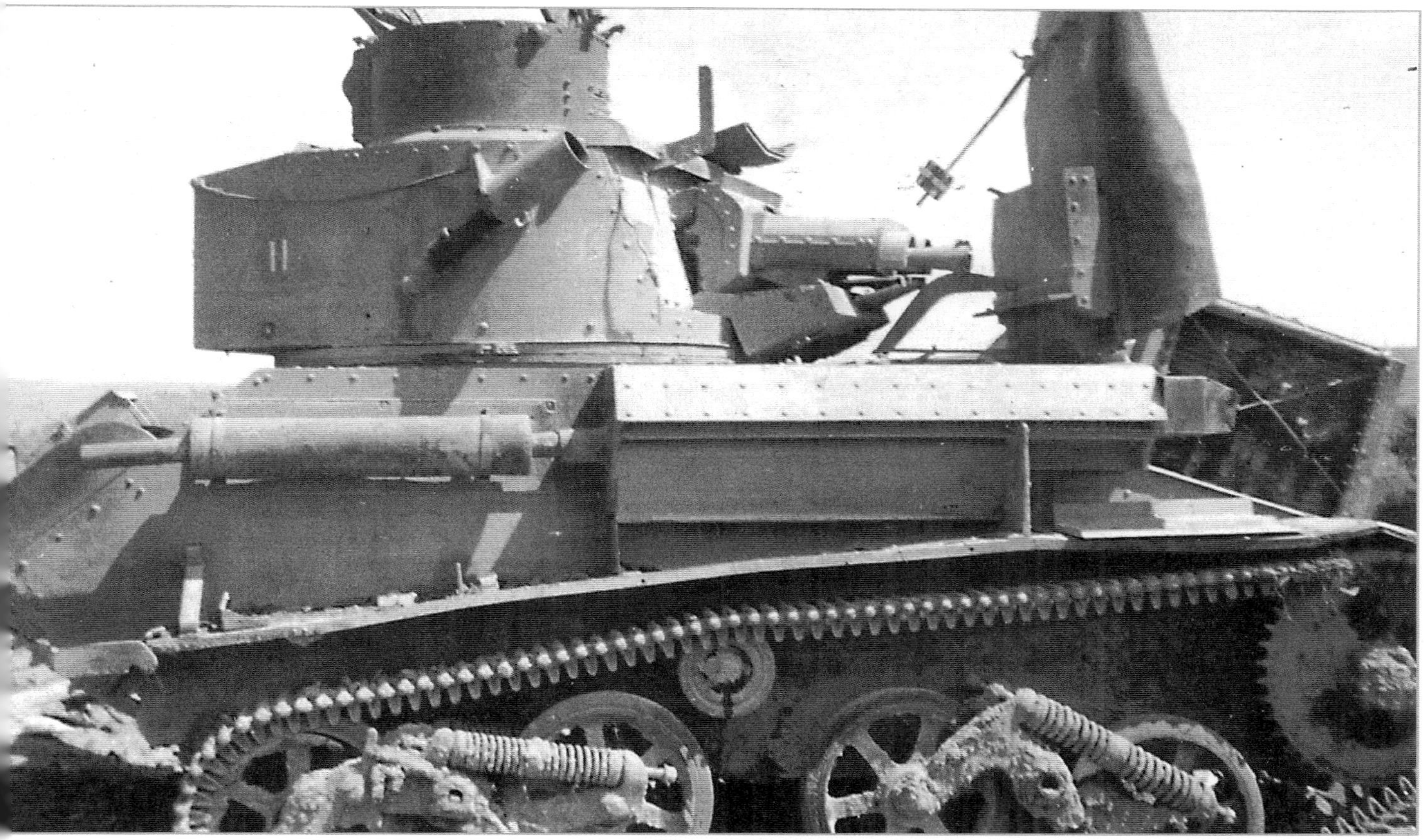

Another British Vickers Light Tank Mk. VI B, from A squadron this time, abandoned in the dunes of Bray Beach.

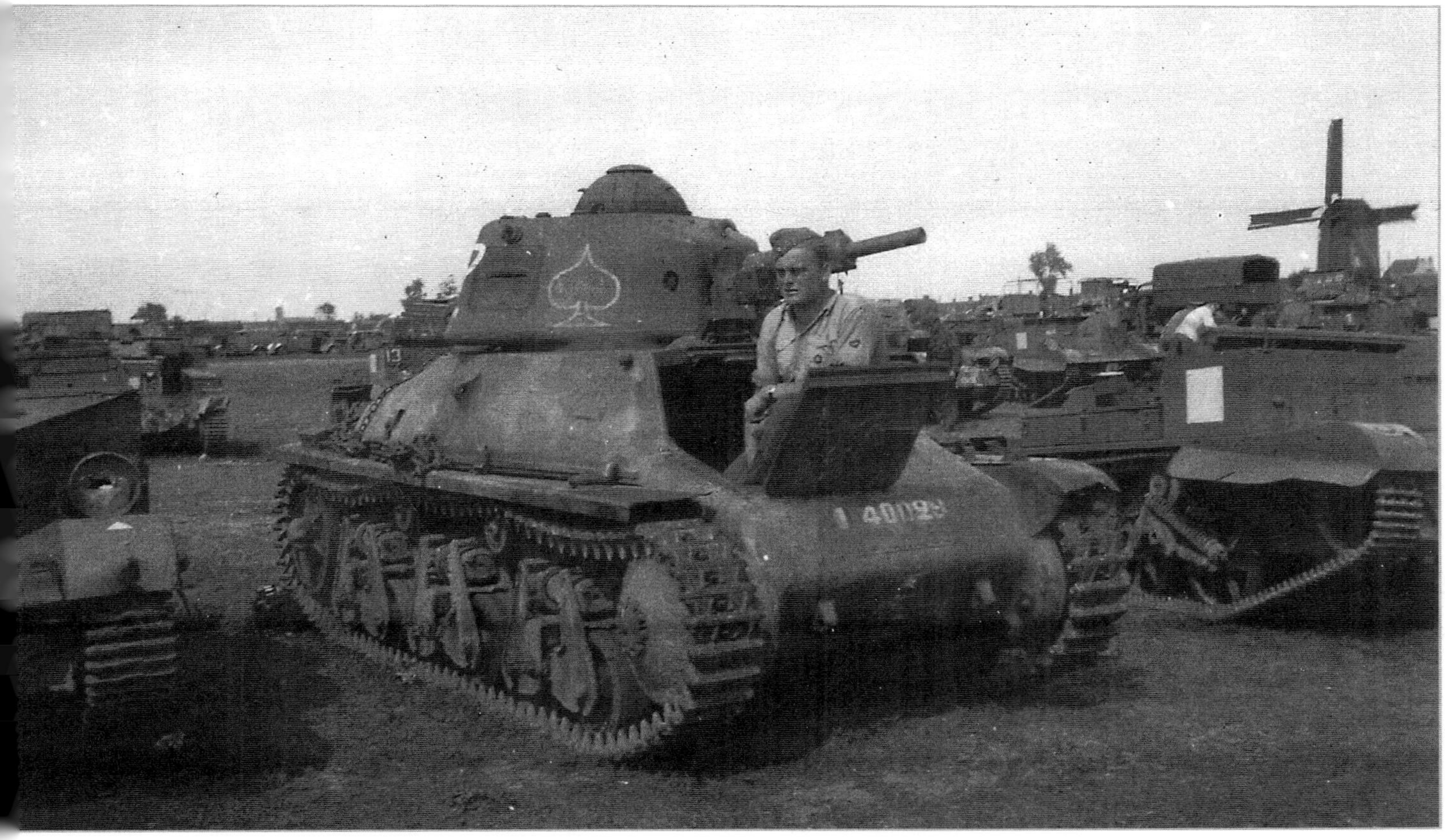

In the farm land to the south of Dunkirk one of the many vehicle gathering stations was set up. Here we see in the foreground, sitting between two British Universal Carriers, a French Hotchkiss H39 Light infantry tank.

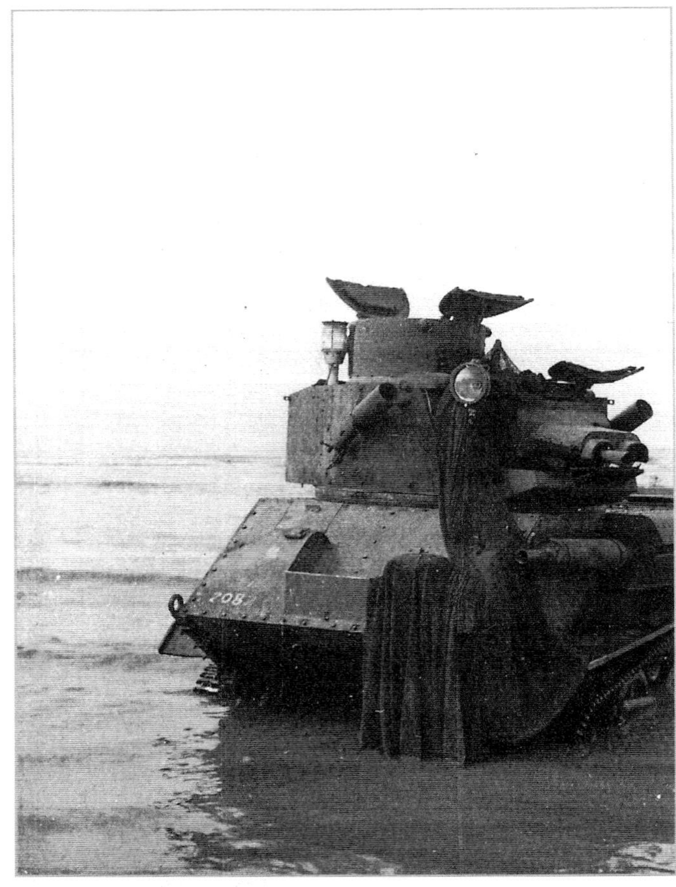

Yet another British Vickers Mk. VI B Left in the surf still fully armed, the Vickers .303 MG can clearly be seen in the turret mounting tube with MG's flash eliminator being prominent.

Another Vickers Mk. VI B from C squadron. Abandoned in the surf but on this occasion it has been disarmed. Many tanks were driven into the surf as a quick and simple way to deny them to the enemy for recovery, a tactic that worked as it was just too much trouble to recover the sunken hulks by the time they had partially submerged in the heavy wet sand.

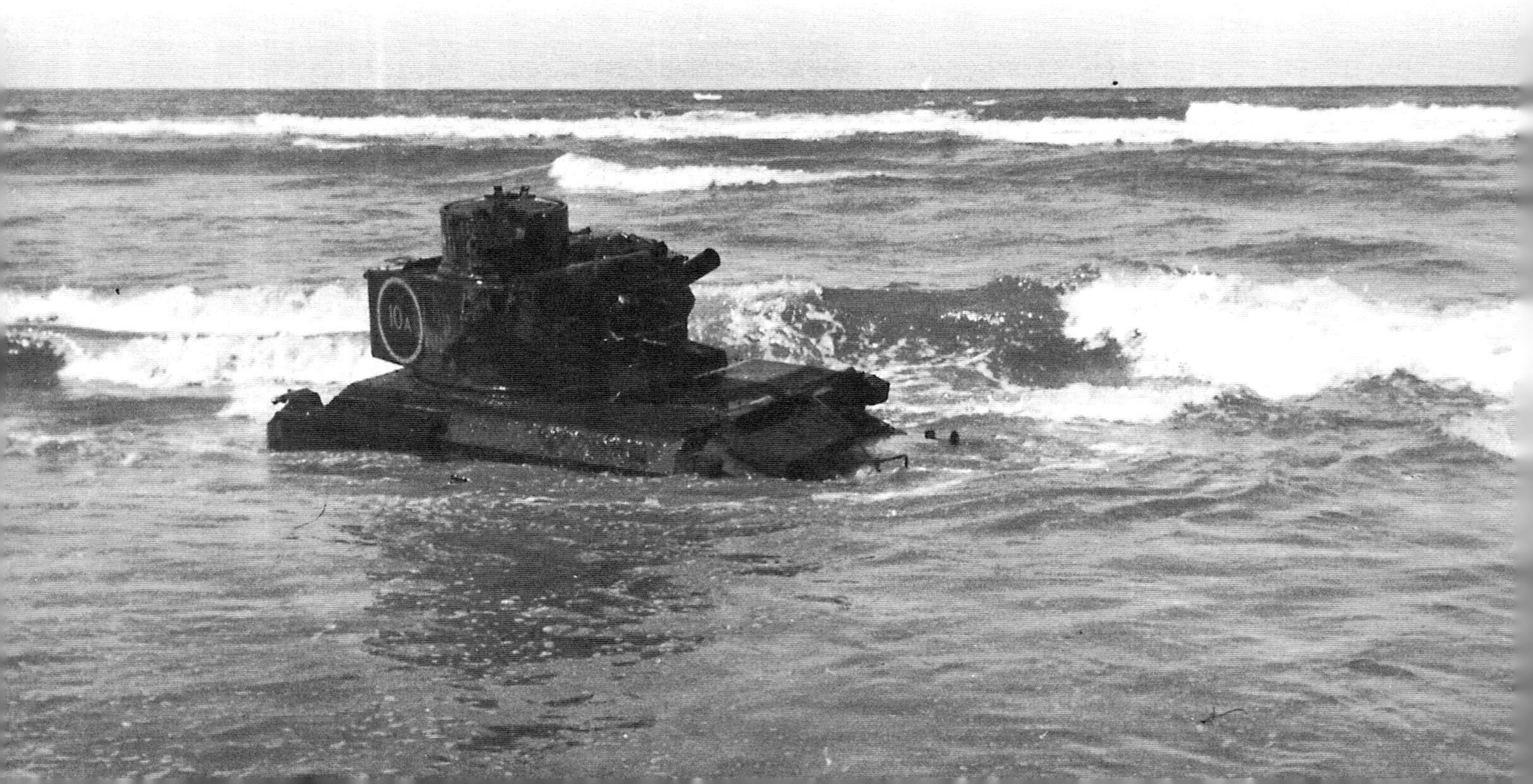

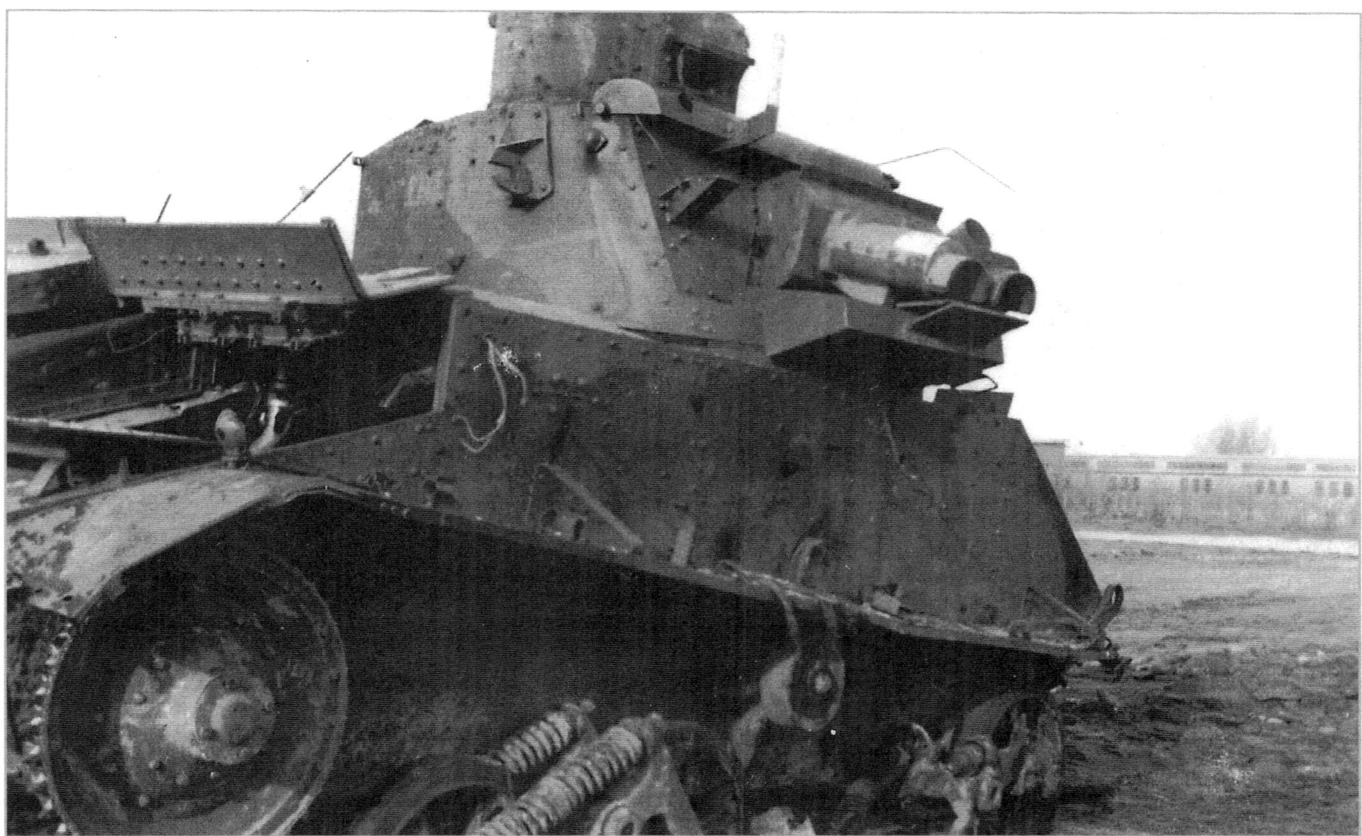

A Vickers Mk. VI B Light Infantry tank left on the outskirts of Dunkirk. This has been badly shot up with both wheels missing and a large hole in the side armour. Whist this may be battle damage, it is more than likely the result of Germans 'knocking up' the tank, a practice whereby an abandoned enemy tank would be shot at by an approaching German tank, just in case it was still in service.

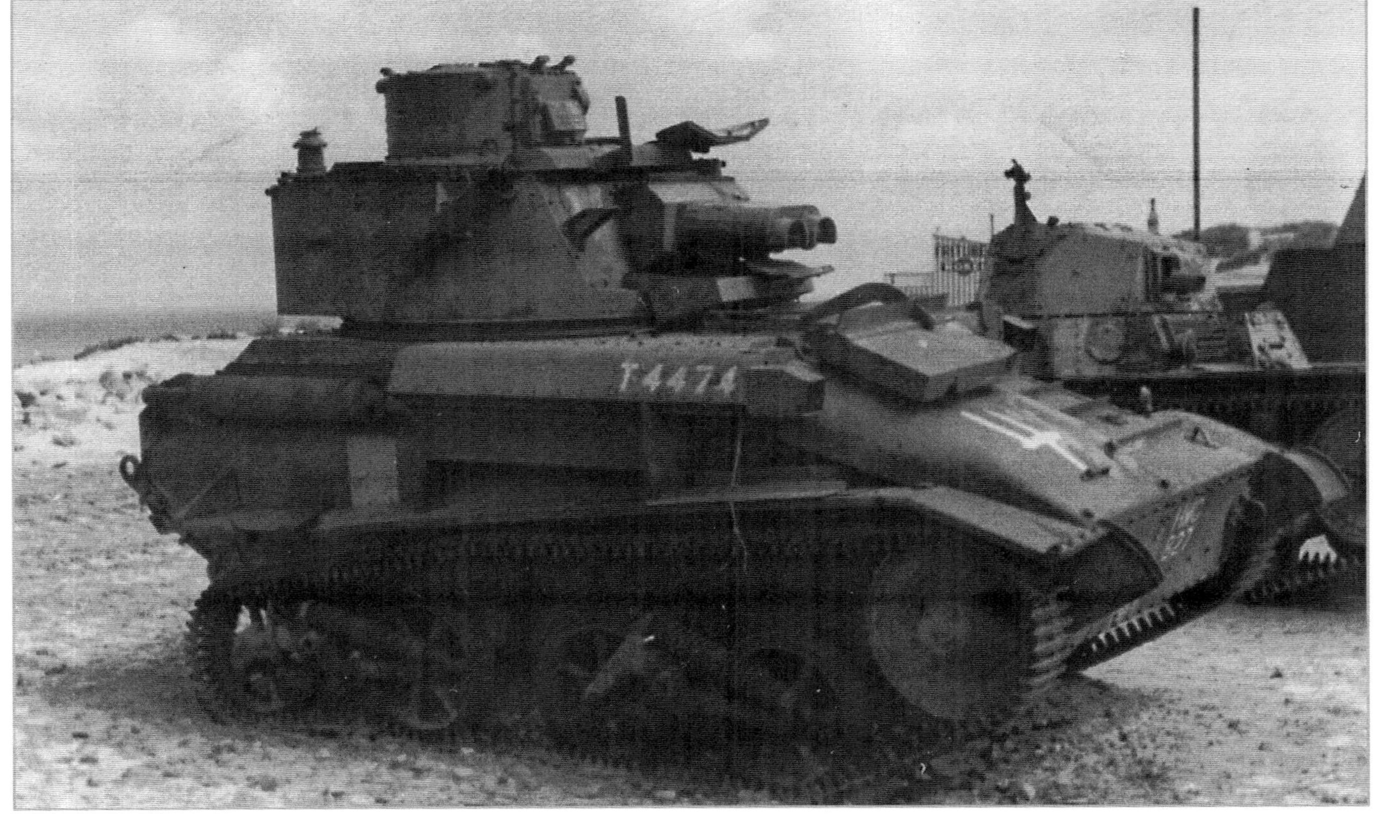

Here in a vehicle recognition collection made up just outside Dunkirk on the road to Calais, one of each type of allied tank was set up for German troops to study and become familiar with for both attack and recognition purposes. Here in the foreground is a Vickers Mk. VI B and behind it is a French AMC 33 Light Tank.

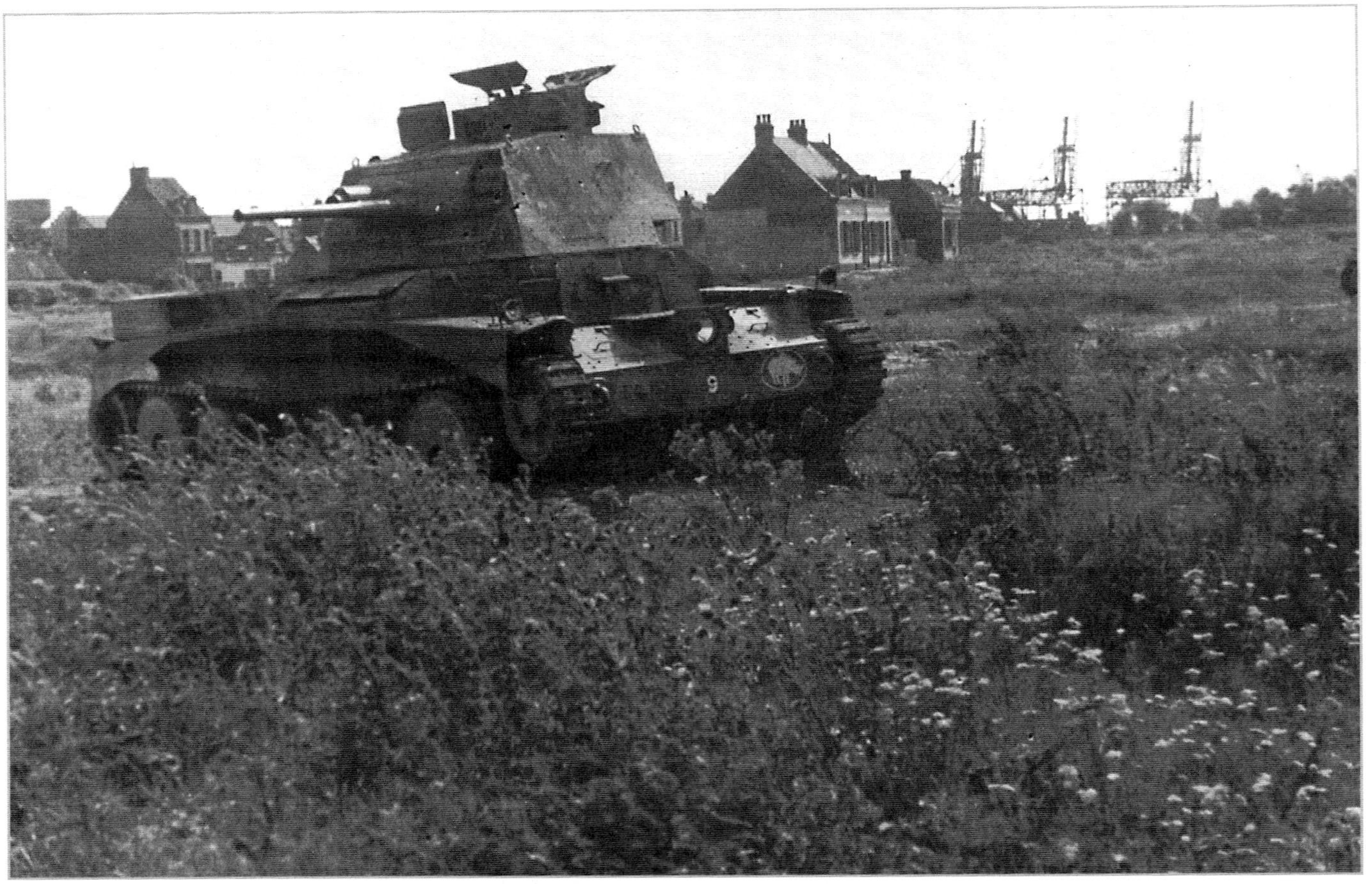

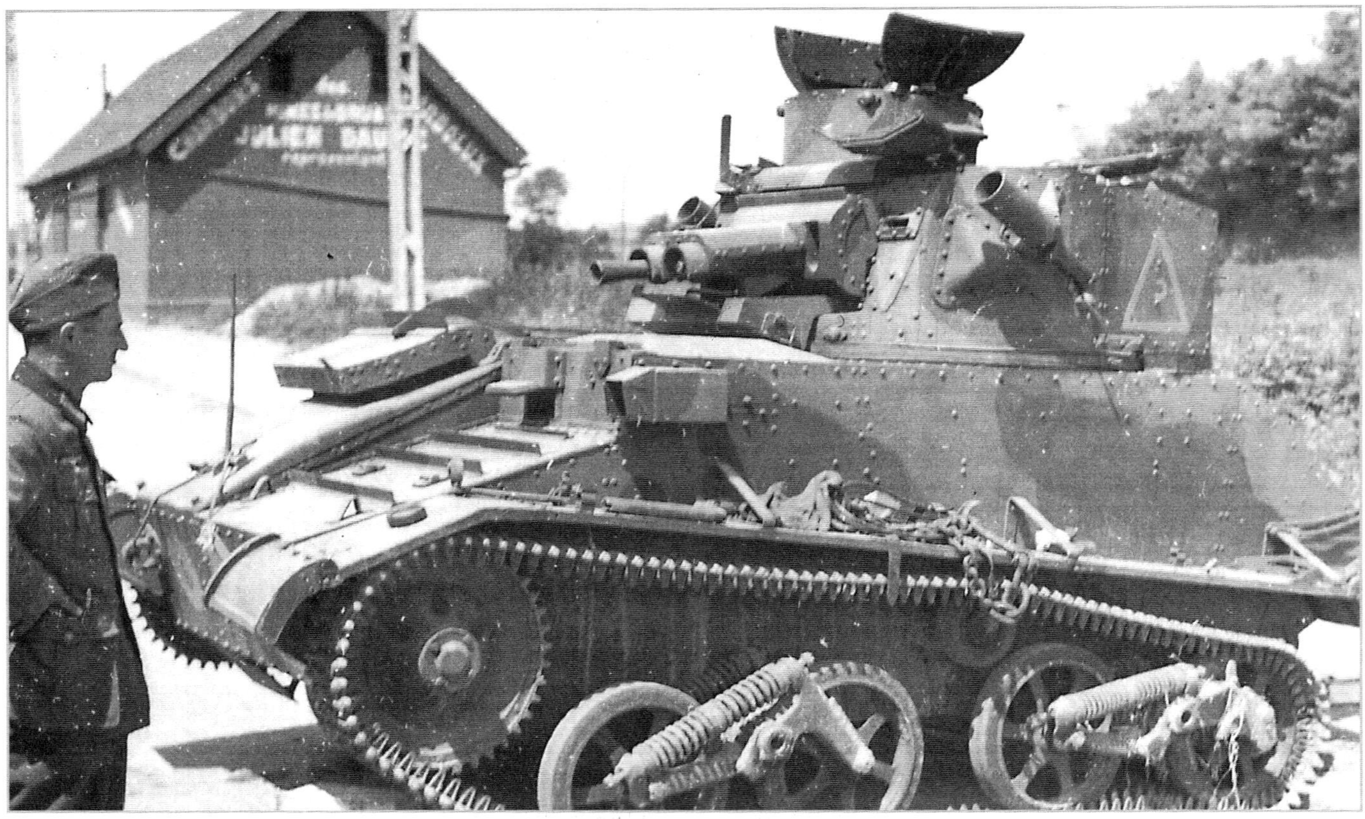

Forming part of the perimeter defence positioned behind an embankment for a hull down position lies an abandoned British A13 cruiser tank of the 2nd Royal Tank regiment C squadron.

On the road to Dunkirk from the Belgium border, another Vickers Mk. VI B Light tank from A squadron is left behind, this one looking in good order. The Germans thought little of the Mk. VI and very few were recovered as no use was seen for them. A few however made their way in to Police units for anti-partisan defence and six were converted to carry an LeFH 16 105 mm field gun.

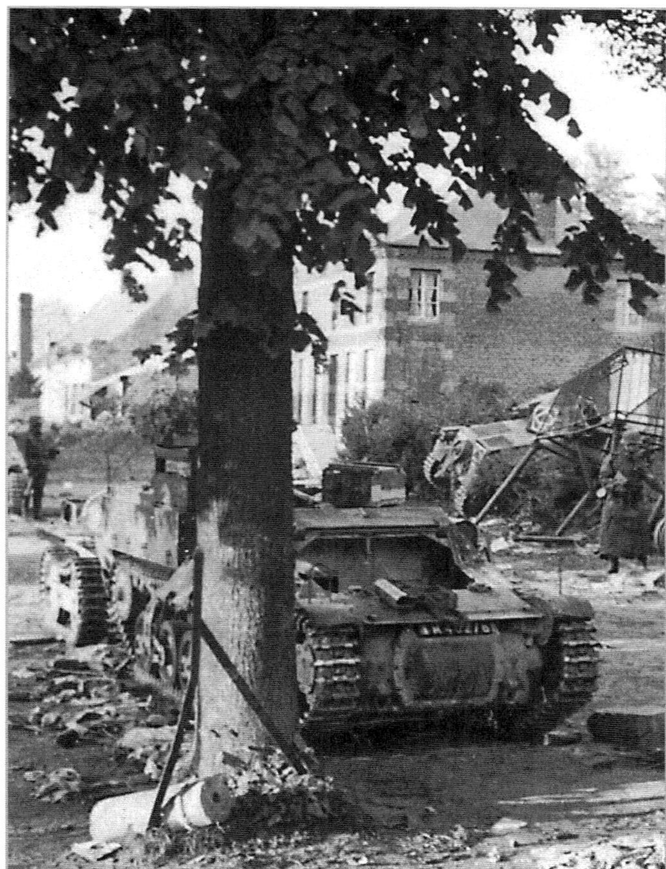 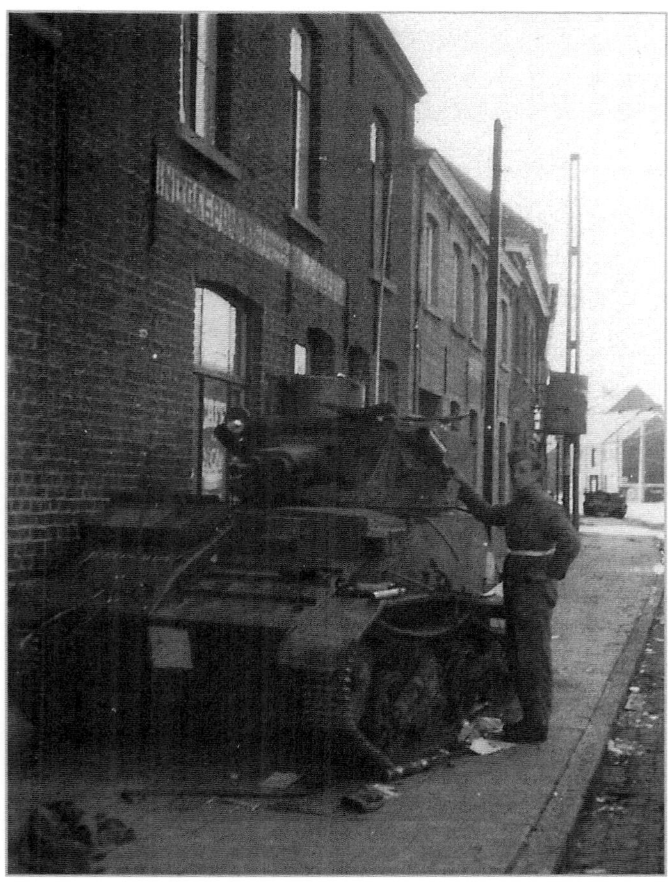

A French Lorraine Schlepper, a fully tracked Infantry support vehicle which the Germans converted into various forms of weapon carriers, including a version armed with the 75 mm Pak 40 and in the background an abandoned French Hotchkiss H35 Tank.

Another Vickers Mk. VI B, abandoned on the outskirts of Dunkirk.

A line up of Vickers Mk. VI Bs, two Matilda Mk. Is and several Universal Carriers abandoned on the western edge of the harbour's western mole.

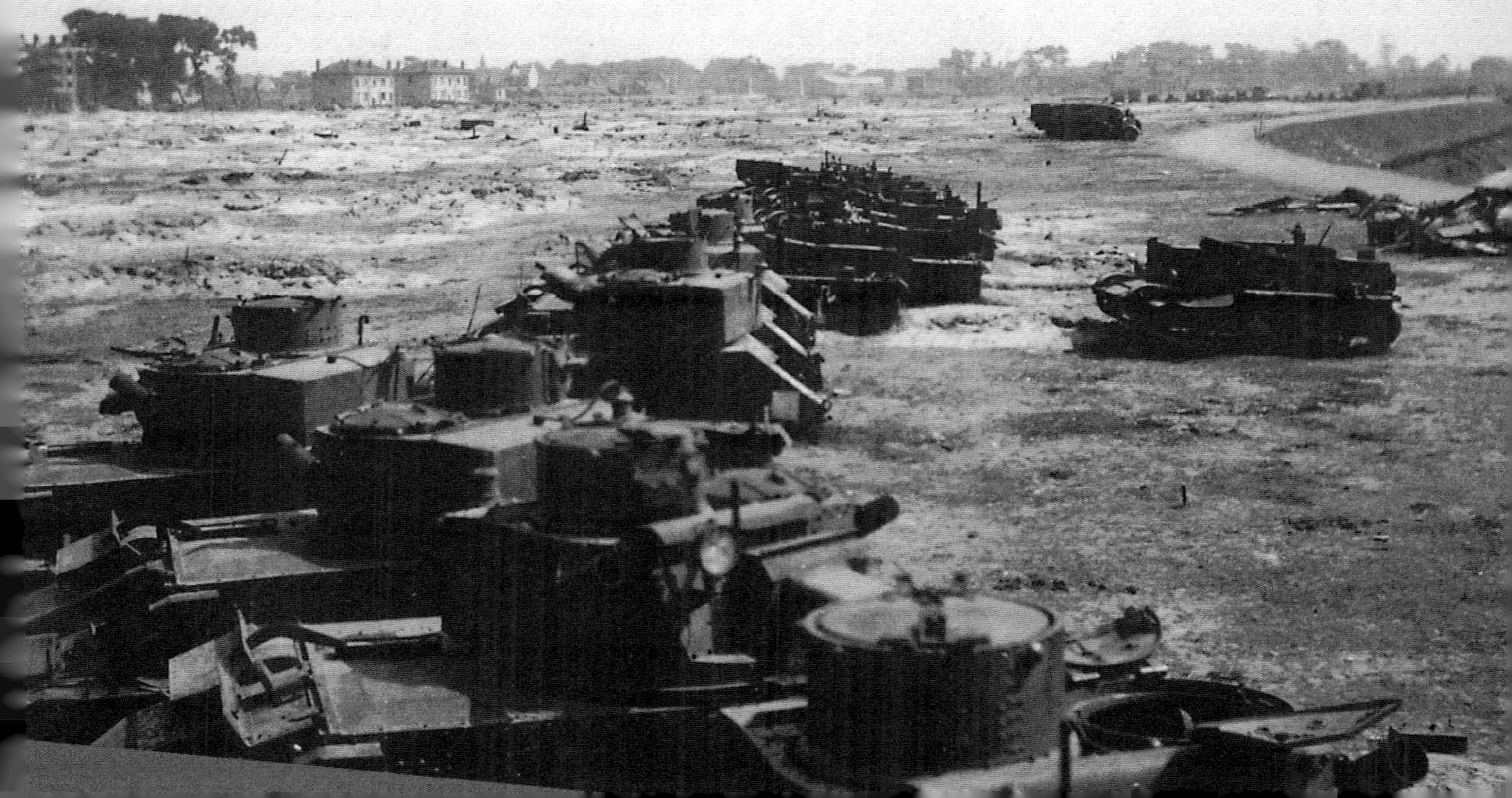

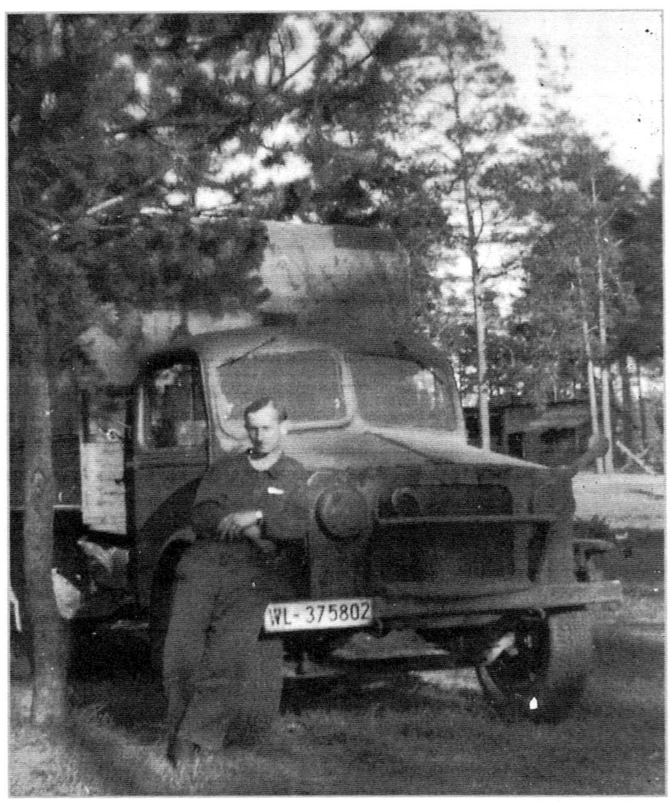

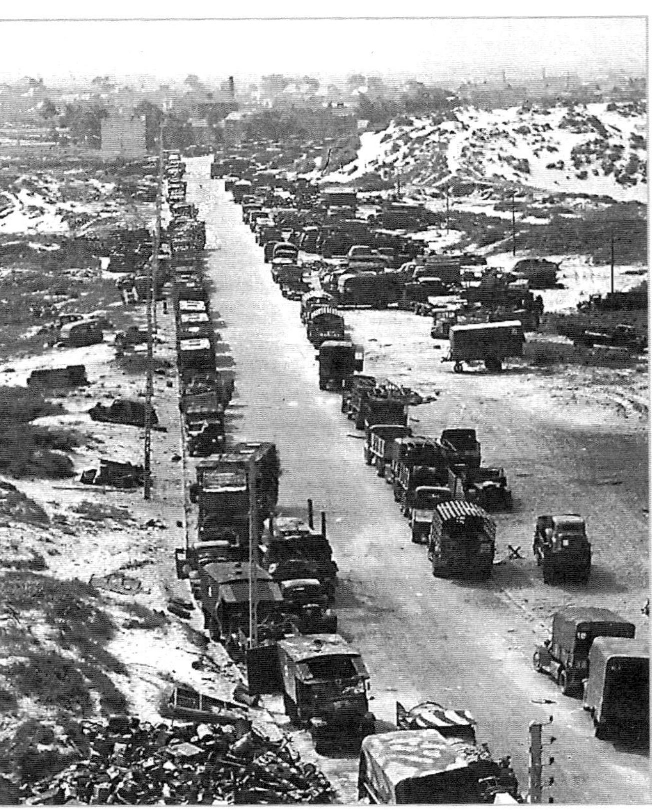

A *Luftwaffe* driver poses proudly next to his new ride, one of the many British Bedford 15 cwts recovered and put back into service by the Germans.

An aerial view of the coastal road to Dunkirk from the Belgian border, which is only a few miles away to the east. Abandoned British and French trucks litter both sides of the road, many looking still to be in good order.

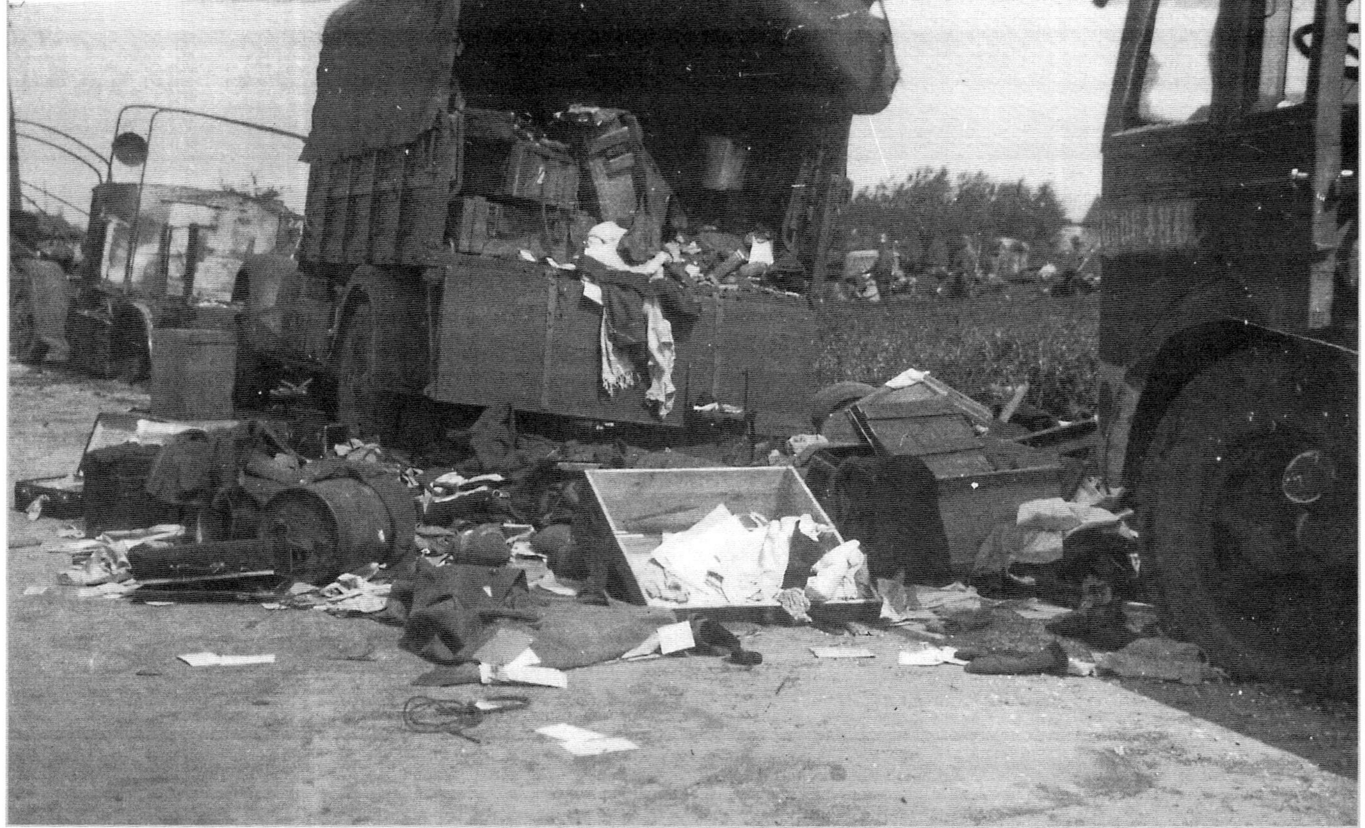

A close up view of one of the many abandoned French trucks on the roads to Dunkirk. Here we can see an example of the amount of equipment and general military supplies that fell into German hands during the course of this battle. As usual the advancing army has rifled through the contents of the truck for contraband.

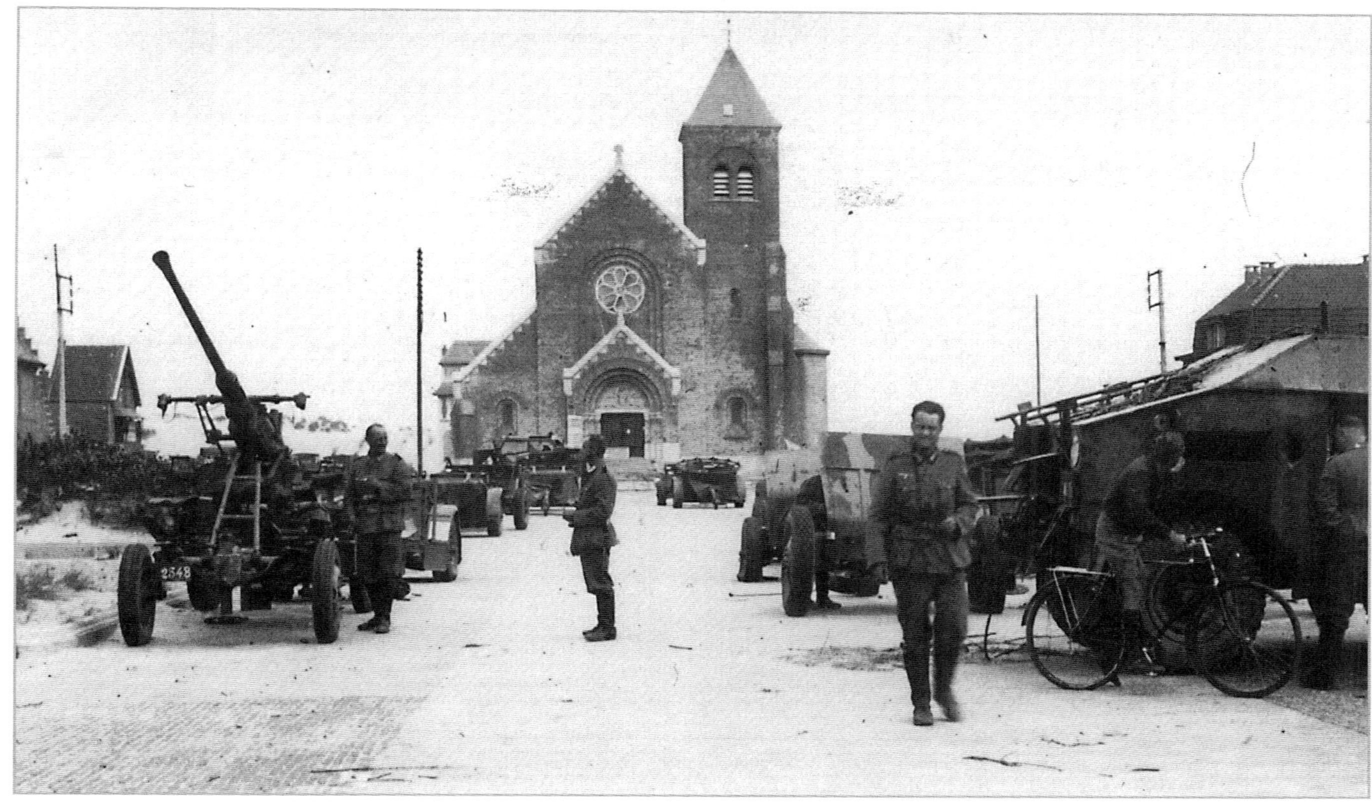

British Artillery Unit abandoned in the outskirts of Dunkirk. Notice the Morris Quad, ammo limbers and the 40 mm Bofors gun also abandoned, all look in reasonable order and not destroyed as the evacuation orders stipulated.

German troops enter the outskirts of Dunkirk after the evacuation and surrender of the rear guard. Note the many home-made German unit location signs nailed to any post the troops could find.

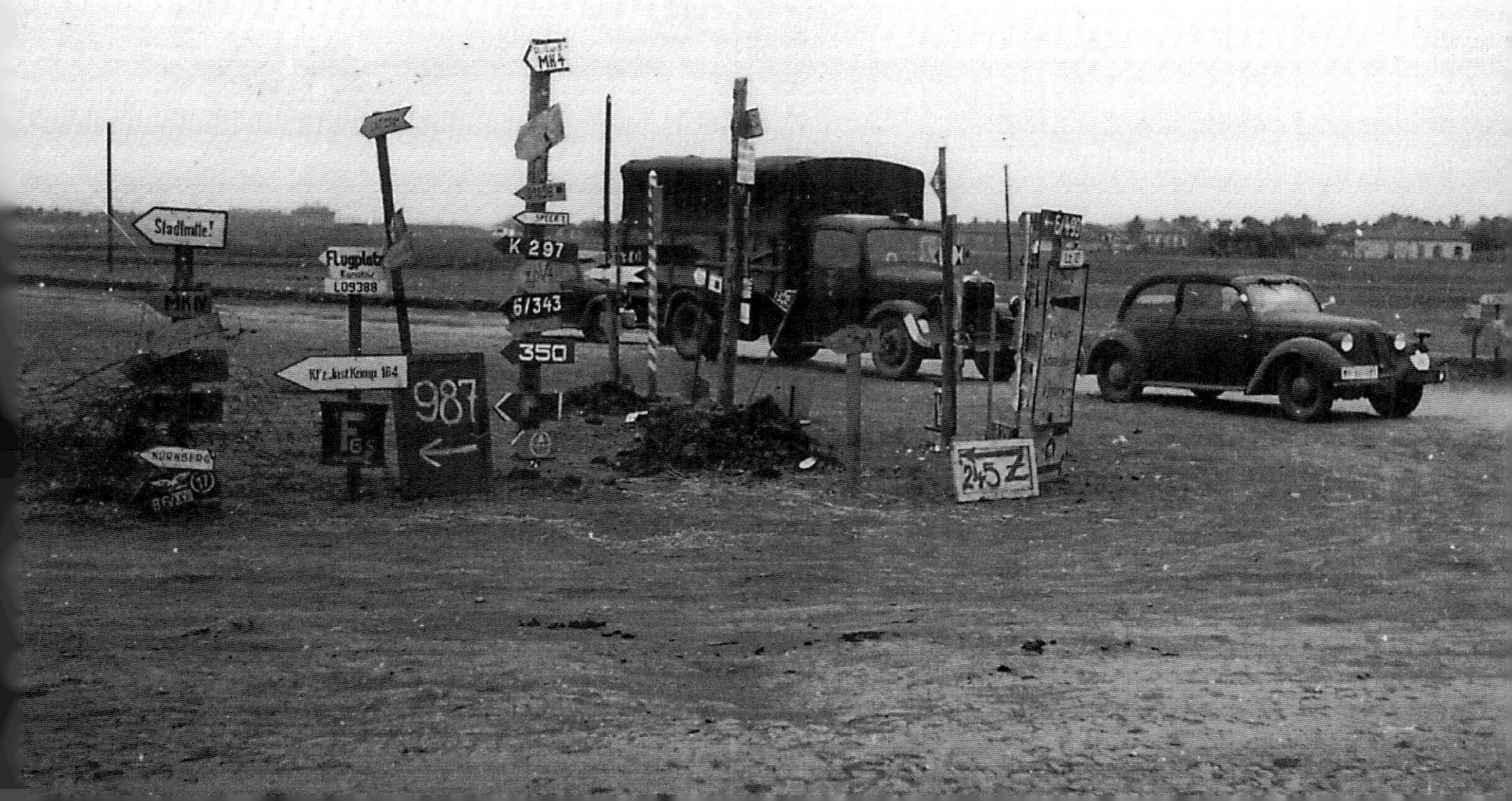

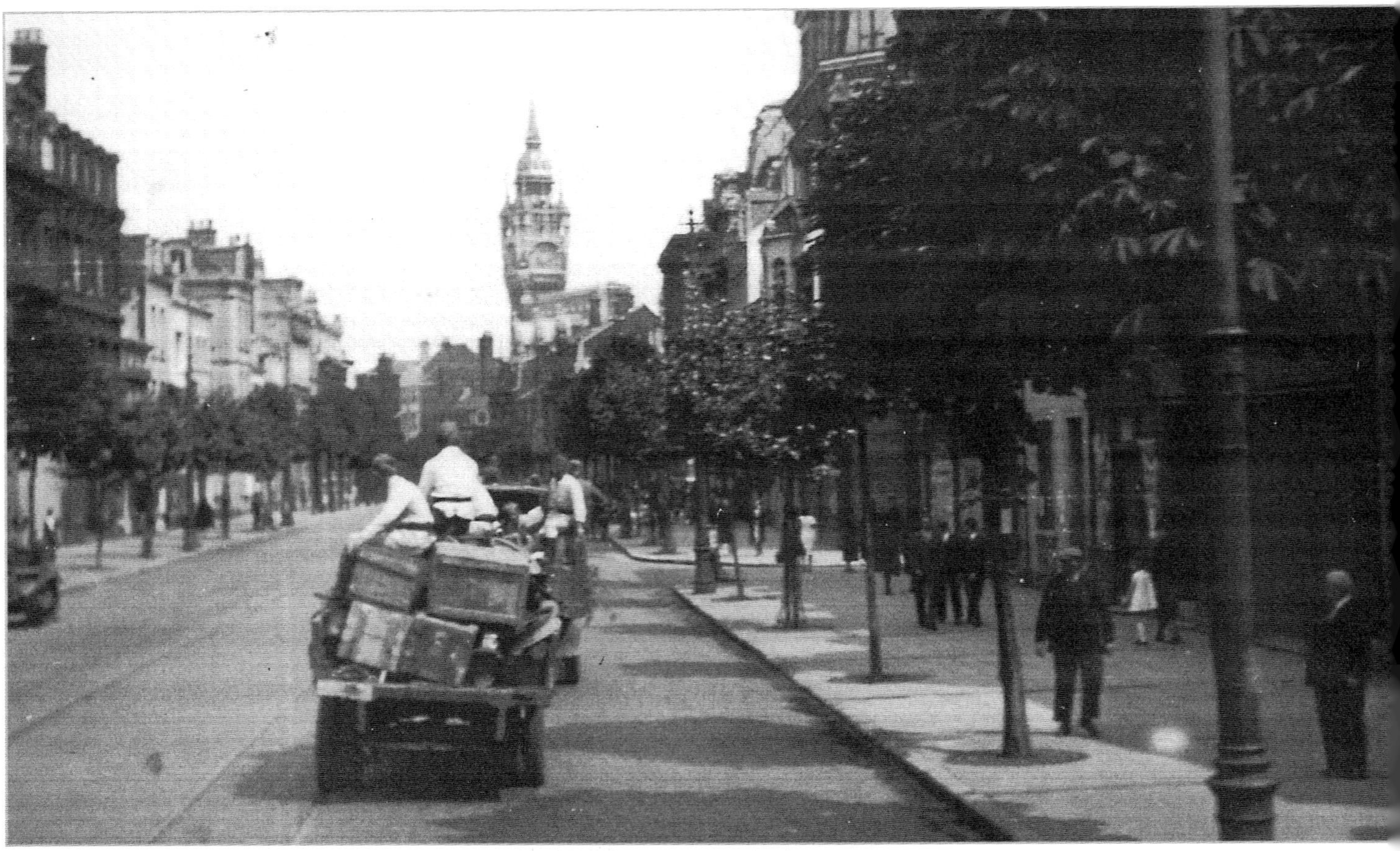

German sanitary troops make their way down Calais high street. Much of the recovered supplies were taken to Calais (only 20 miles down the coast to the west) were they could be sorted and warehoused in undamaged buildings.

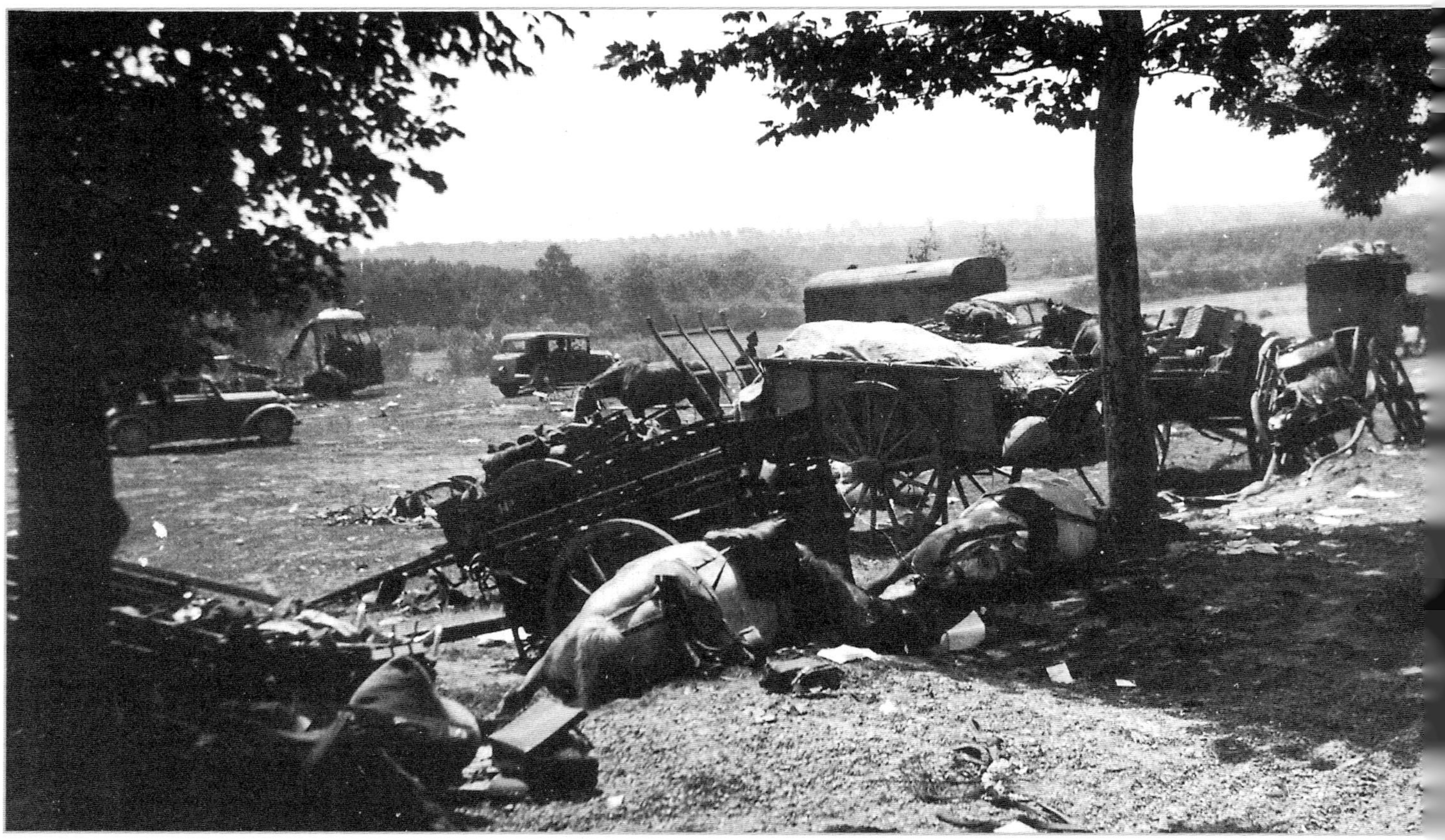

More French equipment abandoned on the roads to the east of Dunkirk. Much of it looks to be left by civilian refugees, who were mercilessly strafed and channelled by German air attacks, to block the roads so that the allied military could not manoeuvre freely.

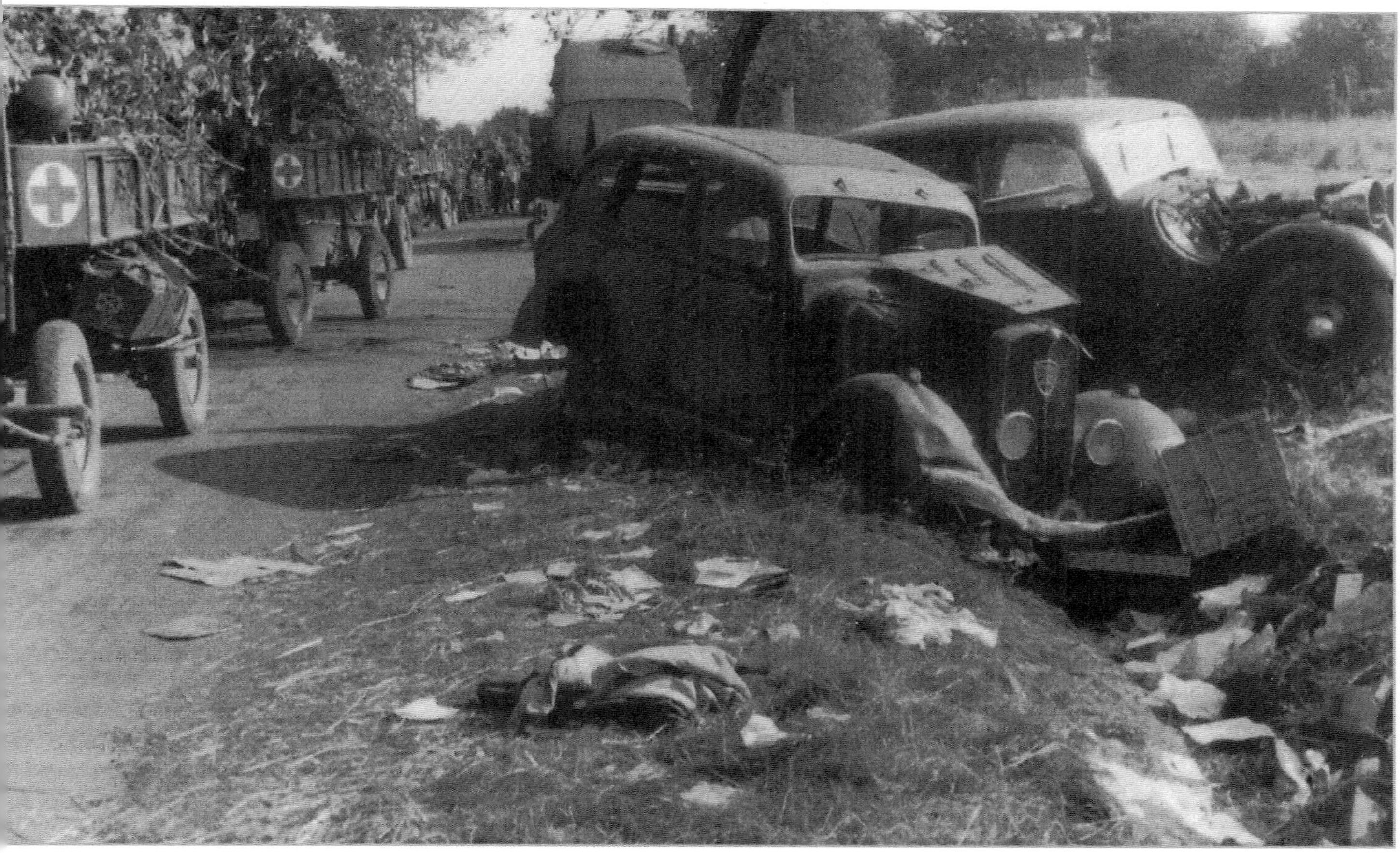

German standard *Stahlfeldwagen*, steel field wagon, (Hf. 7) infantry carts pass yet more devastation on the roadside leading to Dunkirk. Here we see French equipment abandoned with, in the foreground, a Peugeot staff car.

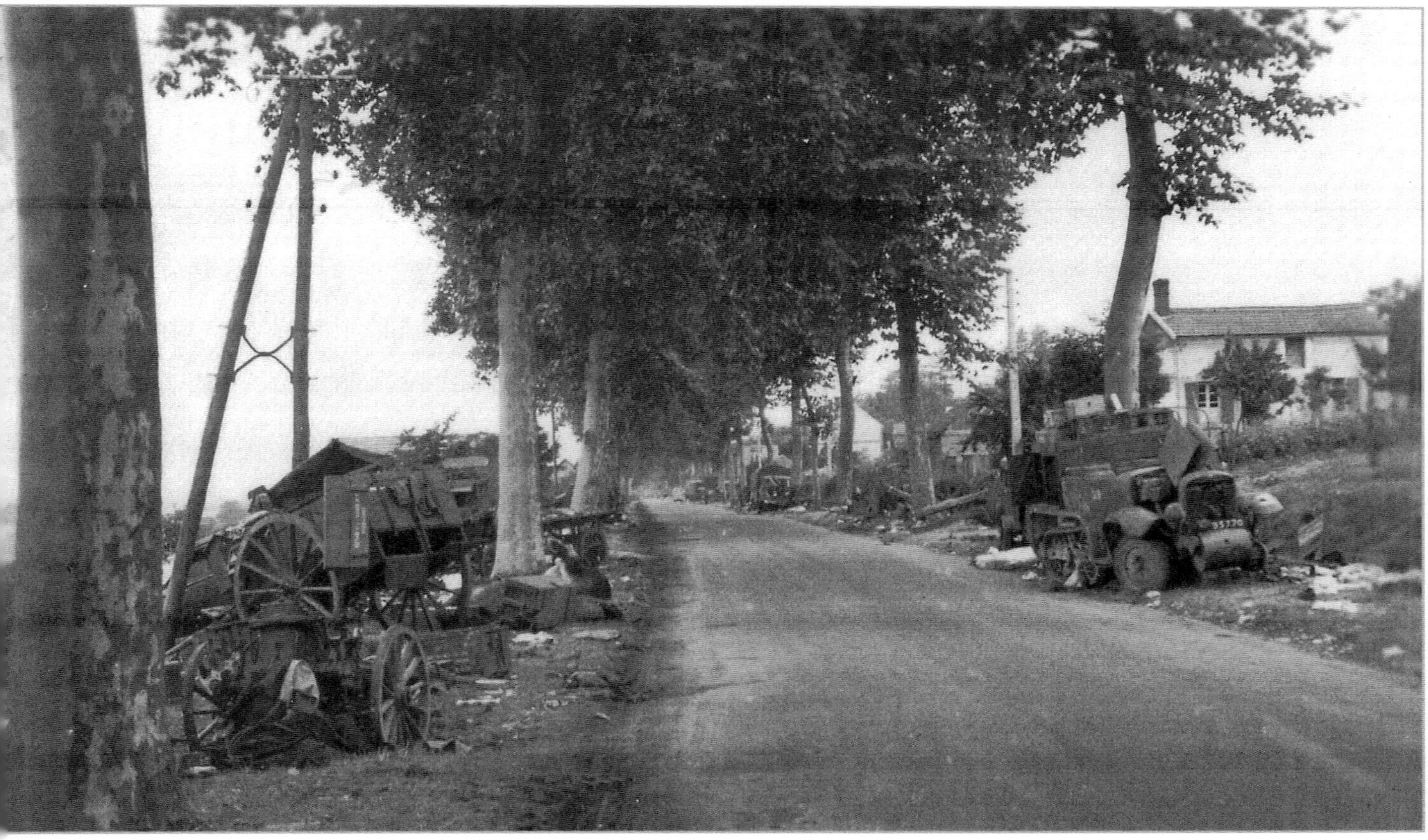

Yet more French equipment abandoned at the roadside. Of note to right of the photograph is a French Unic 304 Halftrack artillery tractor.

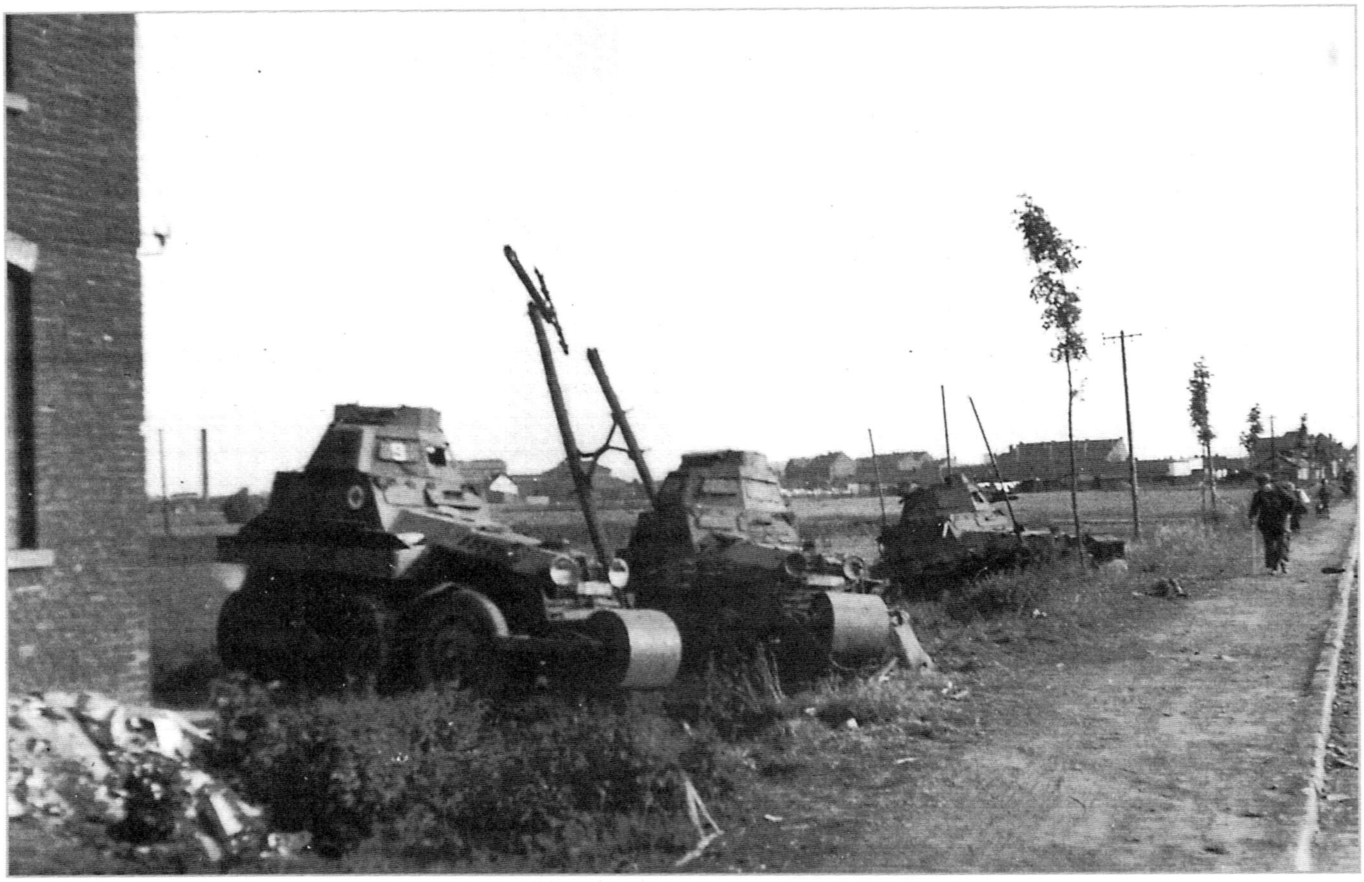

On the eastern edge of Dunkirk we have three French Schneider P16 Model 1929 heavy armoured halftrack reconnaissance vehicles, abandoned by the side of the road.

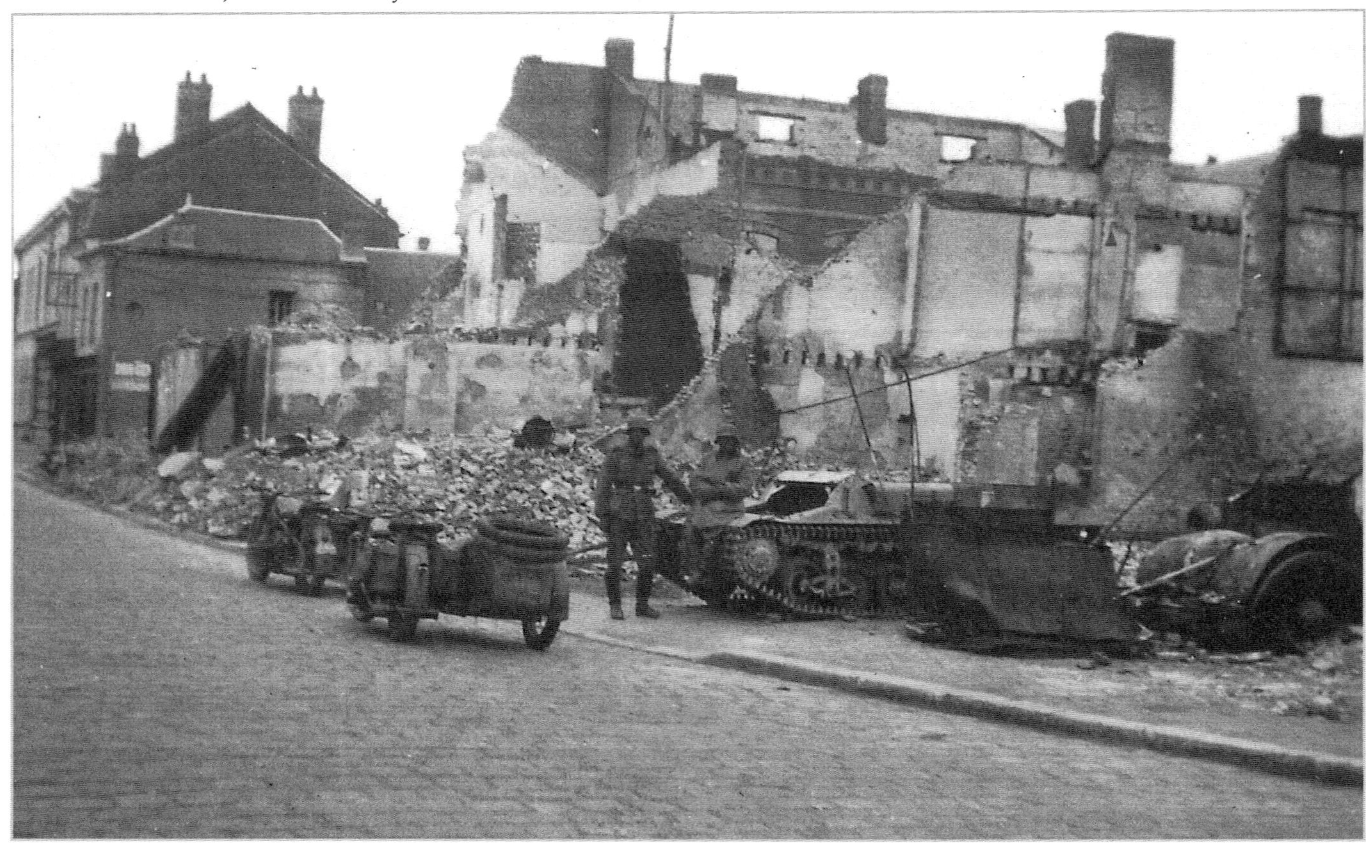

Here amongst the devastated housing of Dunkirk we see a German soldier proudly posing next to an abandoned French Loraine Schlepper armoured infantry support vehicle. Note the two BMW R12 motorcycle and sidecar combinations parked in front of it.

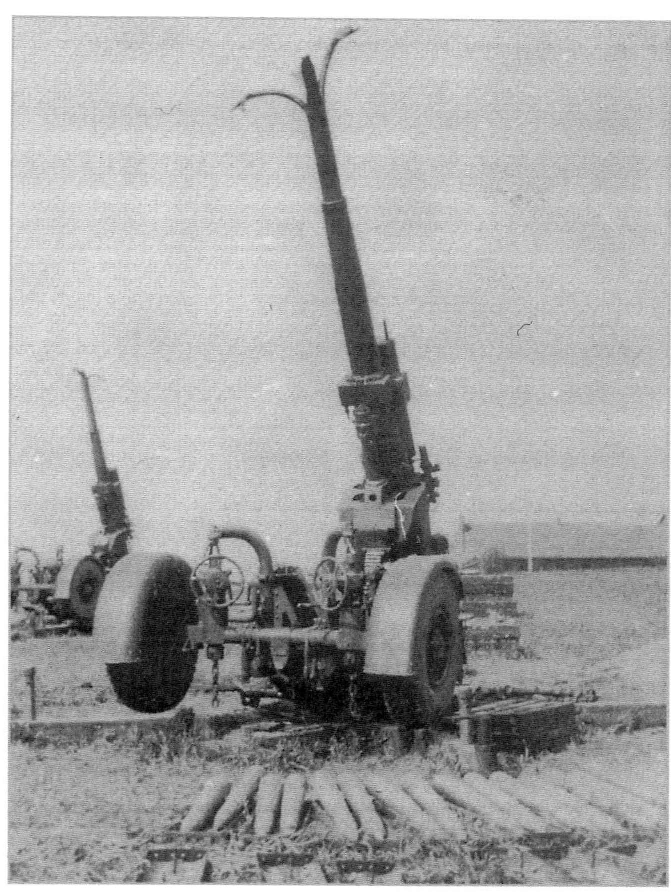

Two British 5.5 inch Heavy Anti-Aircraft Guns abandoned, but both spiked to render them useless to the enemy, lying in a field on the outskirts of Dunkirk.

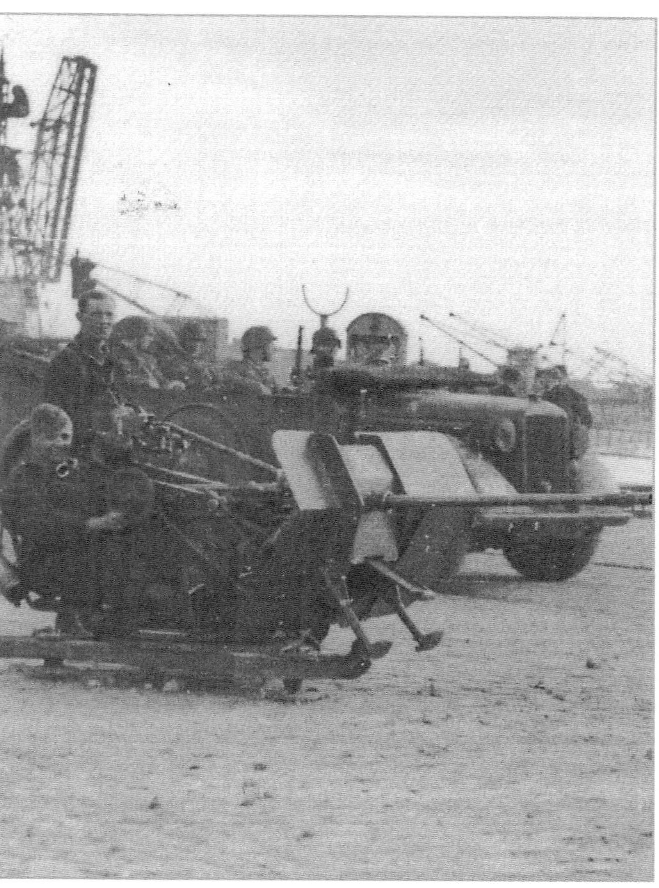

A German 20 mm *Flak* 30 anti-aircraft gun is set up on the inner harbour dock, probably for some target practice looking at the low elevation of the gun. In the background is a German heavy infantry car, a Kfz. 15 Horch.

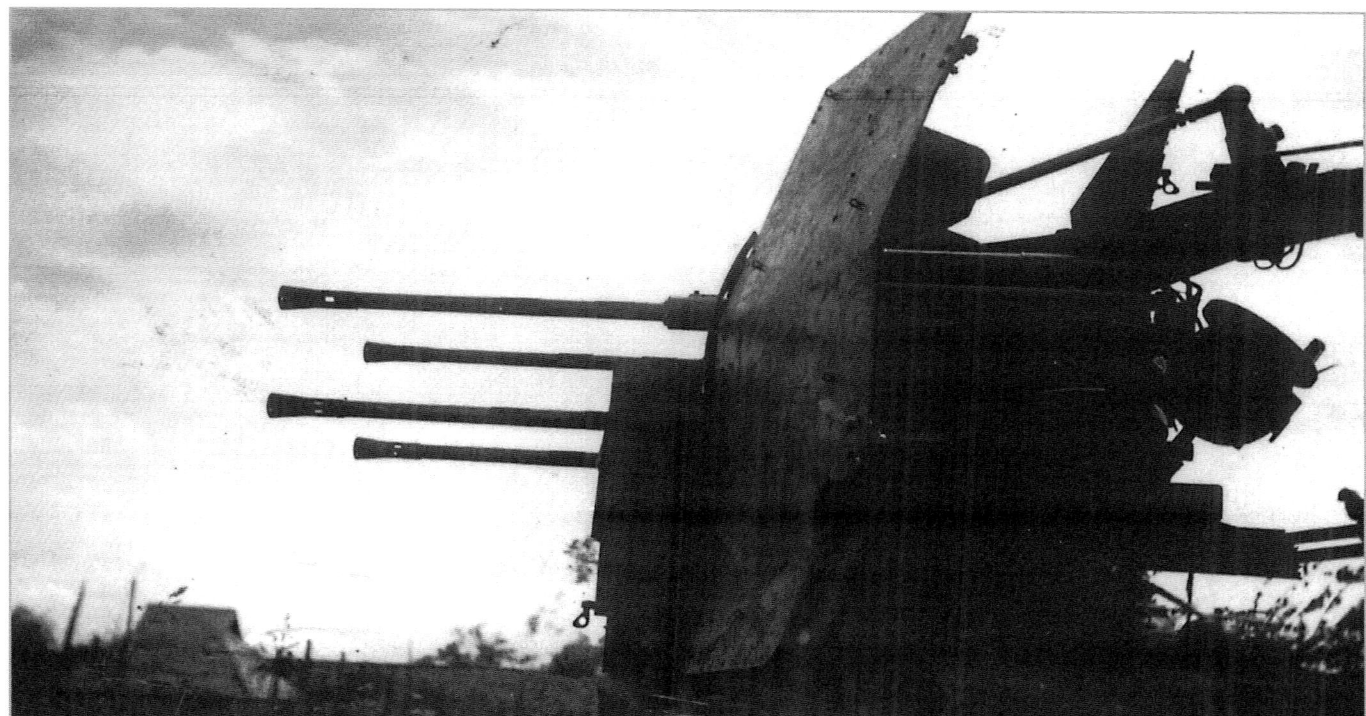

A 20 mm *Flakvierling* 38 set up on the outskirts of Dunkirk and being use against ground troops. This one however was put out of action by the defenders.

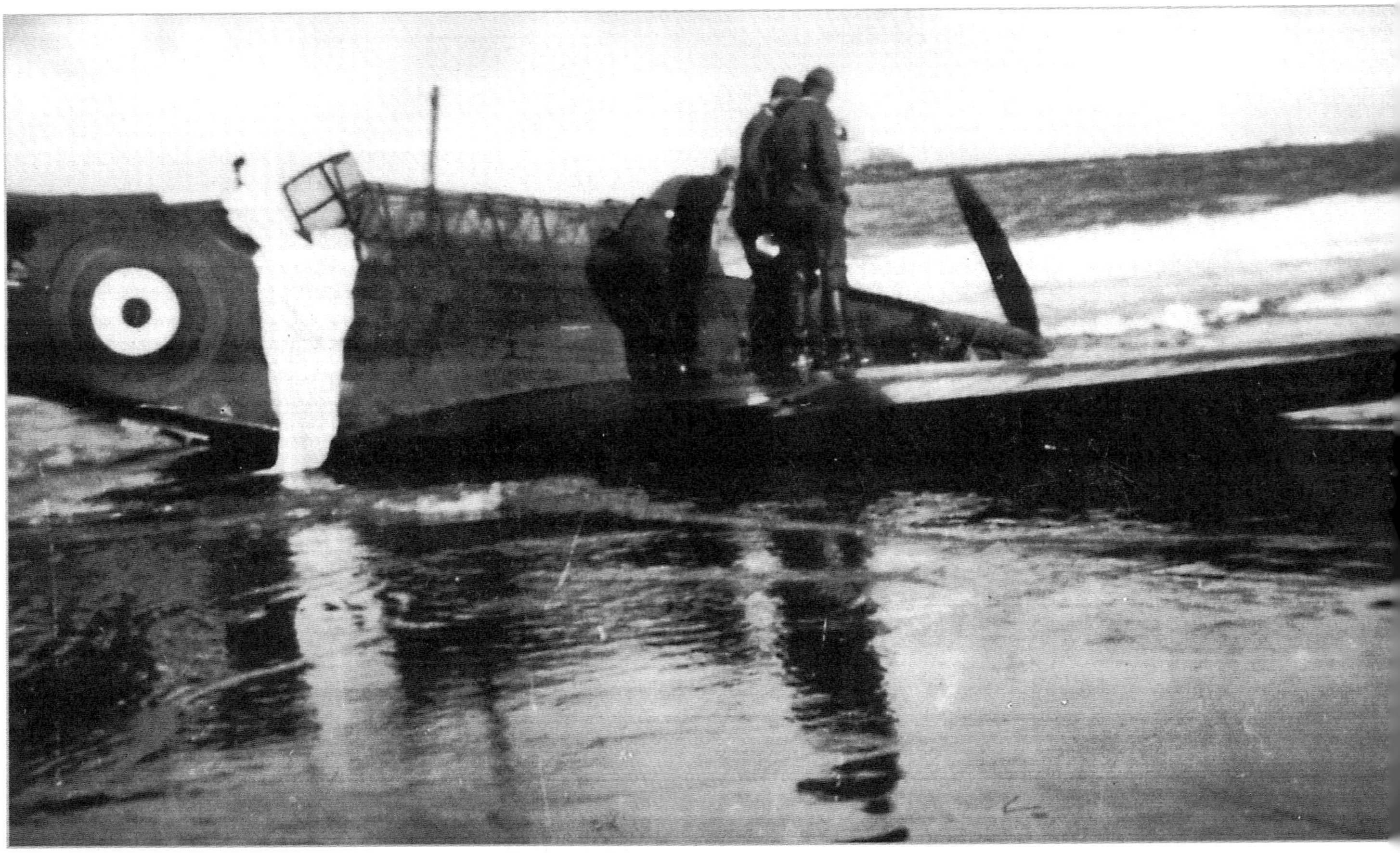

A British Fairey Battle that has been shot down and has crashed in the surf just west of the Dunkirk defensive perimeter and is now being examined (souvenired) by German infantry.

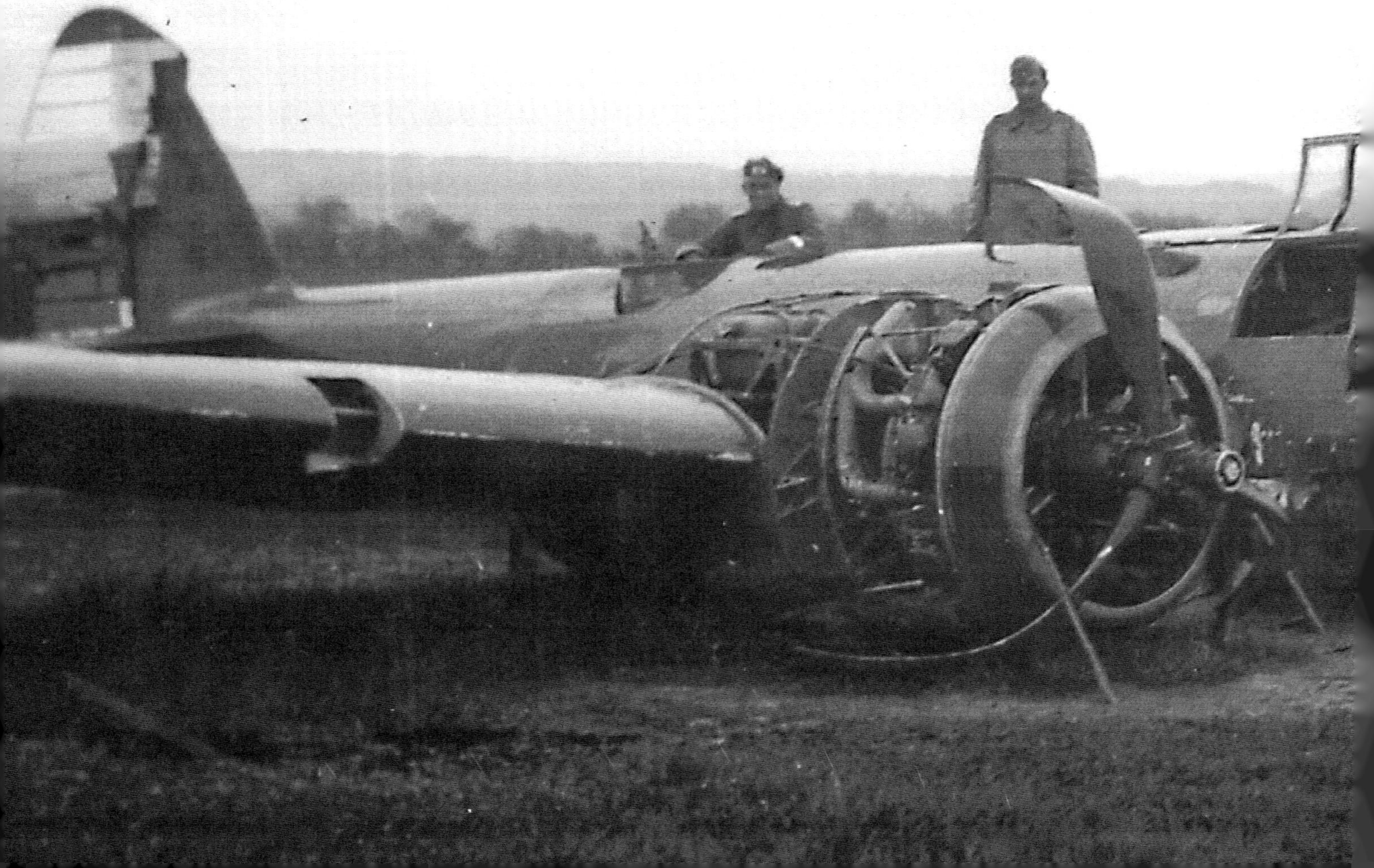

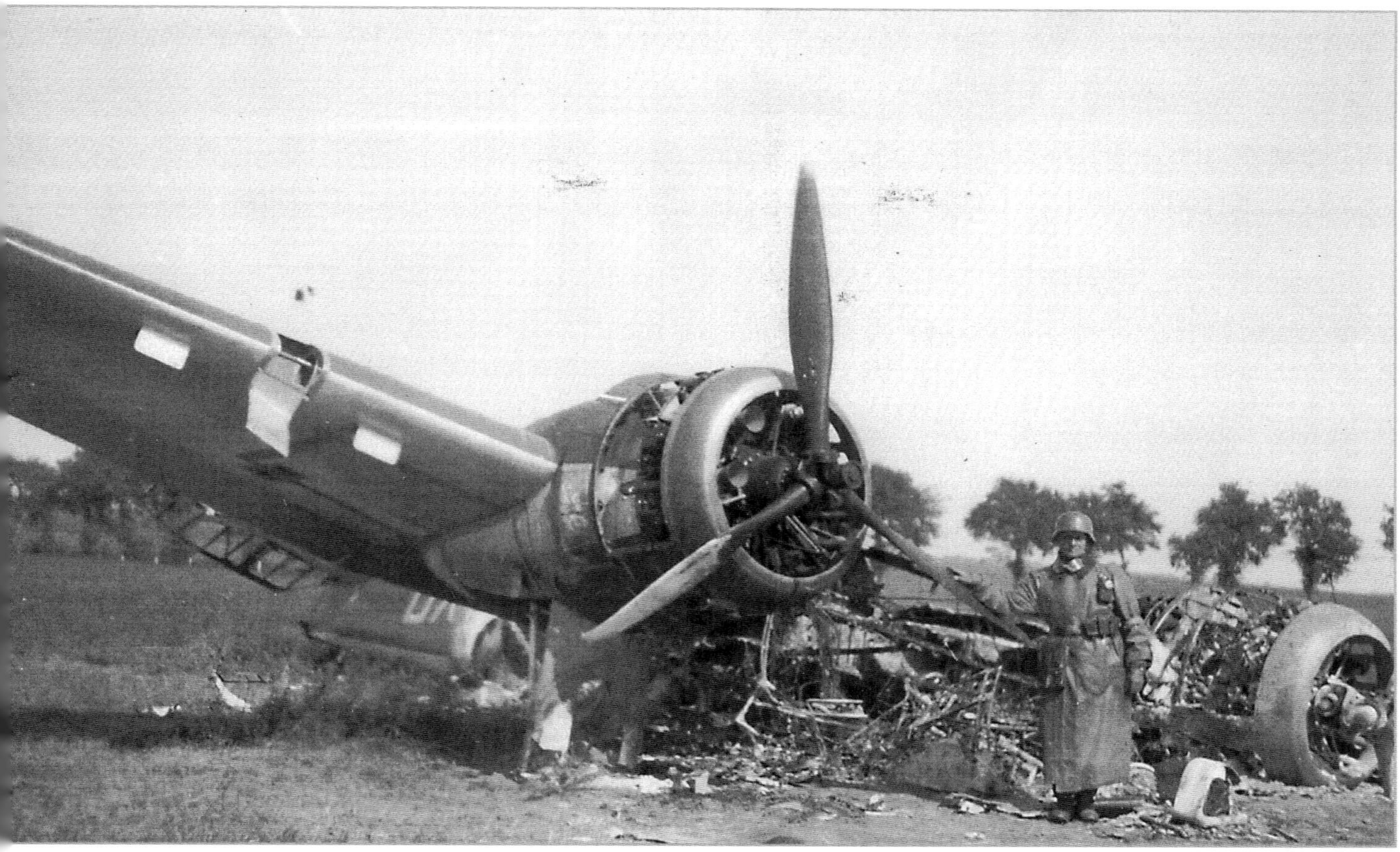

A Bristol Blenheim Mk. IV of 82 Squadron RAF crash landed and burnt out being used as a back drop for a photo to send home to a proud German family.

A Bristol Blenheim Mk. I crash landed south of the Dunkirk defensive perimeter.

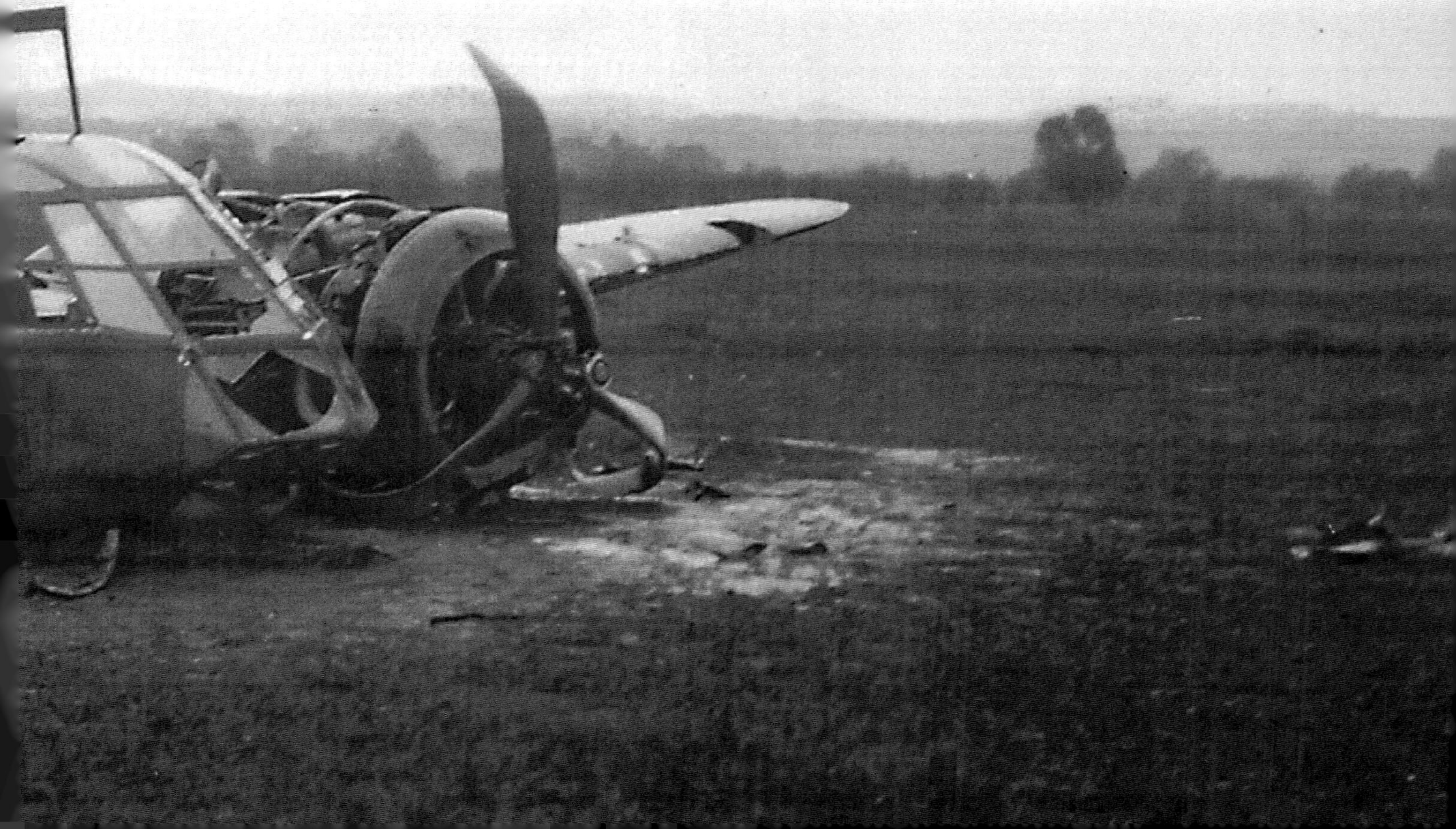

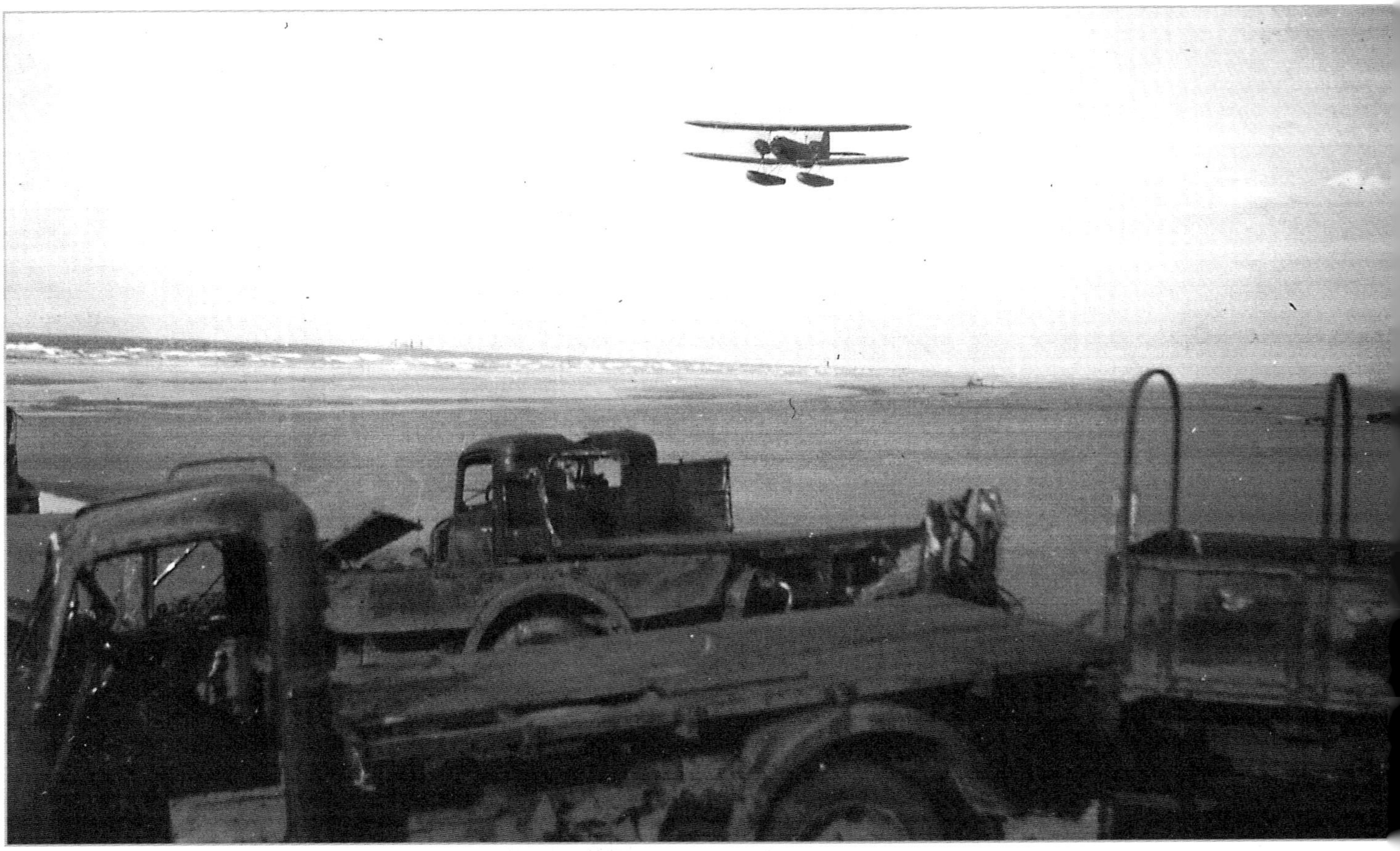

A German Heinkel He 59 *Luftwaffe* seaplane over fly's Dunkirk's beaches. This three seater aircraft was used mostly as a torpedo bomber but here is serving in a photo-reconnaissance role.

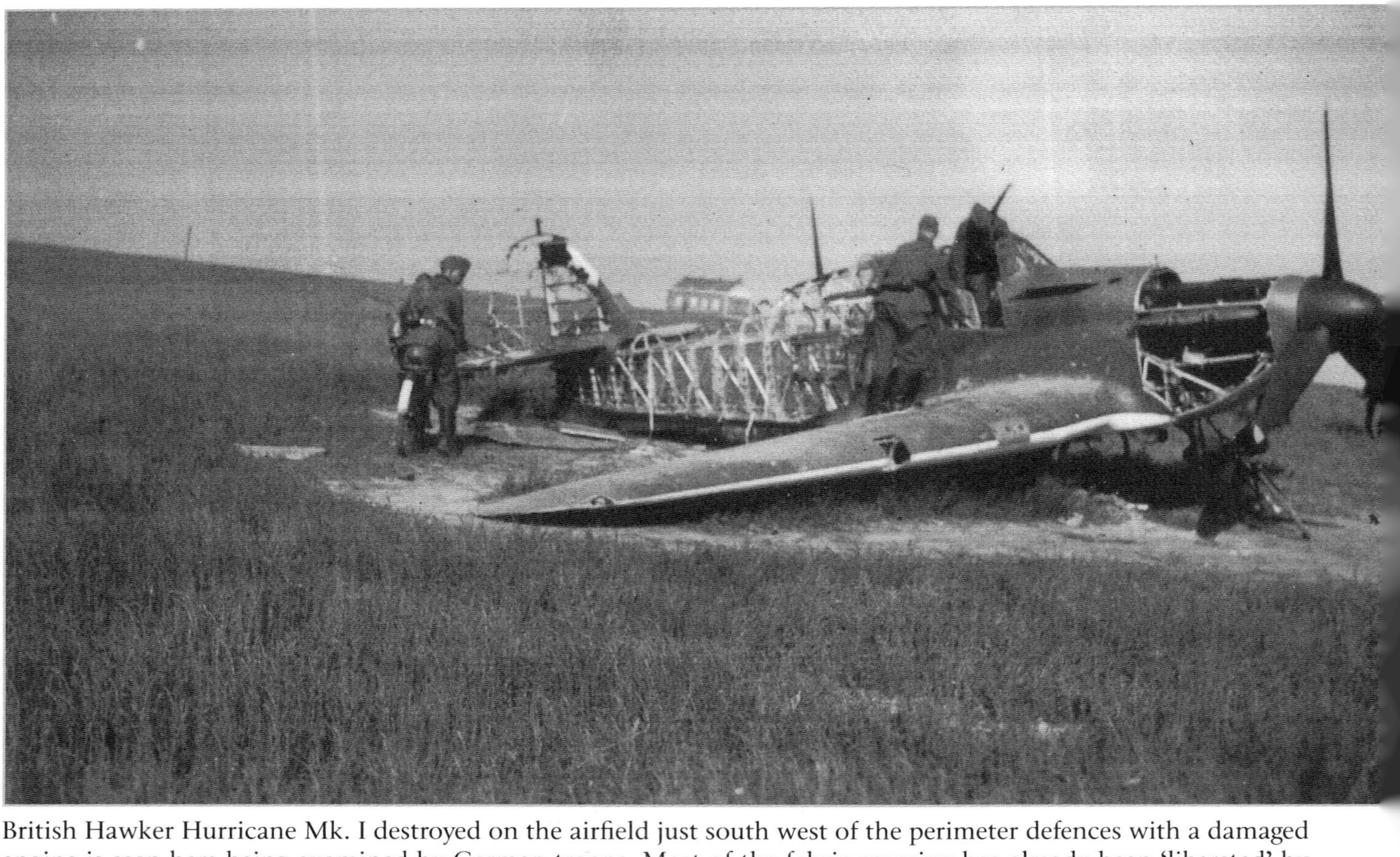

British Hawker Hurricane Mk. I destroyed on the airfield just south west of the perimeter defences with a damaged engine is seen here being examined by German troops. Most of the fabric covering has already been 'liberated' by others for souvenirs.

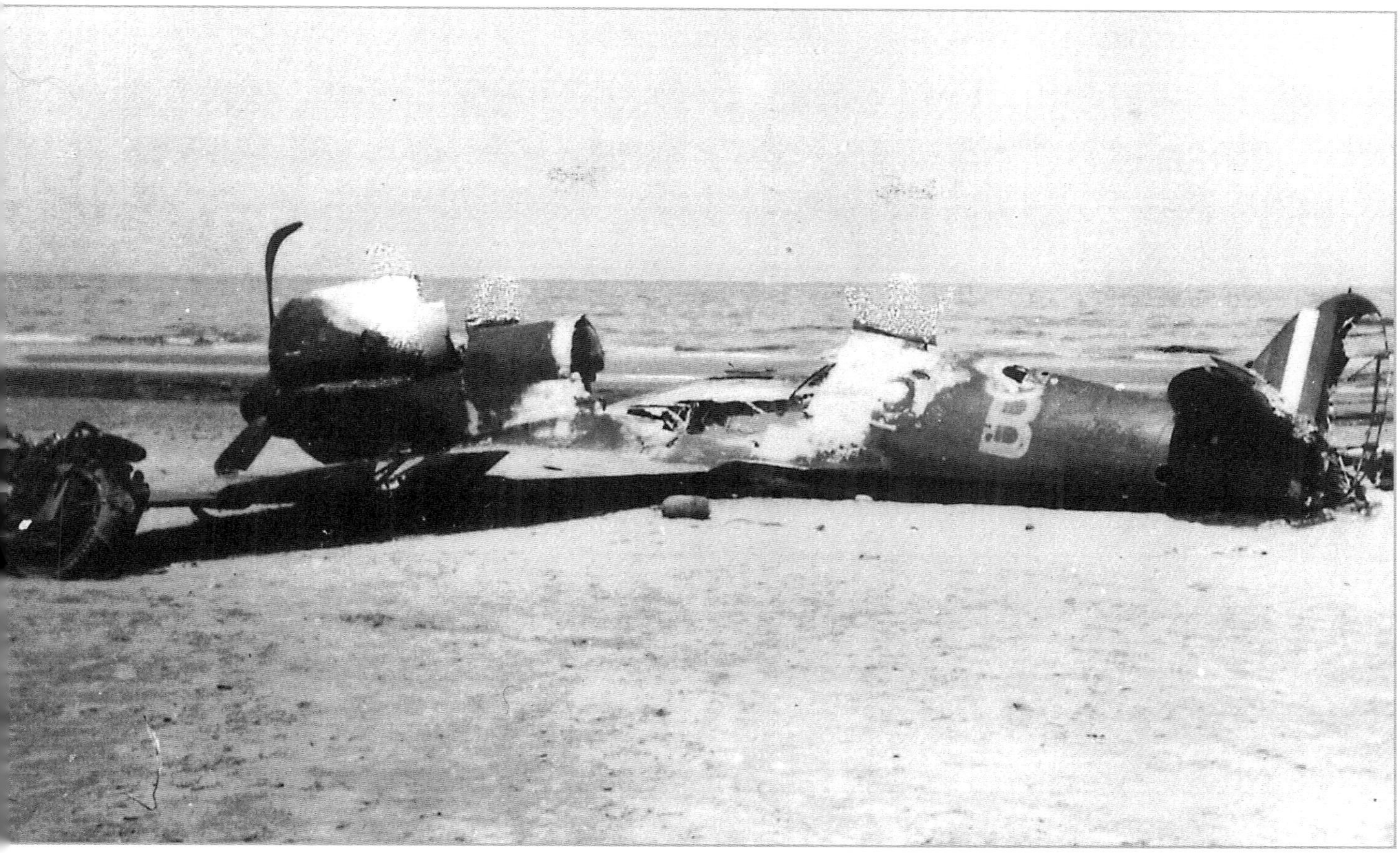

The sorry looking burnt-out remains of a British Supermarine Spitfire Mk. I which crashed on the beaches of Dunkirk during an aerial defensive battle which raged above the whole area at the time of the evacuation operation.

Another destroyed British Hawker Hurricane Mk. I. This one has been thoroughly burnt out and no doubt been 'souvenired' as well. Note the bent prop tip. The prop must have been windmilling slowly as the plane hit the ground.

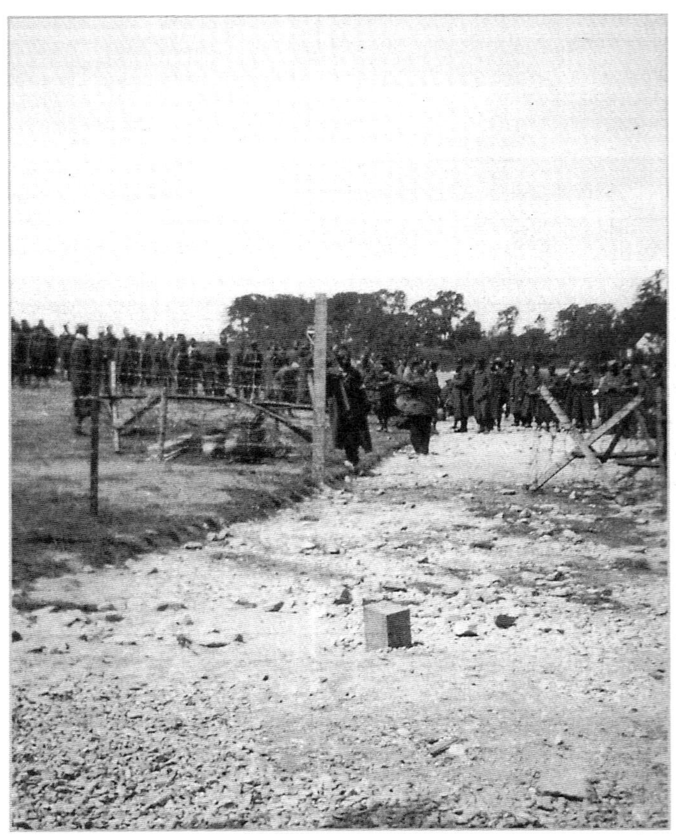

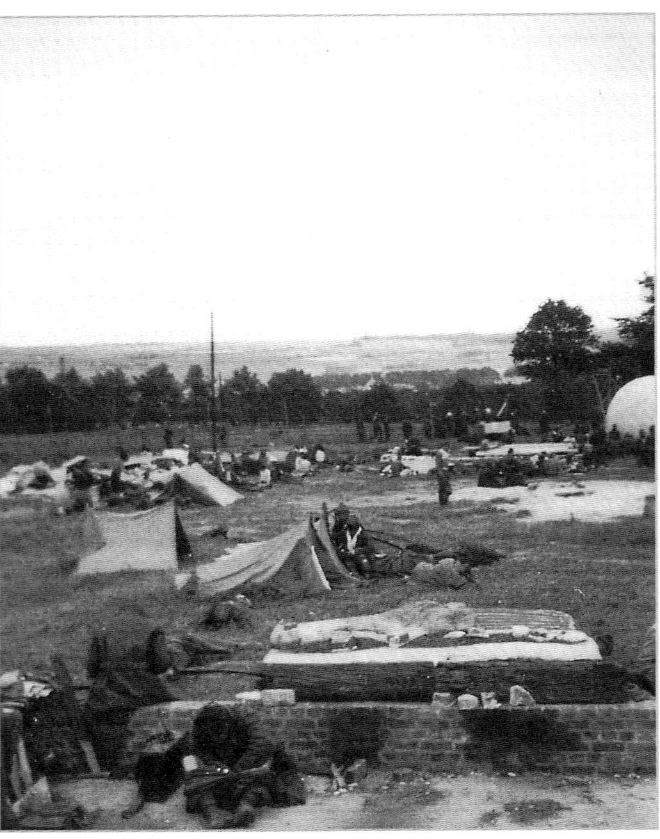

On this page are three photographs showing the temporary prisoner of war assembly camps which sprang up around Dunkirk in the days following the evacuation.

All these temporary camps seem to have been based on various farms to enable access to water and make use of the animal pens as stockades.

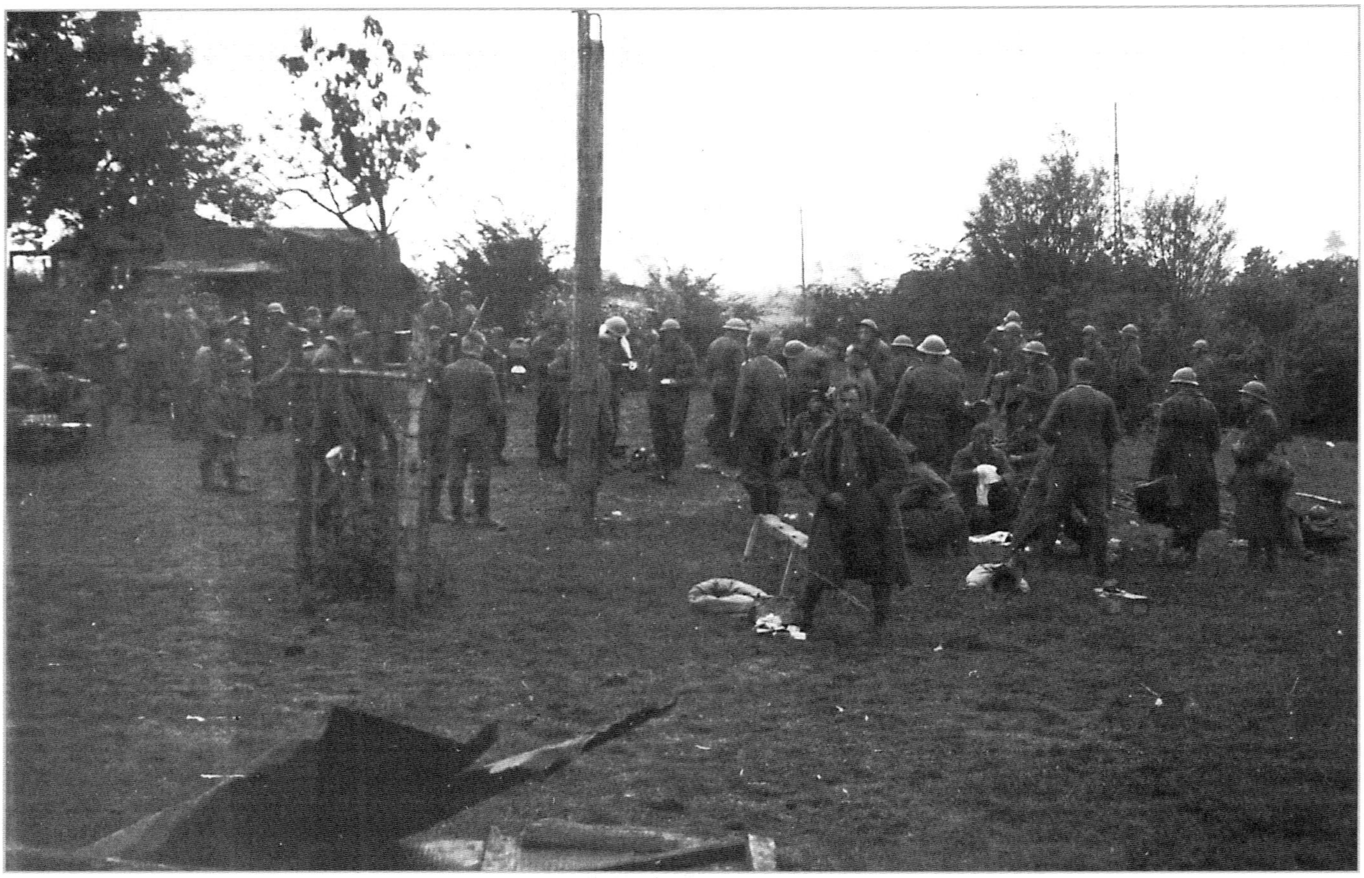

In this camp we see a mix of both French and British prisoners. Luckily these camps were run by the German *Heer* (the regular Army) not the *Waffen SS*.

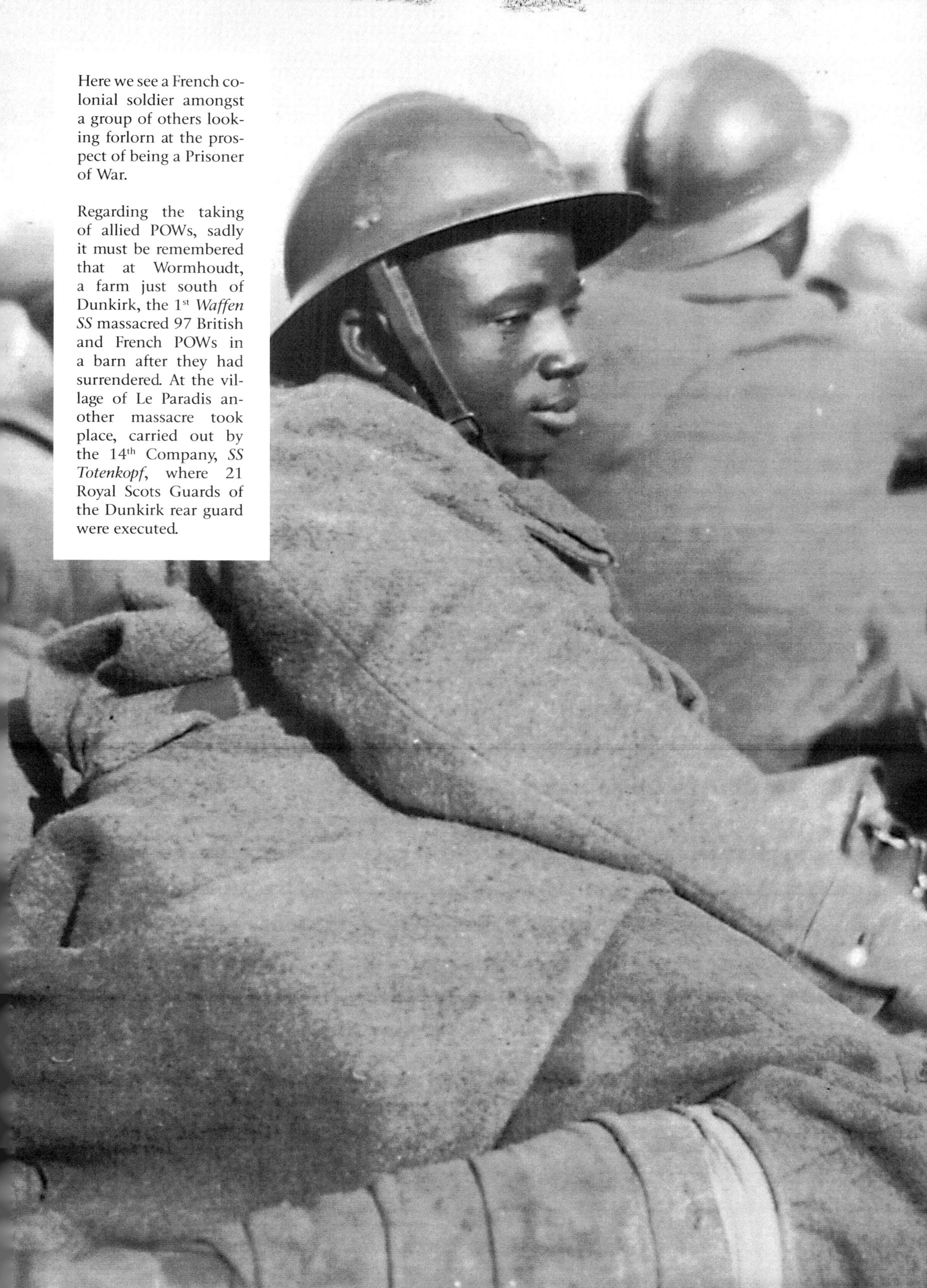

Here we see a French co-
lonial soldier amongst
a group of others look-
ing forlorn at the pros-
pect of being a Prisoner
of War.

Regarding the taking
of allied POWs, sadly
it must be remembered
that at Wormhoudt,
a farm just south of
Dunkirk, the 1st *Waffen
SS* massacred 97 British
and French POWs in
a barn after they had
surrendered. At the vil-
lage of Le Paradis an-
other massacre took
place, carried out by
the 14th Company, *SS
Totenkopf*, where 21
Royal Scots Guards of
the Dunkirk rear guard
were executed.

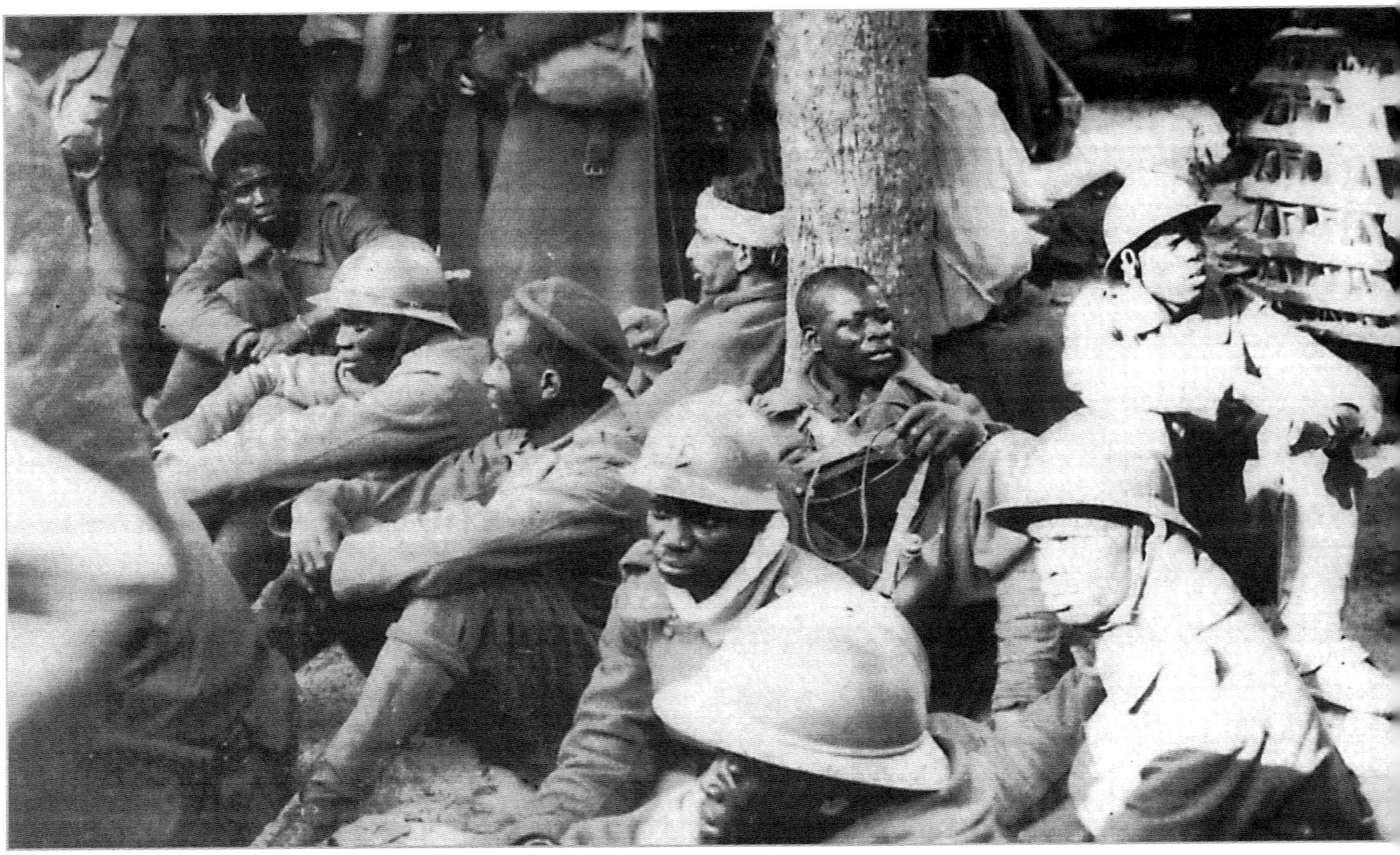

A group of French Colonial PoWs sat behind a PzKpfw IV await instructions.

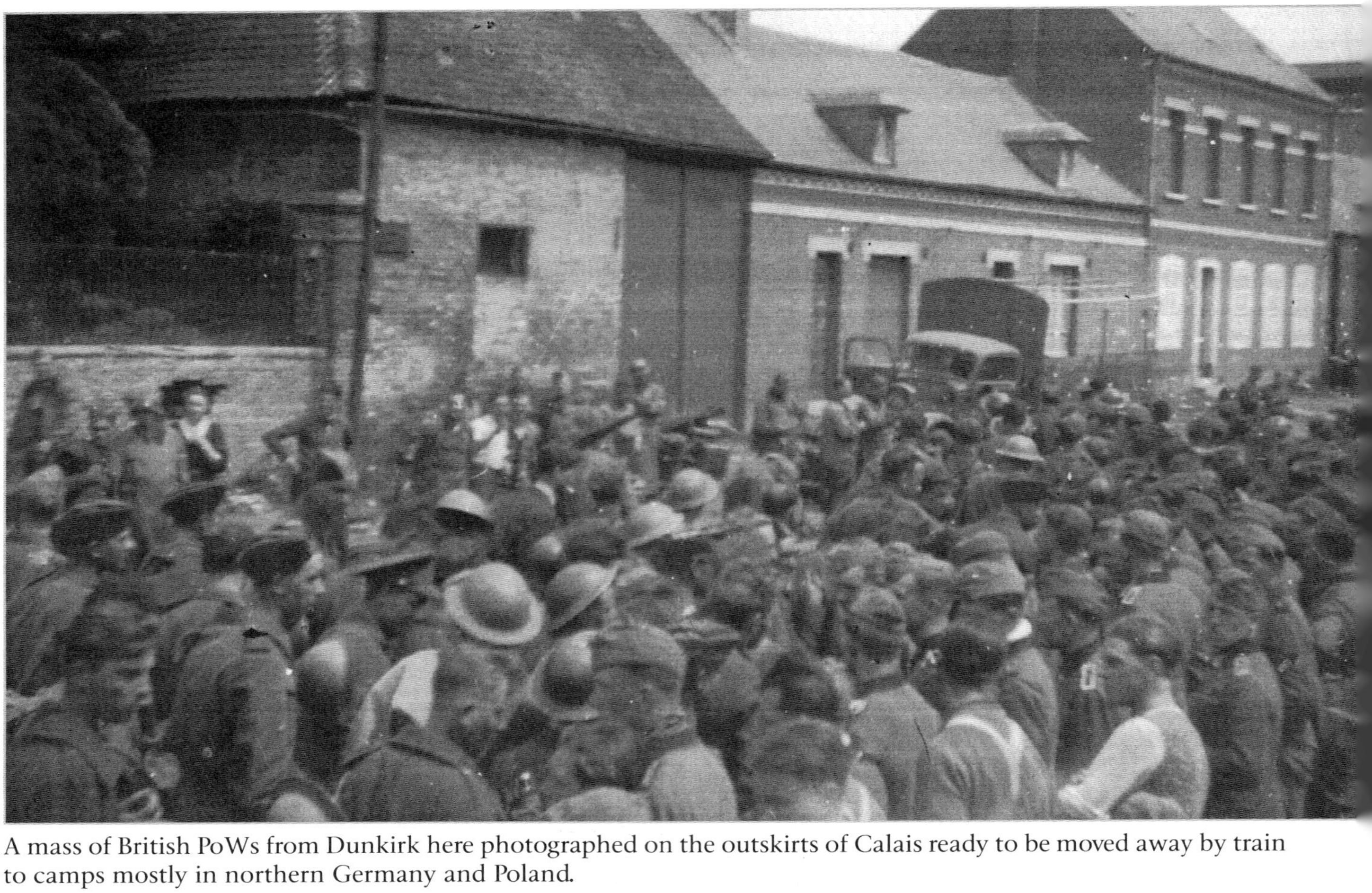

A mass of British PoWs from Dunkirk here photographed on the outskirts of Calais ready to be moved away by train to camps mostly in northern Germany and Poland.

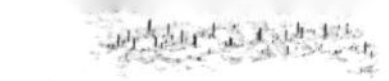

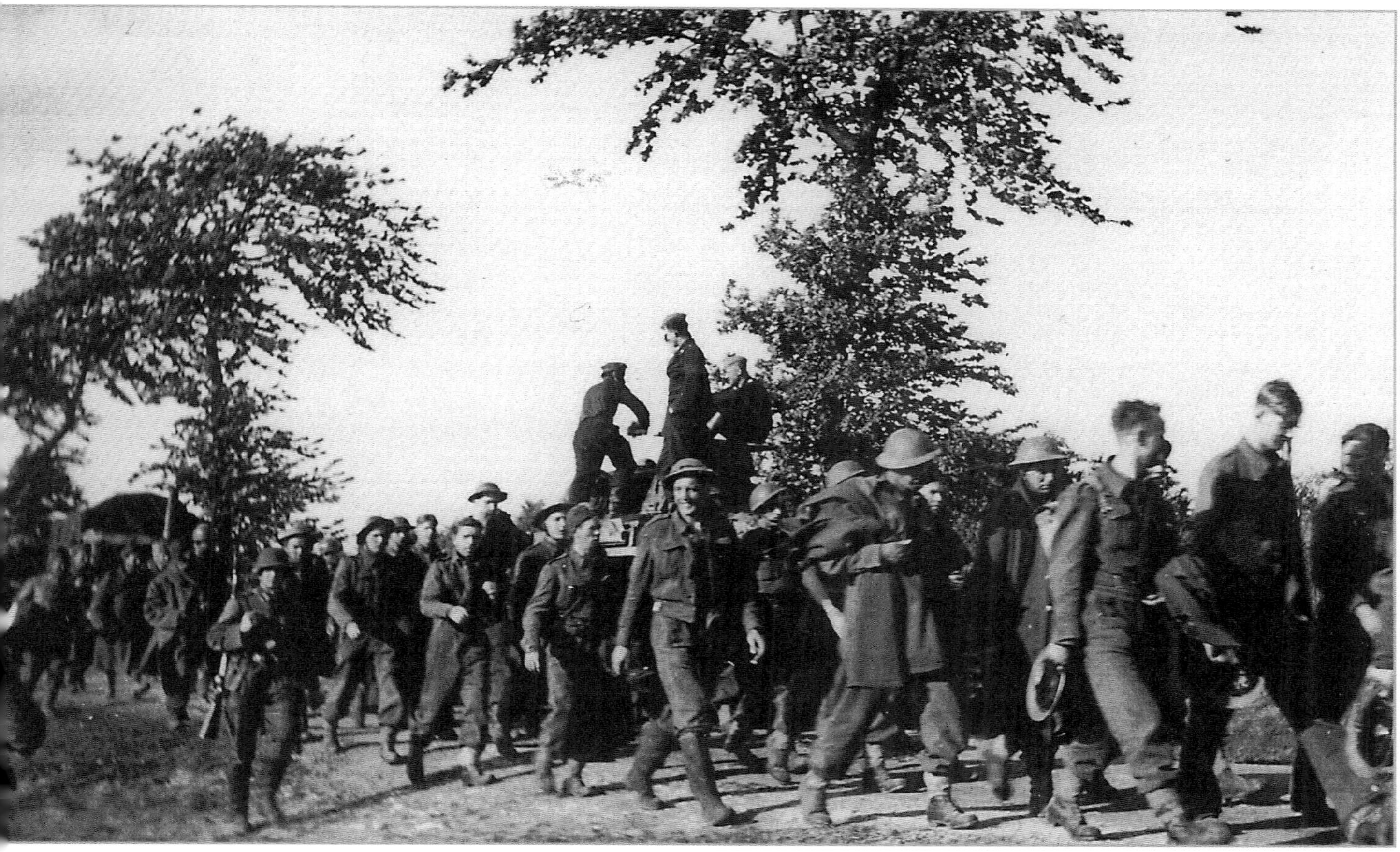

More British PoWs on the move out of the temporary Camps to be permanently incarcerated elsewhere.

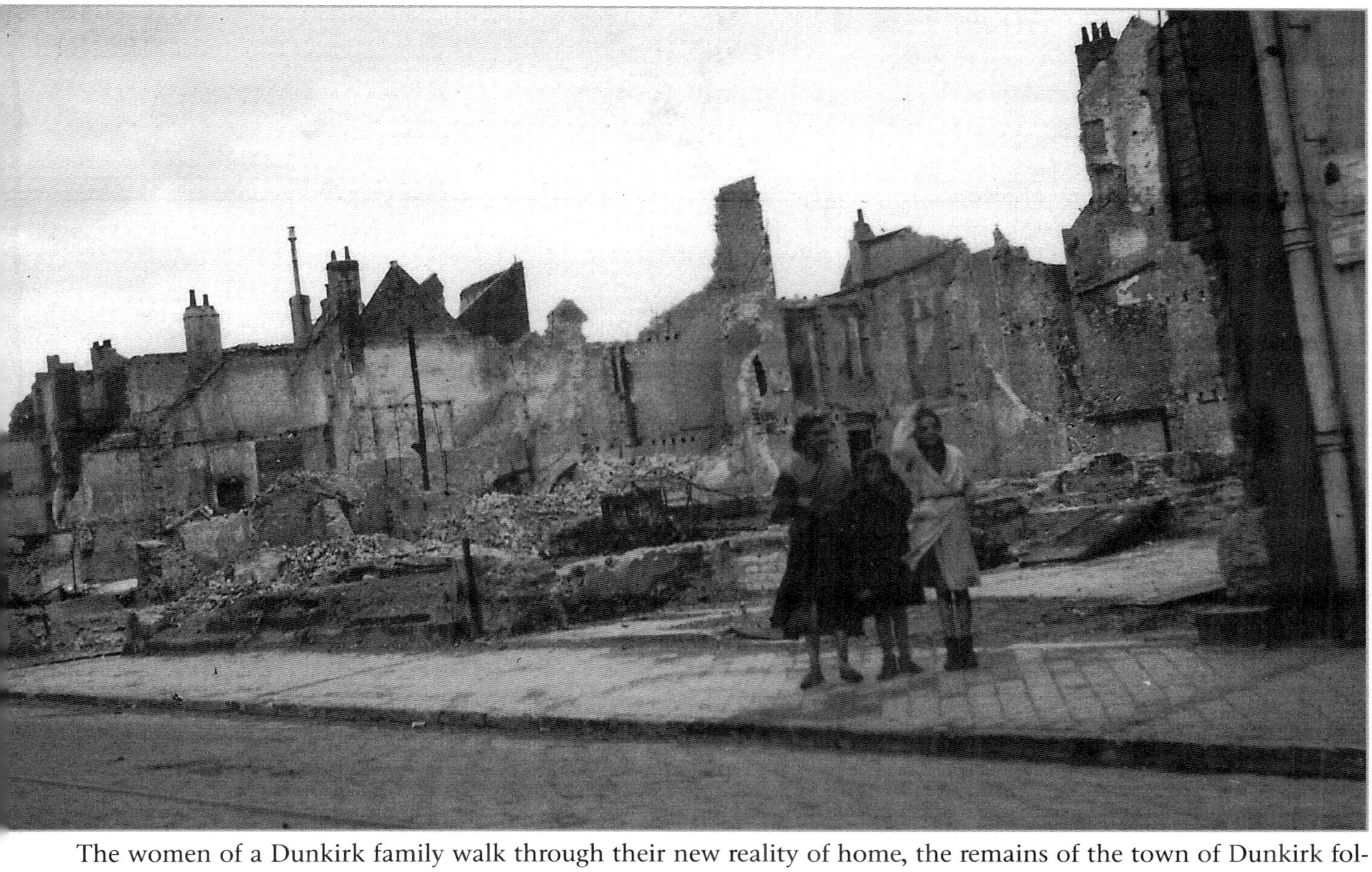

The women of a Dunkirk family walk through their new reality of home, the remains of the town of Dunkirk following the clearing up operation.

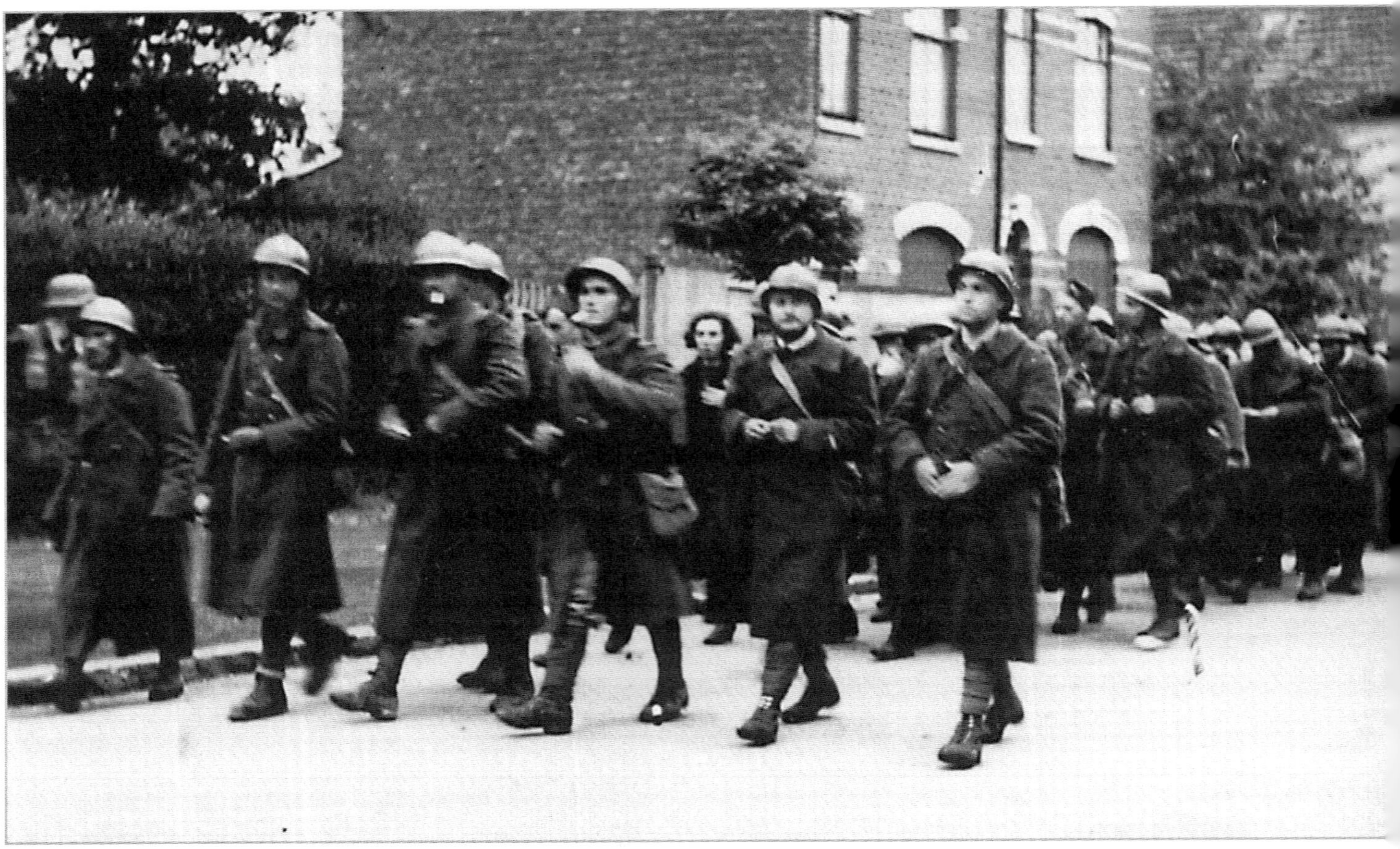

On this page we see French PoW' on the move out of the Dunkirk area; sadly many of these men did not make it to regular PoW camps, many were sent to work camps throughout Germany.

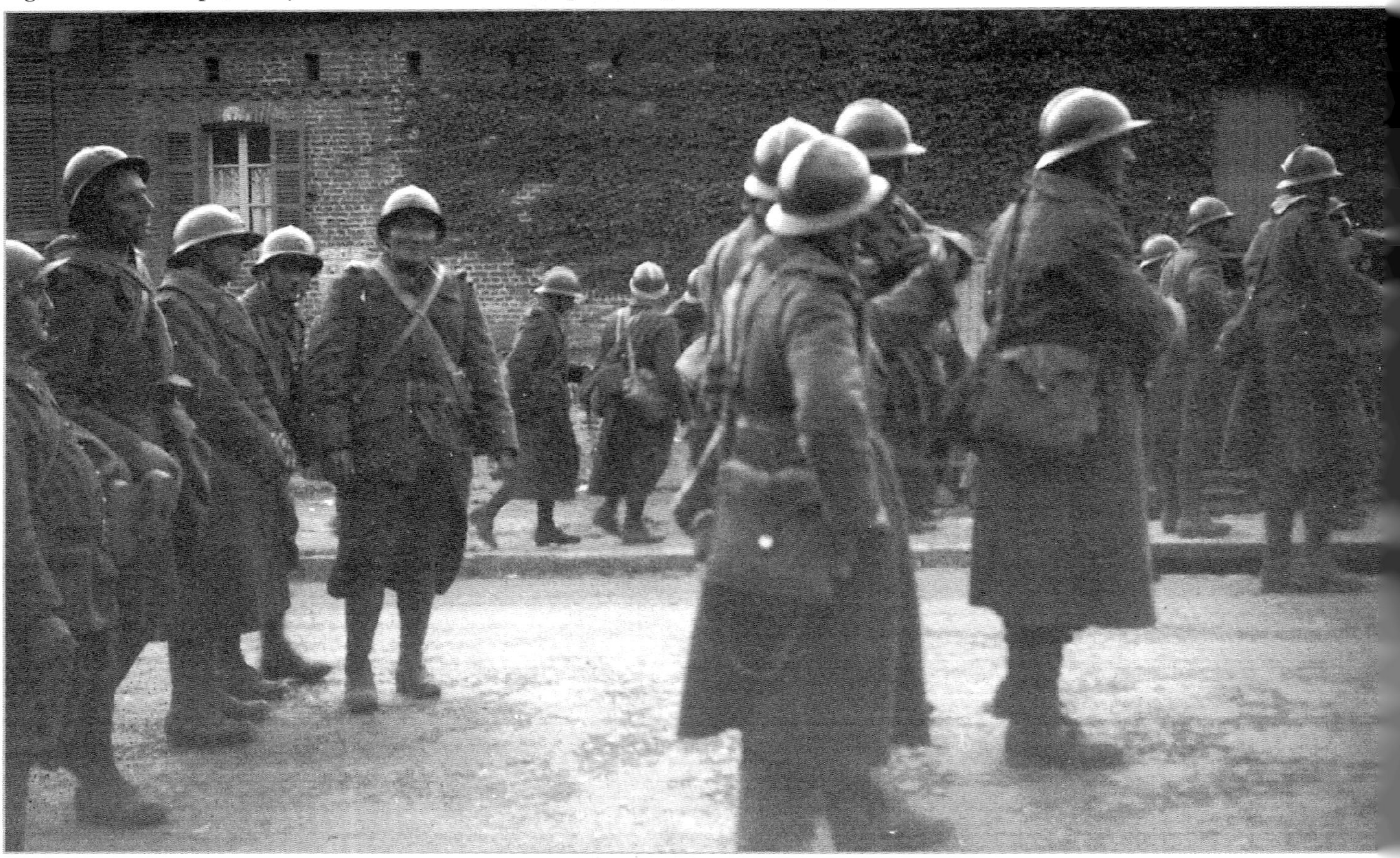

More French PoWs seen here near De Panne Railway Station awaiting transfer to PoW camps elsewhere.

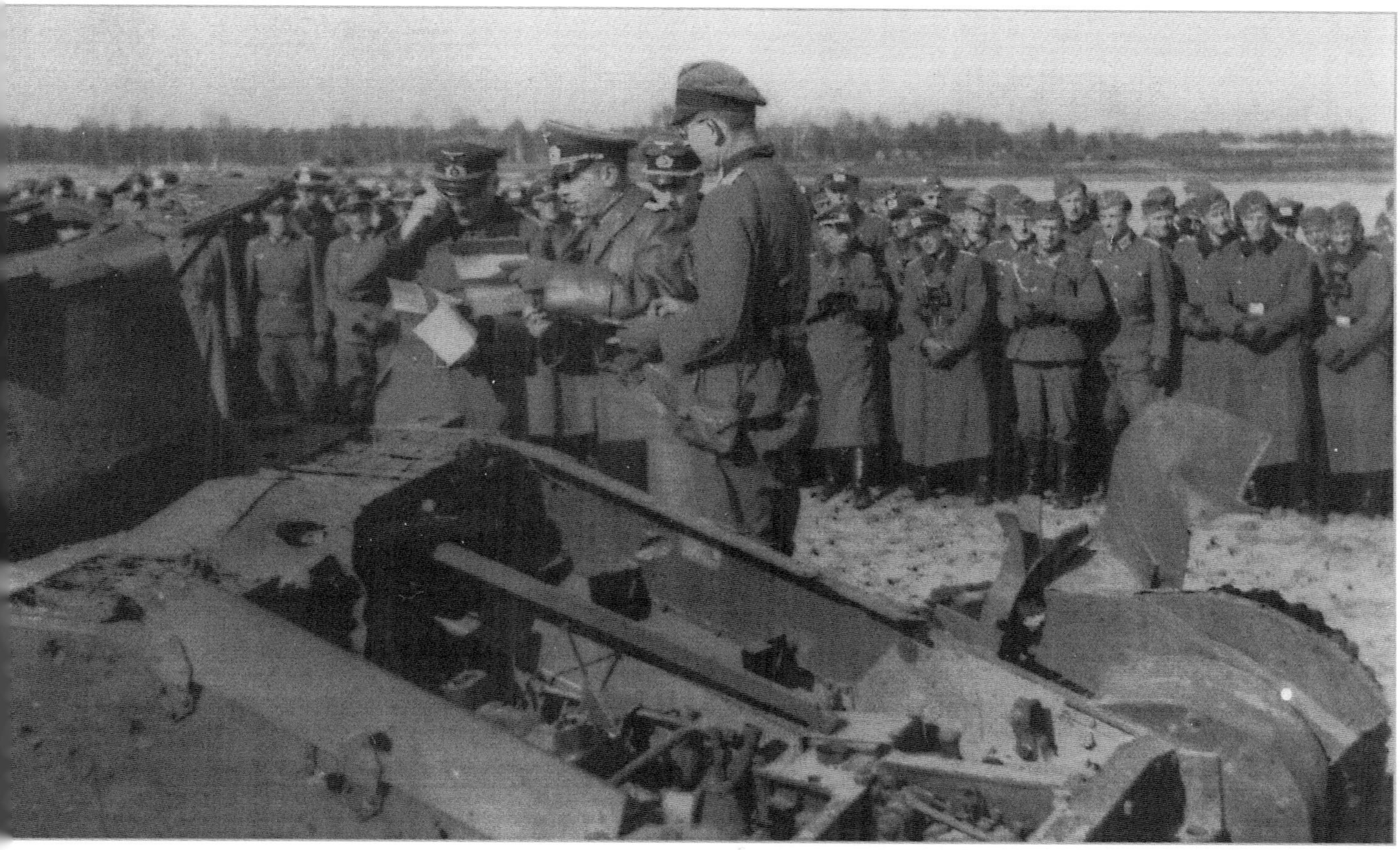

German Officers get ready to address their troops at a medal investiture in the field with the backdrop of a knocked out British Matilda Mk. I.

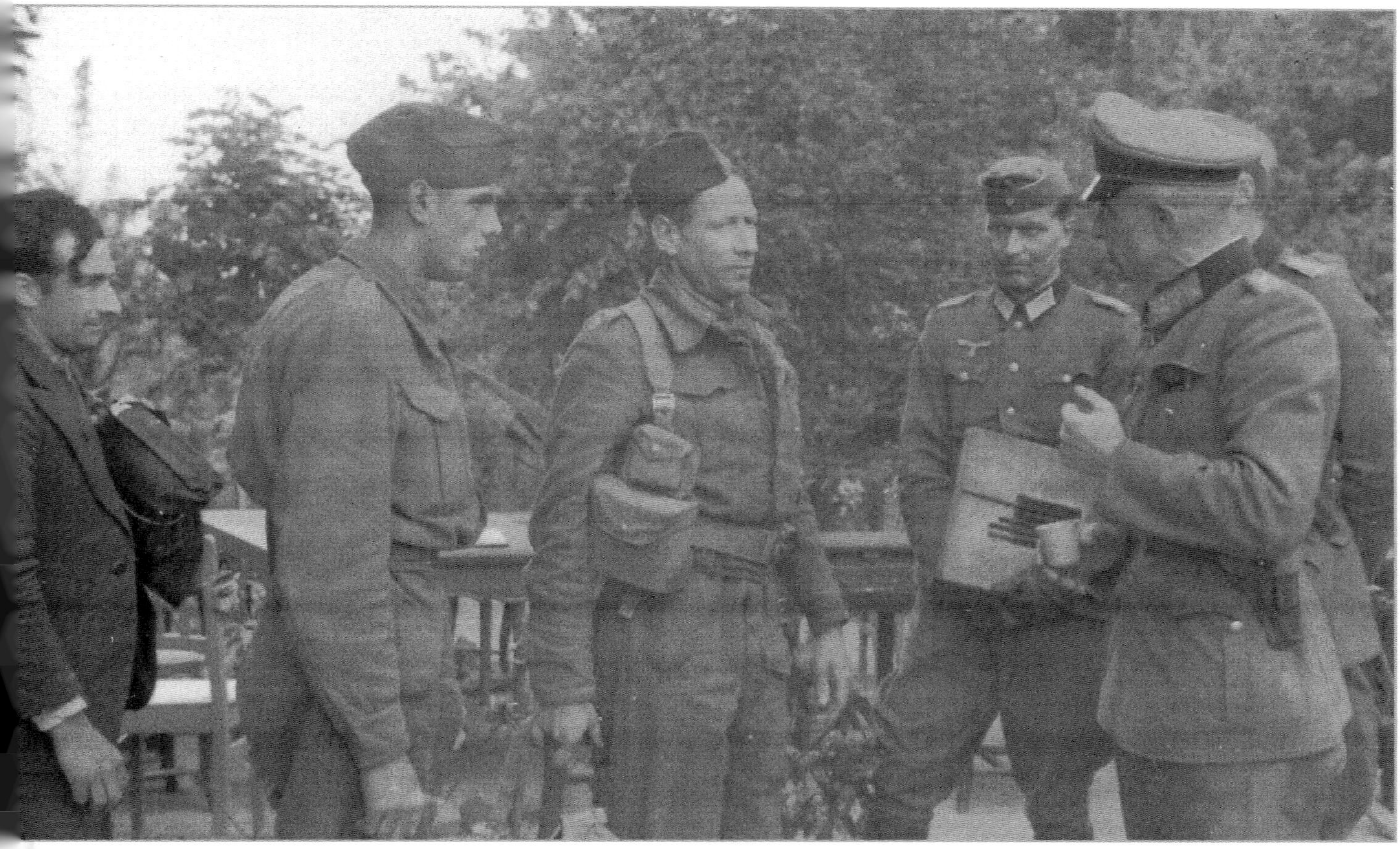

A group of German Officers interview two British POWs in what looks like a relaxed atmosphere. I am not so sure what role the civilian plays in this group photograph though?

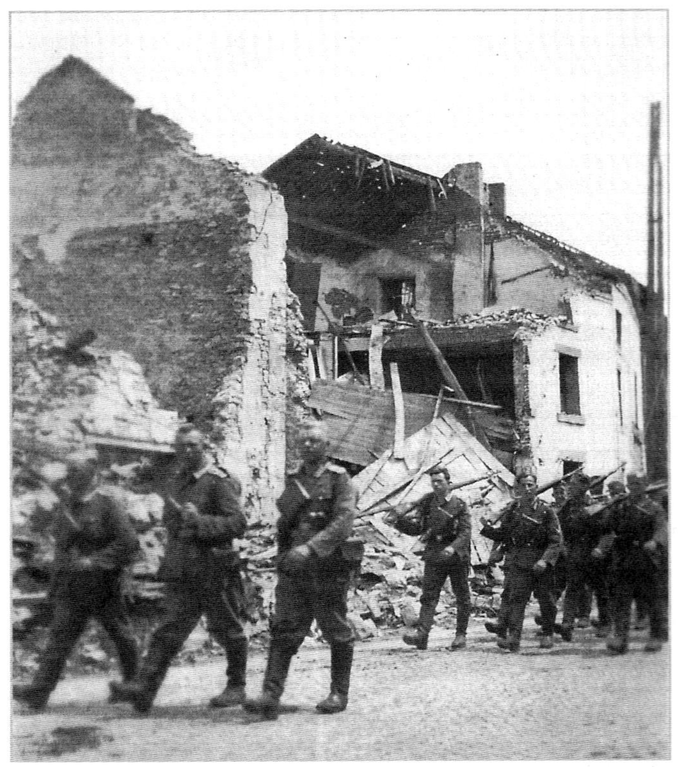

German Infantry march into the battered remains of Dunkirk to witness their victory. This photograph was taken on the 28th June 1940, some three weeks after the end of the evacuation.

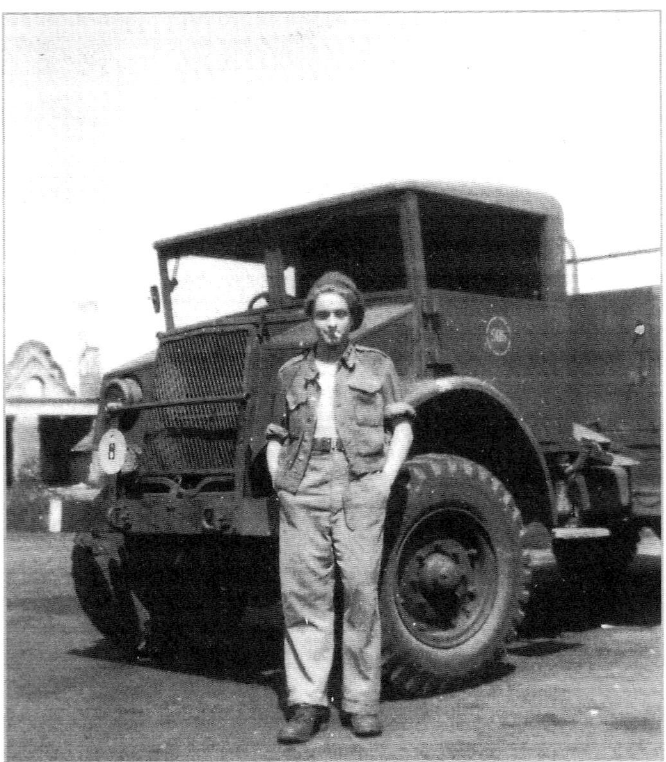

A French civilian mechanic stands proudly next to a refurbished Bedford 15cwt. Note he is wearing a British battledress top. Many local French civilian motor-garages made a lot of money refurbishing great quantities of the captured French and English military vehicles s for their new German masters.

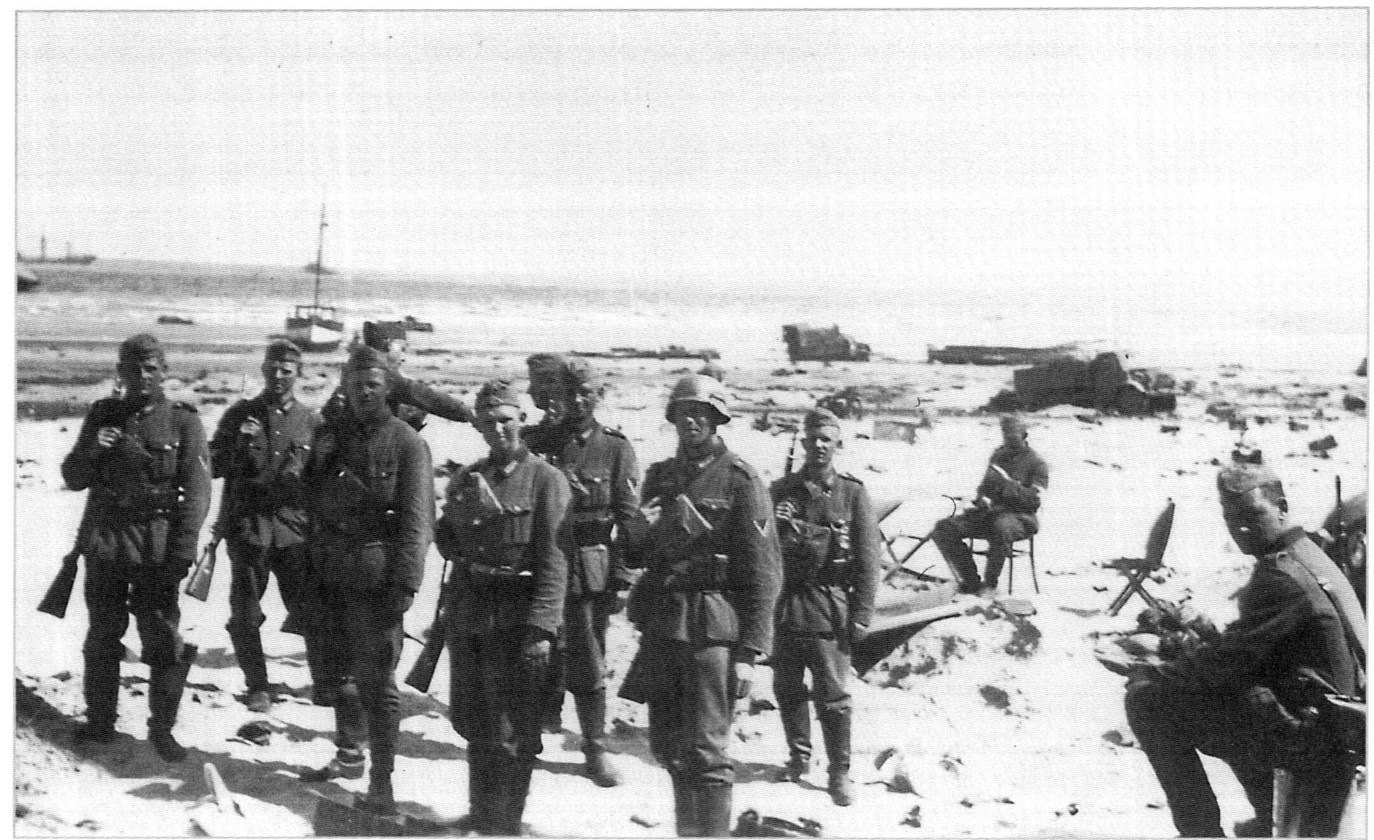

An informal group photograph of a German Infantry platoon at assembled on the beaches of Dunkirk awaiting orders.

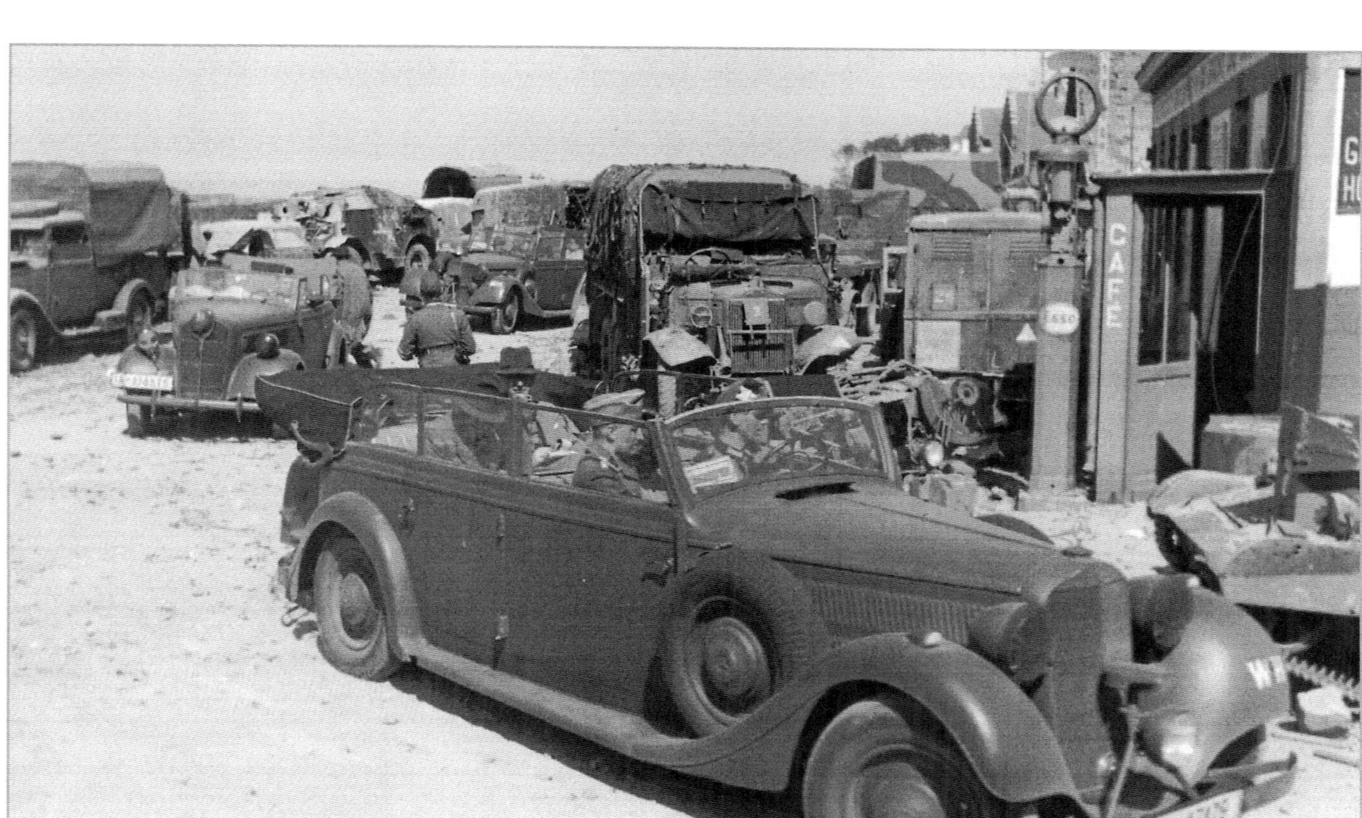

German senior officers drive down the promenade 'taking the tour' in their Mercedes V170 followed by their staff in two Horch staff cars.

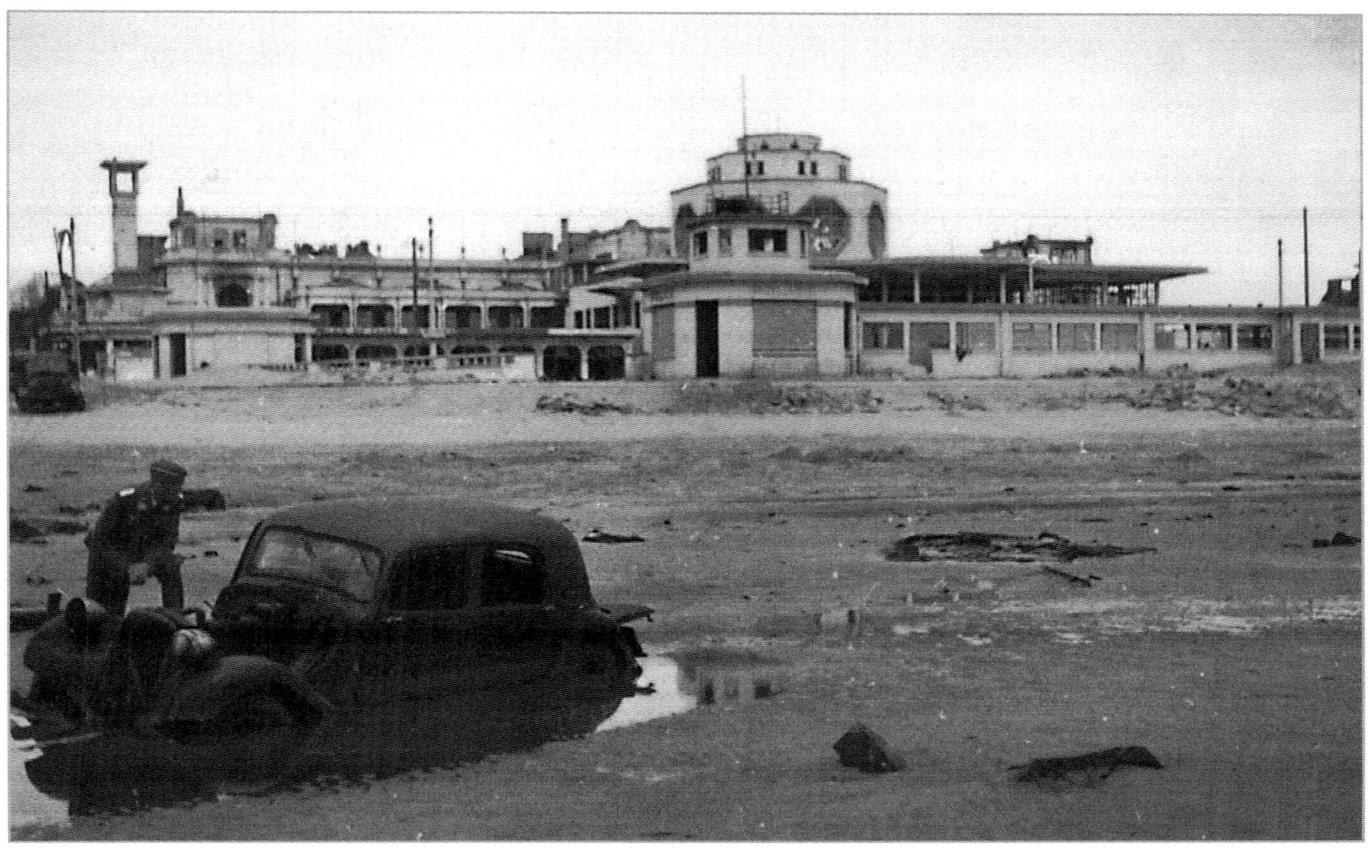

A very good view of the Malo Les Bains Casino a building complex that served a major role in operation Dynamo, that of both a casualty gathering station and Hospital and also its outbuildings serving as control points for the administration of the evacuation.

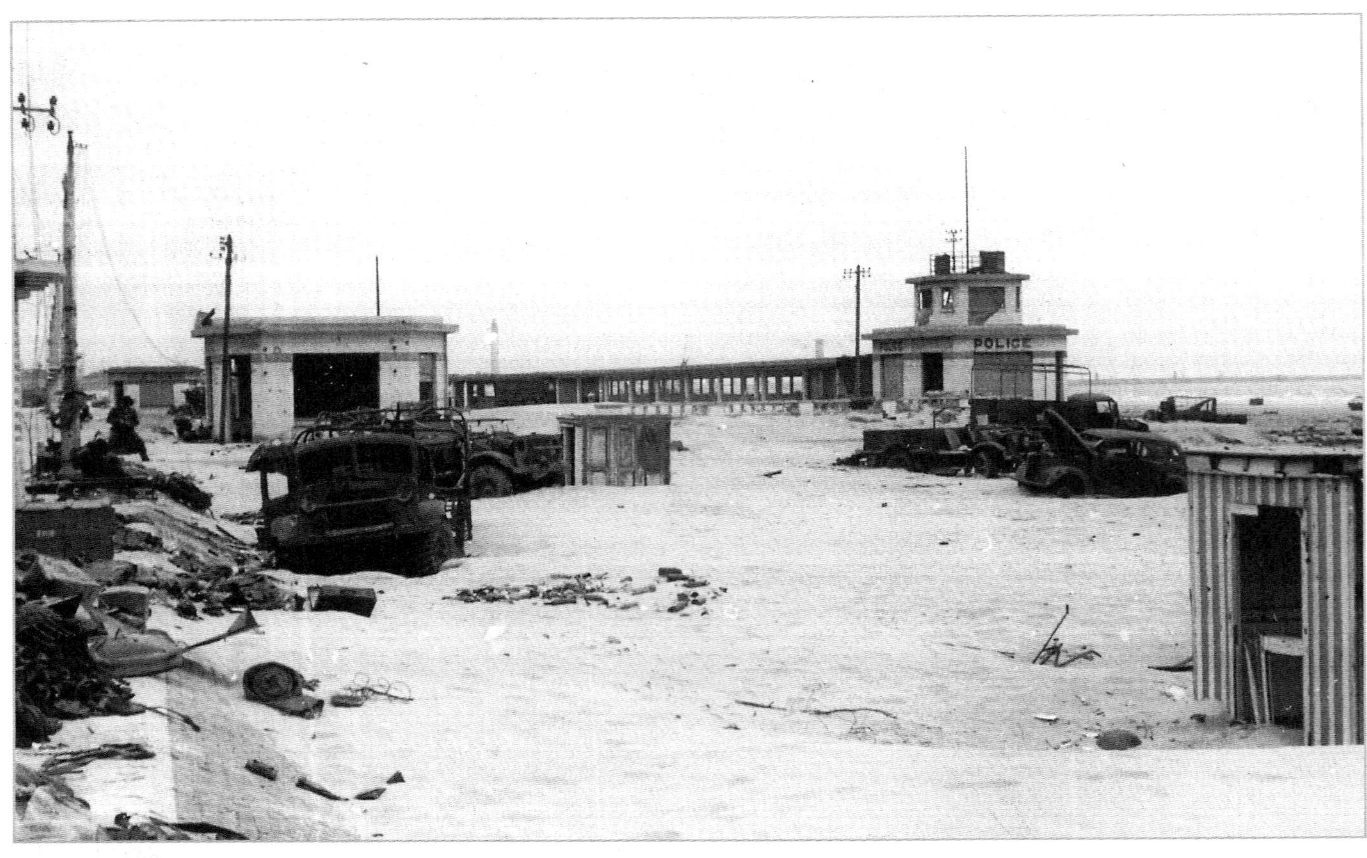

Here we see the Malo les Bains Casino from the east side. In foreground on the right is the ice cream parlour/summer house and to the left is the Police hut, both served as control rooms at some point in the evacuation. Behind them are the cloisters that served as a first add and triage point.

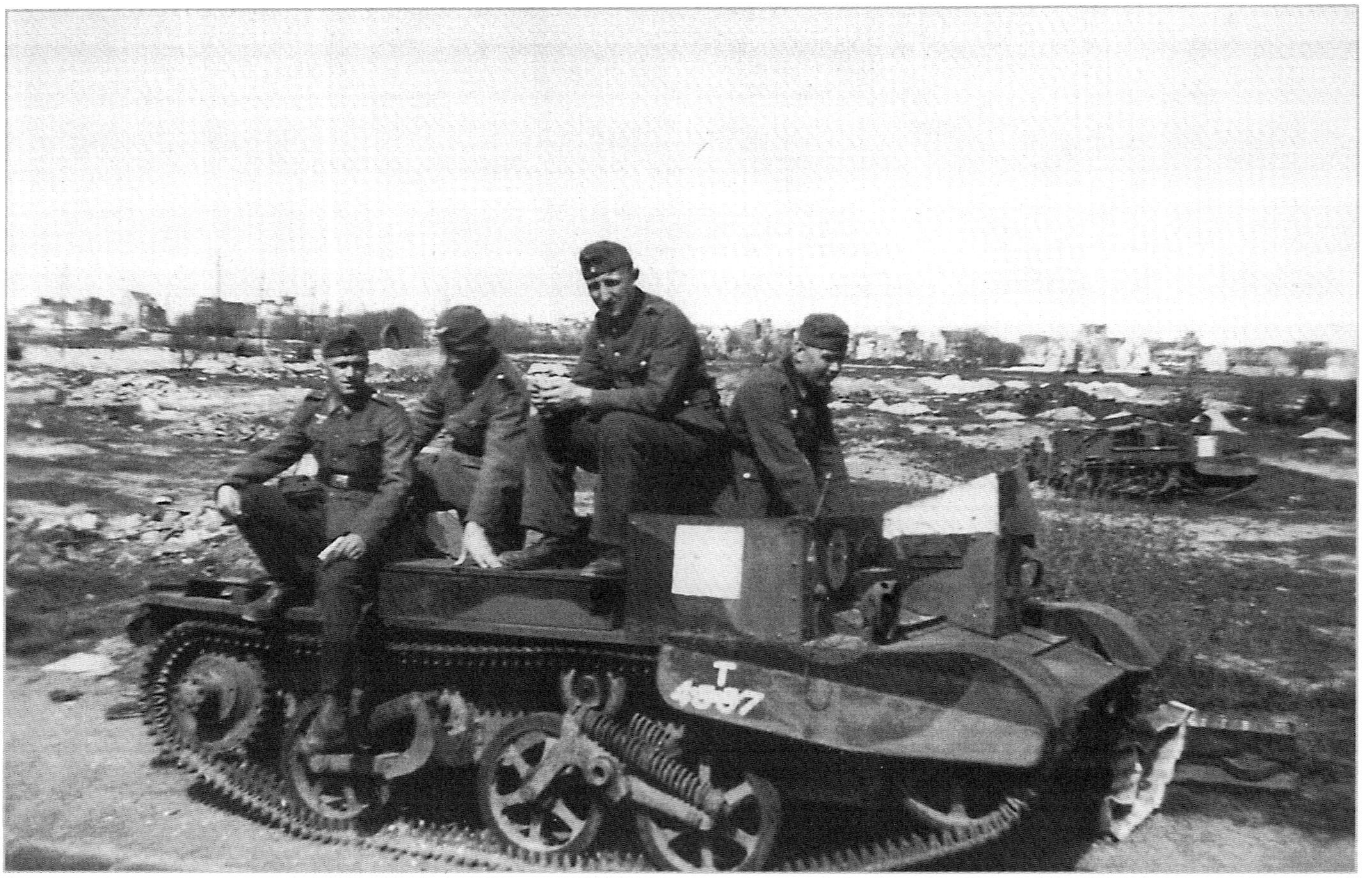

German troops pose on their newly acquired British Universal Carrier, both it and the one behind look to be found in good order.